AYLA'S QUEST

(Adventures with Aliens, Nature Spirit Creatures and Humans)

By

M.Ferguson

Howard,
Love meeting you. Wishing you and your wife many happy years.
Ayla ♡

ISBN: 9781515252030

© 201X by M. Ferguson
All rights reserved. Copyright under Berne Copyright Convention, Universal Copyright Convention, and Pan-American Copyright Convention. No part of this book may be reproduced, stored in a retrieval system, or transmitted in any form, or by any means, electronic, mechanical, photocopying, recording or otherwise, without prior permission of the author.

Cover Art Design, 'Rainbow Wheel', by Carol McCloud@GalacticAlchemy.com
http://www.galacticalchemy.com

PROLOGUE

Until I set out on my guided journey at the age of 41, I had worked various jobs and spent three years as a student in two Universities.
 Years earlier I had expressed the wish to know as much as possible while on this planet. I had assumed that I would glean this knowledge from books, teachers, videos and movies. Assumptions, projections into the future while not knowing if they would or would not materialize, became one of the mental configurations I had to let go of.
 Why did I not embark on my journey earlier?
 I did not volunteer for this quest. When I became forty-one years old, an awareness of the corruption that influenced major decisions that were made contrary to the people's collective well-being, prompted me to throw in the societal towel. Nobody could convince me to continue to contribute my gifts and abilities to a system that benefited a handful of misguided people.
 Little by little, I came to understand how to fight for and regain my freedom from the matrix, and guide others who were pointed out to me. Rather than spending time in ashrams, yoga, meditation or spiritual centers, I hoofed it alone through nature and the cities of Europe as well as the United States with direct communications from my Higher Self and other aspects of Self in the timeless zones.
 Being my own (spiritual) home, clearly indicated in my natal astrological *Signature* that I chose for this

incarnation, over time it mattered not if I rested my head on a rock, in a jail cell or in a castle.

My mother's controlling behavior pattern inspired me to observe others as to discover that there are instigators who apply invisible, electronic means of controlling the population, such as putting people in a trance to make them do things they normally would not consider doing. Hardly capable of remembering or even understanding what it is they are doing in a dream-induced state, it is impossible for the controlled humans to even take responsibility for their own actions, a necessity on the road to Freedom!

With my mother as a role model, initially I adopted most of her pattern. It became the reason for me to tackle and eliminate that pattern to become the true individual I longed to BE.

My choice of labeling those who tried to derail me, the Simultaneous Spirit Suppressors, is based on their hive-mind behavior. That type of behavior has been taken on by many different types of simultaneous spirit incarnations, including such individuals as those who suffer from Asperger's syndrome, or different types of so-called autism, etc. or anyone who is a habitual TV watcher. I used the SSS delineation to differentiate the sequential incarnation from the simultaneous incarnation. The SSS identification is not intended to be an 'all-inclusive' label, or to pertain to behavior patterns as displayed by less mature simultaneous incarnations.

For me, the only way to be able to perceive what is *really* going on in the world is through doing inner work, sweep out the vibrational cobwebs or veils to build up inner strength. Progressively, when my inner battle between the mind and the spirit subsided into a *surrender* to my Higher Self, I perceived the world differently. Knowledge is earned and wisdom is learned. Applying that knowledge in many situations has shown me many new insights.

After my surrender in 1991, with my Higher Self taking over the reins, I lived according to the natural laws as described in The Handbook for a New Paradigm. This marked a total turn-over in my understanding of reality:

Law of Attraction (what you give is what you get)
Law of Intention (placing intent in creation of new experience)
Law of Allowance (releasing control and manipulation of beings and experience)
Law of Harmony & Balance (that which manifests when the others are applied)

Note- *As an aside I'd like to mention that I did this with the guidance of my Higher Self. I would not recommend this path to anyone who is less aware of their own body. I am describing observations made and lessons learned on my own specific path! Remember always, to trust in YOUR own higher self on your journey.*

Definition of terms
Higher Self = True Self
Light sider = Polarity that uses control mechanisms.
Dark sider = Polarity that may cloak itself in Light and uses control mechanisms or may be openly Dark.
Yin yang balance = Blending of Light and Dark energies
TRUE Balance = Optimum state of Being.
Guide = Aspect of Higher Self
OOB = Out Of Body
Chakras = Energy vortexes in the body
Cycle = an action comprised of a beginning, middle and end
Self-determined = Making decisions free from outside control.
Other-determined= Making decisions based on learned behavior or external control.

ACKNOWLEDGMENTS

Above all, I send my heartfelt thanks to John Chastain. Without loyal friends like Hildebrandt Delver, Neil Smith, Martin Ferguson, the late Lenie Thijssen, I would not be who I am today…Furthermore, to all my relations ….

TABLE OF CONTENTS

PROLOGUE
PART I   OTHER-DETERMINED
BEHAVIORS
PART II   THE QUEST
EPILOGUE

PART ONE

OTHER-DETERMINED BEHAVIORS

Many people have asked themselves at one time or another: why did I do that? Incoming negative thoughts or ones that stimulate desires for things or bodies that the mind/brain of the person naturally abhors, are conducted by others. Either electronically or telepathically, they do not originate by the self/Self, thus are other-determined.

ONE

I am a spiritual Guide with a Teacher who is a more advanced aspect of my Higher Self. What is the difference between a Teacher and a Guide?
A teacher in the physical or in the spiritual reality is not the same as a Guide. One can be a Guide in the physical reality or one can have a Guide in the spiritual reality. A Guide gives others guidance on a specific area of their journey, whatever that may be. Since I specialized in diminishing the influence of Suppressors of Simultaneous Spirits (SSS hereafter) I would mainly point out who it was in their immediate environment and how to start dealing with them. Guides can come and go on your journey. Think of a guide that travels with you when you are exploring a new territory. They are with you for that journey and then you part ways to go on new explorations.

A Teacher is more personal. They can be spiritual teachers that are, or are not in this reality. However, with a teacher we, as human beings, develop a personal relationship. They may be a teacher of life, a teacher of a specific aspect of life, or they could be a teacher of what not to do. They come in many forms: *when the student is ready, the Teacher will appear!* A teacher will always point out options without making the choice for you. A teacher will always reveal aspects of self that we might not wish to see.

For the first forty years of my life I received training from my invisible Guides (of whom I was not aware then) in the perception of differences and similarities among people, aliens, creatures connected to the Nature Spirit. I studied their behavior patterns while I learned how to get my emotions under control, a primary reason for incarnating on planet Earth. In tandem with stillness of mind, one will fade out of or extract themselves from the matrix in which we are imprisoned once we manage to master them. An interesting side effect of the 'hollow bamboo' state is the ability to make one-self invisible to others!

I did many different jobs to make a living, spending time with wealthy and poor people and those in between to get an impression of how the nations created a reality the masses would act out. Many books were explored reflecting philosophies in different cultures and times, in several languages, and other skills I needed to do my job.

Application ensued when I spent the next fourteen years traveling through the United States and Europe, making myself available to many people in a variety of situations. I also explored being a rebel, breaking rules of laws written by dark, self-serving politicians to gain access to jails to assist those that were kept out of sight behind bars. As a Guide I became an expert in reading intentions so I could give guidance to others in a specific area of their respective journeys.

In native societies, often animals are Guides for the simple reason they have specific messages or medicine for someone to breathe in and use on the journey at that moment. Many animals came to give me information I needed for myself as well as others but my main power animal or Guide is and always will be the Eagle.

As a Guide I practice non-attachment to people and things in order to be effective so my love/compassion can flow unchecked.
--

TWO

There is a difference between watching, and observing! Watching indicates a total withdrawal that has no intentional reason for becoming aware other than curiosity. Observing is done for the reason of using the knowledge gained for an intentional purpose.

As The Handbook for a New Paradigm states in its description of the Law of Allowance *'the composite of thoughts, opinions and attitudes of each individual generate the experience patterns of living. Through the flow of daily experiences these are filtered through this composite of each one's total collective experience..... When attitudes and opinions are deliberately programmed within a limited set of rigid guidelines, the activity level of the total pattern of experience begins to slow. This means that the guidelines are imposed, not by the individual through knowledge experienced into wisdom but by the beliefs imposed on the individual by those (s)he considers outside authorities. The pattern of each individual as a whole attracts to itself life experiences that resonate in harmony with that pattern. If a person desires some thing or some experience that does not resonate with that pattern, it is difficult, if not impossible to attract it. Two divergent patterns cannot blend cohesively. By honoring what IS, the Law of Attraction is invoked'.*

How is that individual pattern established? Of course, the answer could fill many books if explored in detail. From my own understanding gained from my personal experiences, I could clearly detect patterns put in operation by my parents' belief systems after I left them to find my way in the world. Had I stayed, it would have been virtually impossible to have gained the knowledge/insights I have gotten.

My first ally outside of the biological family, someone who helped me along on my chosen path, was a blind amateur astrologer who volunteered to do my horoscope, the astrological blueprint/pattern for my current lifetime. The revelations were so startling that I immediately signed up for a class to study it on my own which led to an entirely new awareness level. Endless debates about whether Astrology has any meaning for anyone are rendered moot if one takes the time to study it to see if it actually works or not. For me, patterns became visible that led to new knowledge.

That information led, in turn, to the purpose of finding out how to still my mind from unwanted, interfering thoughts; to getting my emotions under control to the extent of being able to choose not to react to situations that on the surface appeared peaceful but, for some reason, would get me upset. In other words, a true inner freedom that would lead to making self-determined decisions that were unassailable by outside mind-controls of any kind.

Alarmed by the nature of certain thoughts that erected real low-life images in my mind's eye that I did not originate, I knew there had to be some advanced technology pumping that into my head so I became determined to put a stop to it. An observing Guide should be free from those interfering controls so that they can be directed without interference by their Higher Self to learn about the mechanics and postures of life on Earth.

It is important to note that *the observer mode is an active one.* The keen observers are aware of the immediate surroundings as well as the role they play themselves; also how it coincides with information that becomes gradually available and its effect on the current reality! As seen from a spiritual point of view, the term re-incarnation only applies to those who live one life at the time which are not members of the human race. As Game players they *appear inside a human hologram* so they can blend in among humans who live simultaneously in different dimensional zones.

The main difference between the two factions is that the alien incarnation arrives with its memory lines open, knowing explicitly who they are while humans suffer from amnesia after entering the Game on Earth. There is no doubt that as far as a more comfortable existence is concerned, the aliens armed with their technologically advanced gadgets, are much better equipped to deal with survival issues than us.

However, it takes them a billion or, at the very least many lifetimes, of doing the same thing over and over again before the new realizations or AHA moments enlighten an area of their ways of doing things as dictated by a beehive mentality. Individualism is not a word that has any meaning in their vocabulary. In contrast, the daring, visionary specimens who arrive with nothing to hold onto but their distinct personalities are on the fast-track path that leads, depending on choices made along the way, to new insights that torch their paths toward a spiritual maturity the aliens can only hope to reach. That does not mean that the aliens are completely dumb. Their ceiling of potential awareness is just much lower than ours.

Basically, the whole Game is one huge arena filled with personalities who are infused by a variety of spirits that operate on different levels of awareness. The agenda of the aliens and their human allies, built upon the model of other planets, has been adhered to from the opening of the Game, thousands of years ago. It goes without saying that those players that have been able to circumvent the traps and boulders thrown on the rocky road by the opponents, by-passing them to a level where the aliens are incapable of following, laugh or shake their heads when they become aware of who is actually installing the mediocre puppets that run our societies. *If the interfering aliens were not here, however, we would not have had the opportunities for such rapid spiritual progress!*

Life is not a Game to the humorless New World Order proponents. They are convinced they live one life at the time (as noted, the aliens do), watch everything to make sure that they are in control, and attempt to prevent the bright rebels from **knowing who they really are!**

NWO proponents among the simultaneous spirits are those of the lower levels of awareness, the ones who are still confused, group-oriented, gophers for the sequential incarnations who put them in prominent positions where they execute their orders. They try to control our existence (the Game), predict everything that will happen, and set the outcome in advance. They are serious and determined about getting that outcome. They try to fix the future based on the past, identify with the body and are easily manipulated by fear and anything that will re-stimulate genetic programming and culturally traditional patterns. They are stuck in 'mind-body' dilemmas, dramas circulating around "life and death", and haven't a clue who they really are and why they're here. More than 90% of the planetary population operates from this perspective.

Spiritually mature incarnations enjoy being (pleasantly) surprised: it is about fun experiences. They know they are spiritual beings having one of many incarnational experiences. *The object of an advanced simultaneous spirit playing the Game is to experience, gain wisdom and leave, without attachment to the vehicles which permit experience to occur, or the emotional patterns which came with it.*

THREE

There are two ways of learning:
**1- The personality learns through doubts and fears. It seeks power through money accumulation and uses it to control through violence and destruction, freedom to buy whatever they want so they can do whatever they want.
2- The soul learns through wisdom, truth, and knowledge. The soul seeks inner freedom, freedom from mind control, DNA-programmed emotions and patterns that can be triggered by ads, music, scents, and thoughts.
3-Combined, the personality and soul create opportunities to have experiences that will eventually lead to the maturity of True Balance, the natural state of the Higher Self.**

In our Western cultures, we get bombarded with pictures on TV, in films and documentaries, according to the points of view of those who put out the material. It is easy to surmise that it is just someone's point of view, someone who may or may not be influenced by factions that have an agenda to benefit themselves rather than that of the individual viewer or society at large. Perceiving the subliminal messages in most TV programs, primarily of a sexual nature, I dropped the idiot box altogether. There are no new insights to be gotten from the ones who operate on the level of the two lowest chakras, representing survival and sex.

Even alternative sources in the media are not fool-proof against indoctrination on sub- as well as conscious levels but they present us with more interesting, intelligent topics that will stimulate new realizations.

One recent subtle AHA moment came when I heard an alternative broadcaster say that there were large areas of forests in India where nobody lives. For years my entire collection of TV images depicted ghettos, overcrowded cities, slums, poverty, Mother Teresa at work among the dying in the streets of Calcutta and just one statement changed that whole picture. It went POOF! A revelation! Even though it was a minor light bulb that went on in my head it was, nevertheless, an important one because it never dawned upon me that there was 'space, room' in India, a country that has not been on my itinerary.

During my quest, two decades of extensive traveling mostly throughout Europe and the United States, I applied/tested my book knowledge wherever I went. Based on earlier experiences with family members described later on, it led to detecting a pattern of identical behavior of reptilians living among us that infected the behavior of humans in every stratum of our societies. They apply their superior technology and use their hypnotic stares to derail weak, insecure people who they manipulate into doing their dirty work, subjugating the brighter individuals.

How many are there? Over the decades, my perception registered the pattern of one in five 'programmed humans or their alien handlers' since all of them had four people assigned to them so we can safely say that at least one of them infiltrates a family. The Fifth Element is a movie about a woman who represented the Creator faction but here we have a *fifth element* that represents the warden to our prisons.

The intention behind their actions is based on controlling the planet and everyone/everything on it. To accomplish this, they cannot allow Earthers (their derogatory term for us is Earthlings since they consider themselves superior) thus they work to prevent us from connecting to our Higher Selves. What better way to do so than to bully one loved member of a family to get the others in line as well.

The people they control and use as our mental prison wardens are not fully aware of their mission but ignorance is neither an excuse (it reflects victim consciousness) or bliss, reflecting naivety. That doesn't make it any easier to deal with them in everyday existence. Case in point was my own mother whose actions and contra-survival decisions actually piqued my curiosity as to why people do what they do:

She controlled every move I made behind a closed door policy of keeping most friends out, allowing only those persons to enter who would be sympathetic to her rules and point of view. Over time I learned to understand that her *Light-sider* attitude of "I only do it for your own good" covered an intent motivated by the desire to control. Why? That became one of the main questions I set out to answer.

When I questioned her about the decision she made not to send me to college, even though a scholarship had been in the offing, she simply explained years later that she did not want me to get too smart. She meant that she was afraid of losing control over me, something that happened anyway because I knew that she would continue to suppress me after she kept thwarting any opportunities that came my way!

I became aware of people who displayed a hive mentality without having any obvious need to develop as unique individuals. Individuality was discouraged by them, the collective order used as a model to kill any imagination, visionary insights or inventive changes. They attracted my attention because they were so different from what I stood for in my life: *promoting individual and spiritual freedom to BE what one chose to BE.*

The sinking feeling about the lack of opportunities for the best and brightest who wanted to actualize themselves, I got early in my teens when I observed the unfairness of the selection process in schools, the job market, the theater. Mediocre youth whose perceptive abilities are of a low caliber so they can easily be manipulated to appear as unstable people are given the opportunities to become stars. Oh yes, they can be talented and do a good job but the thing to remember is the level of their intangible attributes. How often do we see an innocent-looking young girl with a fantastic singing voice, for instance, suddenly turn into an over-sexed kitten overnight to please the crowds to activate their lower two chakras? *We humans strive to open up our heart, third eye and crown chakras!*

As an observer who is *in* the world but not *of* the world I like to say that there are so many human bodies available at present that it follows that there are different types of spirits giving them life. **We are not all the same!**

The main reason why the government of the USA is so successful in taking its citizens' freedoms away so easily, is the influx of masses of nature spirit creatures who were animals in their previous lives and still live by the law of the jungle combined with an exodus from Third World countries of illiterate, irresponsible people who merely come to benefit from the white man's riches. Since their main interest is focused on food, shelter and procreation, all a self-serving politician has to do is to promise those minions what they want to get their votes. No wonder that the beleaguered Americans cannot organize a revolution with people who understand what is really going on and are willing to make sacrifices, right?

The aliens and their human allies select spokespeople of a low level of awareness to reassure the minority of brilliant and fast-track simultaneous spirit incarnations with *the oft-repeated lie that they are here to assist us.* Of course, they are not available to answer questions such as 'why are they hiding? Why are they so arrogant to think we need their assistance? Or, what are they doing here? Since they are polarity-driven by the intent of 'doing it for our own good, they represent the *Light-sider* faction. If they are here to plunder the planet or subjugate us into slavery, well, I know you'll get the point!

One can also comprehend how it would have been possible for groups of them, working together in secret societies or in more overt groups like the self-appointed Illuminati, using Astrology in secret and their available memories to plan out hundreds of years of events that stage a total take-over, planned under the innocent-sounding heading of The New World Order.

Now we arrive at the answer to the question of why are they doing all of that? If you know your Higher Self, like the aliens do, you have a huge advantage over those who do not. But their level of awareness is devoid of compassion and/or empathy, generally speaking, so they can only act out desires and mentally driven decisions that are in tune with that level. Evil? They merely respond to their polarity-driven Dark- or Light-sider nature. If it dictates it needs to be in control, it will do so.

Too bad they resort to such measures as food poisonings, air pollution like Chemical-trails, legal and illegal drugs, unhealthy waters and tampered-with seeds for our food to make our lives as miserable as possible. Anything that makes us happy, mellow, amicable, and considerate is usually outlawed by the humorless people who are assigned to most roles of authority.

Why? They cannot allow us to BE so they cannot apply the Law of Allowance; they fail to understand that a compassionate individual will not pose a threat to them because they can only see themselves and they know what they are like: control-freaks. They act like spoiled teenage children of reptilians…but the 'selfie-generation' nowadays is another wildcard invention, as diabolical as anything...

FOUR

Simultaneous Spirit-Suppressors

My attitude towards these *simultaneous spirit-suppressors* as I will refer to them (SSS for short) changed over time. They are strategically placed among us to ensure that agenda-approved belief systems are instilled in our children, setting the latter on a course to ensure compliancy to their approved programs. They are accurately referred to as *sequential spirits* because they have one incarnation at a time with their memories intact from previous lives. Nowadays they are so desperate to remain in control they feed our youngsters drugs like Ritalin to ensure indoctrination/conformity from an early age on. It puts an end to any inclination a youngster may have to strike out on her own to explore new areas of life.

Being denied the opportunity for people to find out Who They Really Are without mediators in churches or on TV is, in my opinion, the most heinous crime against us; yet it does not show up in any guidance book of any religion. So who do you think has written those books? Writers inspired by whom?

My upbringing was colored by the tenets of The Bible. Due to its incomprehensibly complex language, it created more confusion than anything else. For me, the bottom line was that nobody in my immediate environment behaved according to the Commandments. In fact, they used it to cover their mistakes or 'sins' with mental explanations that defied any belief. It also proved a fairly usable control-mechanism for mother who would delight in putting the fear of God in my younger brother and I. Fortunate for me, abilities such as going out of body steered me away from conformity based on lies unlike my gullible sibling. I ditched conformity in my teens along with its entire belief system to open up to new venues.

That arrived in the form of a blind social worker who had many braille books in Astrology that assisted him to predict a course of action I would have never dreamed possible! Instead of marrying my beloved fiancée I was ditched by him on instigation of his mother, ending up on a plane that brought me to the East Coast of the United States as an au pair girl.

With Pluto in the second House of my natal astrological chart, a position that requires one to re-invent herself every so often (Jeffrey Wolf Green-Pluto: The Evolutionary Journey of the Soul), I intuitively started to let go of beliefs, people, ideas, etc. to open up to new concepts reflecting a different point of view. With a Moon squeezed in between the Sun and Neptune in an intercepted Libra in the fourth house and a South Node in Scorpio, indicating the past in other lives, staying put was not likely.

A few years earlier, a stint in the Dutch Air Force where I acquired some stability and discipline took the edge of my bafflement and fears surrounding others who displayed a behavior pattern similar to my own mother's. I say similar here and not identical because to her it was an acquired behavior that slowly eroded her spirit. As any shaman can contest, people lose soul pieces when they are in traumatic situations they don't want to deal with. She and my father (who was mostly absent during my life in spirit as well as body) lived through WWII in Holland, not knowing for five years whether they would live or die.

The eclectic family had members such as sailors, dock workers, white collar workers, psychics, artists as well as a cousin who became the first female president of a bank. A micro-cosmos, together they offered a view of the different players in the Game. The only one with whom I had a spiritual connection was my maternal grand-mother who died when it was time for me to leave for the United States, freeing me to continue on. (As a side-note, I met her again after she incarnated again at the age of thirteen, one of my guiding numbers in this life!)

As a mature spirit I incarnated with some abilities that allowed me to re-gain memories fast; for instance, when my younger brother arrived I recalled having been in many male bodies before the present female one, a body I had to learn to love and deal with over time. It certainly has more restrictions than a male body and is less powerful in its expression. Once the body surrenders to spirit the whole comparison between the two becomes moot. The idea is to reach a state of yin yang balance, integrating both male and female energies.

It was a revelation to me that strangers behaved in a similar manner as Mom, propelled by fear, the opposite of love or compassion. Mercury in Scorpio, the sign par excellence governing sleuths or nosy people, also positioned in the fourth house trine my Uranus in the 12th House of the Higher Self, was piqued to dig deeper into the matter of the mysterious mass-induced, transfixed behavior by those who were, in essence, spiritually in diapers!

The major choice we have to make in our lives is to side with the 'service to self' polarity or the one that is 'a service to others'. We need to experience, live through, both sides, on our way to the Balance of our Higher Selves which is, in essence, us. It should be obvious that it takes more than one life to be able to do that, steadily maturing to a point where **we are free to leave for good.**

FIVE

Service to Others

The 'service to others' choice I made during this life and my desire to understand my true self resulted in the endurance of unpleasant situations before and during my quest when my Higher Self tested me on my resolve to be free. Whatever we caused in some lives will make us the effect in other ones. How could we possibly understand the pain we cause to others if we do not return to have that done to us so we can gain knowledge of how we are responsible for our own actions? There are no short-cuts.

We cannot buy technological gadgets that will project us into a state of awakening on a permanent basis. Therefore, it is the most rewarding yet most difficult thing to do for a person to remove the veils to find the Truth, to act in a self-enlightening way. You know you are mature when you arrive at the point in the progression where the value of having adversaries, people who give you a hard time, becomes very clear. Instead of experiencing negative emotions such as anger, frustration, grief or apathy one can thank the other for the opportunity to grow. **Try it sometimes, it is really liberating!**

I went through many stages where my point of view changed, a sign of success on the rocky road of spiritual progression, and I had to adapt to the new way(s) of looking at people and situations. After doing extensive inner work for years I saw the SSS type as a pesky fly, a nuisance, boring, and inconsequential, no longer capable of keeping me pre-occupied with thoughts of vengeance. Then, after my quest that lasted close to two decades, I managed to detach myself completely on an emotional level. I lost interest in them, regarding them as another form of human that happened to be living here. They had no longer any power over me and my purpose: I became invisible to them.

Unlike the popular images of ogres, criminals or patients in insane asylums as promoted by the truly insane (this is my perception), they appear as angelic, pretty women and handsome men who are impossible to blame because one can never quite put the finger on what's not right with them. Their auras do not emit vibrations that can be picked up as a warning for the unsuspecting average person, unfortunately. Most of them have prominent positions in our societies, leaders who are disdainful towards the citizenry that pays their salaries and outings. They are parasites who know exactly how to create the image of hard-working, caring cornerstones of the communities. **They are not**.

They went so far as to create a controlled media of dense individuals fueled by fears to fool us: anchors in the daily newsroom who use hand gestures to sway our subconsciously directed opinions, ads filled with sublime messages with the purpose of having a few control the many. It will be the end of the Game of Life as it is, because once we are micro-chipped or constantly stopped in our endeavors, there will be no other opportunities for us to learn anything worthwhile.

They are functioning on a level of awareness where their interests are mired in body-related endeavors and sensations. Earth is the only planet in our galaxy in quarantine; in other words, the average person living here is not aware of what's going on other planets or knows whether there is even life on other worlds! How easy it is then to tell tales! World orders are ruling other planets so it follows that the intention of certain groups of aliens to create another type of human, one that is more docile that acts on a predetermined set of behavior traits, is very real.

How can they possibly control free Beings who have no need of outside authorities? Agent Smith regarded the captured Morpheus in the movie The Matrix as a virus, a contamination because he was incapable of being free! Prince Philip, the Prince consult of the Queen of England said that the 'wanted to re-incarnate as a virus' to decimate the world population! Of course, this remark was presented by him 'to contribute something to solve overpopulation'.

SIX

Mind Control
No peace of mind, no spiritual expression
Without free thought, no free will
Without free will, no spiritual expression
How to recognize a simultaneous spirit-suppressor (SSS)?

Below is the list of behavior traits I observed in humans programmed to function as obstacles to our individual spiritual progression. Thanks to the constant exposure to the ones in our midst, appearing self-confident, intimidating behind closed doors, exploiting our fears, many people have taken on some or many of these traits. Thus, new generations are indoctrinated in what is 'normal' by the ones who are anything but normal as seen from a spiritual point of view.

Fortunately, more perceptive people-and their number is growing- can clearly see how insane our self-appointed leaders operate on a visible level. It is always harder to notice it in one's immediate environment due to the involvement of the personality with its emotions and (sub)-conscious minds unless they are particularly adept to vibrations. It can be fun to discover any of the traits on the list below within oneself so they can be erased or modified to open up to the incarnated spirit.

Behavior Traits of the SSS
If number ONE does not apply to you, read on.
1)   They are perfect in their own minds.

2) They use gophers to do their dirty work.
3) They rely on technology.
4) They are control freaks.
5) They are master manipulators.
6) They hint. This way the person will think he/she does something voluntarily.
7) Sex and money are their prime control mechanisms.
8) They surprise you at inopportune moments.
9) They are gossip mongers.
10) Their reflective, glassy eyes transfix their victims.
11) They are very convincing.
12) They are petrified of being exposed.
13) *They are bound by rules*!

SEVEN

1.   They are perfect in their own minds.
How can it be different? An inability to take responsibility for one's own actions is near absent in those that seek power and control to command the rest of us so they can tell us what to do and not to do. It is a direct violation of the Law of Allowance.

In comparison, a person who knows himself for who he truly IS, has no ambition or need to use his fellow men as servants: his friends will voluntarily assist him. Only ego-centric people with a malefic intent make others labor to pay for the horrors of unnecessary wars in which he does not personally participate, while he lives on easy street. Heroes like the King of Rohan in The Lord of Rings, fighting in front of his troops usually only appear in fantasy novels.

In my own visions I see circles where two people are standing next to one another, looking alike; they may even be twins. One journeyed around the circle, her balanced outlook colored with patience by the many experiences she gathered; her knowledge turned into wisdom. She remains silent. The other has yet to get started but is loudly proclaiming how she is to be trusted by anyone who puts his faith into her because she is perfect, she knows it all.

Aside from the occasional exceptions especially in indigenous tribes and non-Western societies, the current reflection of our collective psyche is represented by the emperor without clothes: politicians whose mouths work better than any other part of their bodies, spouting promises they never fulfill once (s)elected to their respective offices. Make no mistake about it, the control freaks at the top of the corporate pyramids will not allow an idealistic person who takes his responsibility to the people serious, to become the leader of any country. It follows that the voting process is a hoax and that a vote goes to evil or lesser evil, something I forfeited in favor of renunciation of the government altogether. However, I will use my right to vote in the Galactic Federation where, kings and paupers alike, we each have **ONE** vote.

It would be helpful if the SSS would hang a sign around their necks but no such luck; just the (fake, reflective) light in their eyes is there to see for those who cannot be hypnotized by their stares! Even our intuition or gut instinct can lead us astray as they do not emit warning vibes to alert the potential victim because they mostly appear as intelligent people who are *very convincing*. But intelligence without compassion is insanity: it has to be connected to the heart!

Tomes have been written about how the 'Devil' looks anything but the hoofed, horned creature when its energies work through people as well as charming children. Thus, most of us are 'attracted' to the ones who are depicted with a halo around their heads even though their personal stories are made up of lies, distilled from stories of others who earned their integrity. Once we awaken spiritually, we can no longer be led by the nose like *sheeple*, believing the lies they tell!

Since we are plagued by personal doubts, insecurities, guilt complexes, actions we are not proud of, emotional outbursts, all weaknesses that can and will be exploited by those 'who are perfect in their own minds' it can be stated that someone who chooses the rocky road of individuality rather than the smooth road of conformity, can look upon them as reversed role models: how not to BE. A yardstick that may lead to the question Shakespeare asked: to BE or not to BE.

If it would be that simple, there is no reason to elaborate on this dilemma but, of course, it isn't. Since we are operating on different levels of awareness, it follows that the denser varieties of our species, people who are mostly influenced by the vibrations of the lower three chakras will be far more at risk than those who earned an expansion of their awareness, a higher more joyful vibration.

Regardless of the failure of intuition to immediately sense if there is something awry, the more astute person will in time pinpoint the intent of the angelic creature, male or female, when it is composed of fear. Since we are prone to 'giving others the benefit of the doubt', disbelieving that a malefic intent exists if we have never explored our own, the time span of recognizing the difference between us and 'them', varies. Someone who awakened spiritually to put their True Self in control of the personality rather than vice versa –which is the case in most people- can almost immediately spot that intent while the next step up is a total lack of interest in the subject. Since it was part of my individual journey to go through all of these phases

I can state that one will reach a point where their presence (aura) simply makes the simultaneous spirit-suppressor (SSS) leave the area, never bothering them.

Their rate of success in collapsing the present day reality where visionary, individualistic people still can choose their experiences, is notably with weak-willed people or youngsters who yet have to discern whom to trust. For that reason, they can be found in charge of governments, corporations, schools, hospitals, court rooms, jails, and mental institutions. Unfortunately, many people suffer from their spirit-suppressing actions without having a clue what is happening, blaming mostly themselves for their problems and misfortunes because 'the ones who are perfect in their own minds' tell them to do so.

Nurse Ratchet in the movie *One Flew over the Cuckoo's Nest* is a solid example of the simultaneous spirit-suppressor: Jack Nicholson plays Randall McMurphy, an upbeat inmate who is put in a psychiatric institution where he attempts to make his days bearable by putting the fun back into the lives of the miserable motley crew of men incarcerated there. Nurse Ratchet, played by Louise Fletcher, is in firm control of the ward. Soft spoken, agreeable on the surface, she has three assistants (her gophers) who do her bidding to keep the men under control.

Randall makes the men laugh while Ratchet puts the fear in them. When a vote is requested to see a baseball game she manages to let them think that she will finally consent to it in a 10 to 9 vote, then she turns around to point out that the rules will not allow her to turn on the TV.

At one point a patient asks for his cigarettes. She berates him and refuses to budge. He protests saying "*I ain't no* little *kid.*" She merely smirks at him like the underling she considers him to be. Billy, a young man who stutters whenever she addresses him, kills himself after he had a romantic interlude with a woman and she caught him. For a few minutes he lost his stutter but it returned when she asked him what his mother would think of him? "Don't tell her," he begs her. "But, your mother and I are good friends," she explains softly. He goes on his knees to beg her to reconsider (giving his power away). She sends him to the doctor of a special treatment. He cuts his wrists.

Later in the movie we learn that the men, with exception of Randall, are in the ward voluntarily. Most of the audience had assumed they had to be there, there was no choice. Questions arise that will be answered by studying the list of behavior traits that nurse Ratchet displays: What is keeping them there? Why do they go there? How come they allow themselves to be mistreated by one female control freak? Did she know exactly what she was doing or was she programmed to promote a hidden agenda?

Another glowing example of a simultaneous spirit-suppressing representative is a woman who shows up in the fifth Harry Potter movie:

At Hogwarts, Harry learns that Dolores Umbridge, played by Imelda Staunton, who is an employee to the Minister of Magic, Cornelius Fudge, will be the new Defense against the Dark Arts teacher. Umbridge and Harry clash, as she, like Fudge, refuses to believe that Voldemort has returned. She punishes Harry for his rebellious outbursts by having him write "I must not tell lies" with a blood quill that carves the phrase into his skin with his own blood. She also refuses to teach her students how to perform defensive spells, prompting Harry, Ron and Hermione to form their own Defense against the Dark Arts group, called Dumbledore's Army. Many students sign up, including Neville Longbottom, Fred and George Weasley and Luna Lovegood. The club meets in the Room of Requirement to learn and practice Defense spells at Harry's direction.

    As Dumbledore and Harry are not matches for Dolores, she gets expelled from the school grounds only to pop up once more in the next movie, presiding in a court room. Again, Harry disables her.

    Since we are not walking around with magic wands we shall have to create other methods to silence them or get rid of them.

EIGHT

2. They use gophers to do their dirty work.
In order to maintain the illusion of being the ideal role model, perfect in their role of citizen, there is little to nothing the SSS will do overtly against the rules of society. Thus, in order to continue their work unnoticed and unobstructed they need weak-willed people to do their dirty work even if it involves violent crimes. Of course, as they are bound by rules they are not free to do so themselves. Thus they pick humans who gradually mimic and adopt most of the collective hive-mind traits, one who is used to further demean the others.

The real crime here is on an inner level: making it difficult, if not close to impossible, for someone to advance spiritually. Actions that include gossip to ruin one's reputation, to manipulate the victim's (*always* a simultaneous incarnation) attention, to play on their weaknesses, and to introvert someone to the point where guilt for bygone mistakes disables them momentarily, are part of their endeavor to halt the progress of others. This form of mental blackmail glues the chosen controllable 'victim' to the SSS, a handler the person will never be able to get rid of, unless there is a drastic change of point of view based on inner work. Since the perception is suppressed, the victim will not be able to recognize the need for inner work so here we have a catch-22. However, once ready for inner freedom, there are plenty of perceptive counselors, astrologers, and other professionals who specialize in empowering the individual.

Of course, there are many control-freaks in these professions so one must be careful in the selection of them. Going from one handler to the next is not uncommon. The Law of Attraction is at work here!

NINE

One simultaneous spirit suppressor's influence
The following is a description of my first experiences dealing with a girl who befriended the cousin I grew up with in the same neighborhood. She entered her life at the age of thirteen to demand her undivided attention. No longer could I exchange a few words privately with my family member as she popped up every time I visited her, with my cousin's "approval." In other words, my cousin became *the perfect gopher*.

In my teens, struggling with raging hormones and developing womanhood, my perception unveiled an image of an upright turtle without shell, standing on her hind legs, behind the new girl's pleasant-looking face on a shapely figure. My cousin's pet was a turtle so it was acceptable for her to have a girlfriend who resembled one, my mind illogically concluded.

The intrusion of this girl in our private lives may be compared to a cuckoo whose egg hatches in a reed warbler's nest, only to grow strong to twice the size of the bird who is feeding it. My cousin metamorphosed from a caring, shy girl into a sarcastic, bitchy gopher for her seemingly self-confident friend who proceeded to coerce her into using her resources and monies to support her. The clincher was that the latter's ability to transfix her victim with a particular gaze made my cousin think that she was doing everything of her own volition.

For me, not so easily enchanted by the new arrival, her presence opened up the new area of having to withstand her and my cousin's newly discovered bully sessions: they cornered me like an animal to probe and harass me till I broke out in tears. No matter what I said, they found something funny about it that translated into hysterical laughter, the kind that gave you the feeling you had 'loser' stamped on your forehead, born to provide amusement to superior people.

With mixed emotions, sad to lose my cousin to this stranger, angry at her failure to perceive what she got herself into, I mentally tried to soften the blow of the shock-effect emanating from her perpetual presence. *If the mind does not have a frame of reference for something, it invents an explanation to appease itself in order to be able to function within the confines of the illusion we commonly refer to as our reality.*

Feeling ashamed for no plausible reason, I asked several people what they thought of her. She was generally liked, the light of the party, a fun person to be with! They alerted me as to not to pursue the matter as a topic of conversation. Besides, the turtle-image I saw inside the human body I assumed to be imaginary as nobody else could perceive it. Only many years later, after perceiving many of the reptilians, I accepted it as a fact. **My curiosity limited itself to the unmistakable clue that her behavior pattern resembled that of my mother's.**

I began to watch her. According to the beautiful woman du jour image, she came close: fashion carefully duplicated from girlie magazines, make-up ditto, no visible scars or asymmetrical body-shape. How could a gorgeous woman like her make me feel so bad about myself? She reinforced my mother's constant judgment that I was an average-looking woman, nobody special, but it was purely based on my physical appearance. To further imprint on my psyche not to get any ideas about being special, all of my clothes came from the pages of dated sewing magazines, their patterns used by mother to stitch them together on her machine.

    My initial attempts to inform my cousin of the possibility that she was being bamboozled by the new girl-friend, totally backfired. For starters, I was not sure what I was looking at so I could not explain it fully. I did not even get a bad feeling about her yet I knew there was something radically amiss. Later on, after years of dealing with this type, it occurred to me that it all boiled down to intent! And how many people are capable of reading intent?

    The new girl laughed a lot about hapless, bewildered people, the type of humor I could not share with her. I reasoned that my cousin preferred her company to mine because she was happier and better-looking than I so the negative emotion of jealousy became an issue for me to deal with. Her mental cruelty, cloaked in the ever-smiling face, seemed acceptable to most people who came briefly in contact with her.

    When I felt bad, the only person I could talk to was my maternal grandmother but she was not around a lot. She was just a sounding board because she would never say anything bad about anyone, including my mother who had lost my trust after some devastating incidents. She provided me, just by being herself, with a terminal of comparison: *I felt safe in her presence.*

My own mother reflected the same behavior as to how to drive others, especially her own husband and children, to depths of despair. Thus, I stood on the verge of the abyss of plunging into the same pattern that was held before me as the way to be and act were it not for a gnawing feeling inside that persisted. This feeling alerted me to the idea that all was not well, definitely contrary to my own sense of wanting to be treated with kindness and love. The constant verbal harassing by my mother that put me in a perpetual no-win situation- because I could never do anything right in her eyes- got exacerbated by the bully sessions by my hypnotized cousin and her new sidekick. The feelings they evoked were awful, dense, like sinking in a mudflat.

People changed around the new girl and mother and not for the better. My alcoholic uncle hugged her a lot with abandon while my aunt, suffering from narcolepsy, a disease that made her fall asleep at odd moments, stayed awake when she came to visit. Then my uncle, whose courage was fueled by a daily quart of whiskey, got brazen enough to extend his new hugging hobby to me while, on one horrible occasion, he gave me a French-style kiss as a bonus.

Talk about shock effects and a betrayal of trust to get initiated into the realm of sexual desire by a drunken relative; it is an emotional whammy at the tender age of 13. The whole affair left a bitter taste in my mouth. It occurred to me then that the reason children do not get adequate sexual education in school is to prevent them from identifying their pedophile predators' actions and intentions. Speaking entirely for myself, the contact made me shudder. No one witnessed it; I didn't have a word for that kiss but my gut instinct classified it as an assault.

My cousin's individuality slowly but steadily eroded under the pressure of the SSS's demands of conformity to her own behavior pattern. Since then my cousin and I grew up…..apart from each other. She never shook the monkey off her back and, until this very day forty-some years later, is the reed warbler who keeps feeding the cuckoo, not suspecting her friendship is a one-sided affair. One by one, she adopted the behavior traits I put on the SSS behavior list.

Twelve years later, after I had moved to the USA for a decade, I naively asked for her assistance for the first time ever. As a trained accountant, she used her financial expertise to become a loan shark. After all, she needed extra money to buy whatever the SSS desired. Unaware of this, thinking she would be finally free from her, I accepted her offer to pay for a one-way ticket for me to fly from Florida to the Netherlands. She charged me twice the price of the ticket. Awaiting me at the airport with her gopher-husband she ordered me to give her my passport as collateral.

It was nothing short of amazing what unfolded over the next few days. In hindsight it made me decide never to borrow any money from anyone for reasons of limiting my freedom. That decision curbed my desires for luxury items to 'do with whatever I got', discipline myself not to want for more, to not allow anyone to exercise control over me with a piece of identification that meant little to my True Self so the cousin became a catalyst for me: *her actions created the adverse effect they were designed to do.* Instead of feeling bad or guilty, I became determined to set boundaries for the people who I would allow to get close to me so; in other words, I started to reclaim my own power!

Staying with a friend from London in a rooming house on one of the canals, I experienced the following scenario with my family after my extended absence: My cousin called my British friend at his place of employment to let me know that my only brother had perished in a car accident. It is debatable whether my friend did not get the message right but, later on, after having absorbed the first shock of grief, it turned out to be her brother: my other cousin. In the southern part of the country, he died in a freak accident two days before the birth of his daughter.

Grasping the opportunity to further alienate me from my family, my mother had spread the rumor that my presence in the country had caused the accident. My crime consisted of the audacity to leave the dysfunctional family to carve out a life of my own and the crabs were busily pulling me back into the bucket.

As I had dedicated myself to healing my past to open up to my spirit more, I was convinced that my Higher Self, appearances to the contrary, would take care of me. That type of surrender has never failed me because it has shown me who *really* is in charge of my life.

    Reconciling myself to the idea that I would have to stay around for a while, working a temporary job in a bank to repay my cousin her money, I answered an ad in which a man asked for suggestions on how to travel through the United States. He liked my pointers and paid my debt after I consented to being his companion for a couple of weeks on his trip: I got my passport returned and left.

    The SSS mindset is remorseless and cruel. For years I witnessed my cousin fall prey to it. The result was an arrogant control freak devoid of any compassion or remorse; a cold-blooded and cruel predator in search of her victim's weak spots in order to energetically destroy him or her.

    We met for the last time about forty years later. Time has a peculiar way of disappearing when one meets people from the past. I changed a lot but it remained unnoticed by her because she had remained the same. People on a higher advanced awareness level can see the ones that follow, having been through the stages on those legs of the journey but, vice versa, it is impossible for them to see the higher expression.

    She contrasted sharply with my simple style of dress flashing an unnatural, salon created suntan that left parts of her neck lily-white. She wore a beaver fur coat, and formed fists to show her eight fingers bedecked with gold rings somewhat reminiscent of a street fighter who is ready to hit you in the choppers.

She bought me a cell phone so I could keep in touch with her, or so she said. The real reason was that she enjoyed hearing about my misery while I had to stay in a home for the homeless, a place upon which the Dutch do not look kindly. Never mind, I went where I felt I had to go, following synchronicities, heart, and feelings, at the tail end of a long quest that changed my life.

One room in the place had been designated to women. Besides myself, there were two others, one of whom was schizophrenic. The latter would search through my possessions and run over the beds in the middle of the night. I practiced the Law of Allowance without protest. She considered me her best friend for the time we spent together.

Every day my suppressed cousin/gopher called to find out how my days were spent, fishing for details she could relate to her handler. Without asking, I knew that the SSS girlfriend monitored her, ensuring my cousin's method of victimization which was now ineffective. And, yes, her proposal of moving me to her summer cottage on the coast sounded too good to be true, but I went along with it, knowing it to be the only way I could get reacquainted with my estranged brother.

And, who just happened to have bought the summer house behind the one my cousin owned? 'My girlfriend will take care of you', she told me, looking for the missing signs of anxiety on my face like the old days. When she noticed my eyebrows lift in amazement she quickly added that there was another couple who would assist me as well. I nodded, wise to the fact that they would also be 'enemies' who would report every move I made. As soon as she lifted her heels I chose my own contact to assist me in case of need.

After all those years I noticed that her laughter after humoring me now included the sharp shriek of a soul in distress. She was so walled off by her arrogance and disdain for me that it would have been moot to attempt to assist her. She chose a life marked by service to Self. Kindness does not resonate within the reptilian brain; it is regarded as a weakness. Affinity or Love is a higher vibrating emotion that is out of reach for them. That does not prevent them, however, from speaking the words many of us like to hear: I love you.

During this stay her gopher husband was allowed to spend some moments alone with me as long as he reported everything we did together via the cell phone he carried along. He attempted to mimic the two women's habit of ordering me around (in vain) and actually gave a treat I had bought for myself, to the girlfriend living behind the cottage. I observed!

It became an extra-ordinary exercise in patience for me to be with them until I realized that I did not have to tolerate them anymore as I had passed my Higher Self's test: no matter what they did to solicit a reaction out of me, I remained neutral.

She took me shopping. I had to sit in a chair, watch her parade new outfits, and then tell her which ones to buy in an upscale department store. She spent a fortune on a new wardrobe. Later, when we passed a market stall with inferior grade clothes, she asked me if I cared for a cheap t-shirt. This tactic was meant to make me feel like an underling but I was no longer the mentally abused teenager; I was now a mature adult with an integrated personality who looked upon her pathetic actions with a sad heart.

One of the easiest ways to control people is to keep them poor; then make them believe they cannot have a life if they're not part of a consumption society that charges money for everything. When my cousin offered me financial assistance I smelled a rat, recalling my prior experience with the airline ticket. She let me know that she had found a room for me and drove me to the house. The place was a mess- a pile of dishes in the kitchen, half of the carpet gone in the room that was empty, hardly any furniture in the living room. A Moroccan girl with bleach blonde hair and a huge cleavage, French-speaking, and a Moroccan man with shifty eyes met with us.

    Any sensitive person would have immediately concluded that, maybe, it was a house designed for shady dealings, prostitution, and drugs? Never one not to take control of a situation where she could get the glory of attention, my cousin took pen and paper to hand to jot down what pieces of furniture to take out of her late mother's worthless heirlooms. "So, what do you think?" she asked me, cheerfully, on the way back to the car. As if that matters, I thought, but said: "I don't trust him." "Oh, I do," she countered, wanting to move me in fast.

    She had kept in touch with my brother who showed up at the right moment to save me from a precarious, illegal move by pointing out a couple of clauses in Dutch Law. Fortunate for me, he showed solidarity with me after all those years. One practical observation became the definitive factor: all the Moroccan had to do for me to become instantaneously homeless without any recourse to redress, was to change the lock. I agreed, and sighed with relief when she was finally forced to abort her absurd plan.

Nevertheless, she retaliated by stealing the money I had gotten from welfare for moving, regardless of the fact that she knew me to be penniless and that her own monthly income exceeded ten times the meager amount I had been allotted. The only reason I did not get into an argument is because I knew I would give my power away rather than endure it. *This moment too shall pass*, I reminded myself.

Every weekend my cousin and her husband moved me from the summer house to their apartment where I was expected to do cleaning duties like Cinderella while they cavorted with the girl-friend and her hapless, weak-willed husband. Then, on Sunday night, I had to take the train and bus back to the cottage. Rest was not permitted on her agenda of re-introducing me to Dutch society.

Next I had to deal with her proposal to buy a summer house that was too decrepit to be lived in and marked for demolition as her solution to my housing 'problem'. Without blinking an eye, she proceeded to offer me a loan to buy the cottage in the exact amount she had dis-appropriated from me for moving. How crazy can someone get without knowing it, I marveled? No, I said simply, knowing that the rest of the day would be ruined for me. Her inability to accept my refusal to any of her insane suggestions or "self-sacrificing" offers of help, led to more irrational behavior.

    Soon she stopped near another cottage to initiate a conversation with a blonde woman, letting me stand there as adornment on our way to a market. Then she proceeded to make me wait at almost every stall where she feigned interest in trivial items, picking them up to show off her gold rings/manicured nails, then insisting on ordering a glass of wine for me instead of a cup of tea or coffee at 11:00 a.m. Her latest parade of victims for my cousin the victimizer, now acting as the gopher of a SSS, she found in AA gatherings. I refused to drink the wine.

    Curious, I asked her husband why he stayed with her, enduring all the putdowns, staged plays of sexual coyness, where she actually imitated the SSS girlfriend by trying to hypnotically transfix him with her eyes: then if he was behaving like the pet she mistook him for, she rewarded him by squeezing her body lengthwise against his while placing tiny kisses with pouted lips on his mouth, and... here I have no clue what went through her or the other ones' head.

    He answered that he liked the apartment, daily food on the table and her car. Besides, she does better financially than I do, he added with a wink as if none of us knew that as an unskilled laborer your income was in a lower bracket than that of an accountant. He probably missed most of the innuendos, putdowns, and sarcasms directed at him, or he simply didn't care, like the free-roaming wolf who turned into a trained pet to get a bite to eat. People have sold their souls or given their power away for less.

The bully sessions were still in full swing. Recalling the insecure teenage girl who would burst out in tears, I marveled at my detachment when they did it again. The whole identical scenario played itself out again:

"Ah, and my cousin is here, too," I heard my cousin shriek, opening the door for the girlfriend who wore the same type of clothes as in the past. I imagined the winks they exchanged anticipating their little show. Led like a calf to the slaughter, I sat down on the couch between the two tormentors. I felt remarkably cheerful and listened to the clichés they exchanged so I remarked upon them. My cousin lowered her head and, not missing a clue, the girl-friend continued the conversation with me when my cousin could not fulfill her old role. The shrieks of laughter had died!

Two days later I invited the girlfriend over to have a glass of wine with me. My prior resentment at giving the SSS-type items or gifts I had overcome. We had almost the same conversation as forty years before. She even used her old trick of leaving an item behind, her sunglasses. All of them sport a certain modus operandus, a gimmick if you will, that they keep repeating. This one left items behind and then would complain about it being stolen or not returned. I ran after her to return it before she set me up for another unexpected visit to "catch" me.

During my last weekend in my cousin's apartment something happened that was quite out of the ordinary. A stained glass door, separating the hallway from the rooms, out of the blue, broke into pieces. There was no draft, no ghost, and I sat quietly on the couch in the living room, reading a book. Amused, I imagined how that story would come across: well, it just shattered. She mentioned before how it had shattered several times before, a gale of wind responsible for the carnage. My spirit-guide shattered it, to punish her while matching her reality since it had occurred before!

"What happened here?" they asked before crossing the threshold into a sea of broken glass. Their blank faces registered little as they tiptoed over the pieces. They expressed disbelief, of course, at my honest version of how it occurred. "Glass does not break in smithereens by itself," I heard her think, where is the sledgehammer? Without missing a beat, she claimed that the restoration would cost the exact amount of the money she had taken from me as if she would have been inclined to return it to me later on. Yeah, right. Since she was insured for that type of damage, it meant double the money for her.

I shook my head, glad that money would never get that kind of hold over me. Glad also that I could perceive the spiritual quicksand in which her true self sunk deeper every day, oblivious to its position, while she lived under the illusion she was in charge of her faculties, her environment and her life, a life of lies.

TEN

3) They rely on technology and controlling others with it.

Faster and faster do the electronic gadgets get launched to a human population that is spiritually not ready to integrate them into its existing form of society. Over the past five decades I went from a manual typewriter to computers that defy the imagination, taking over just about everything we used our brains for: adding, subtracting, etc. In most stores, we now have operators who are completely dependent on computers. Once the computer goes down, the person behind the cash register is helpless as simple arithmetic is a skill she did not develop.

We went from cable, to satellite and now High-Definition TV's that may become mandatory in every home. Why? The psychotronic technology known as *Silent Sound Spread Spectrum* (SSSS) will combine HAARP transmitters, GWEN towers, micro wave cell phone towers to induce severe physical, emotional and psychological effects that will be used against the couch potato, TV-watching population.

The technology of the micro-chip, now the size of a grain of rice, to be inserted into the back or neck with or without their permission during surgery and intravenously, links the brains of people to satellites controlled by ground-based super computers.

It follows that spiritual progress is rendered impossible once that type of control is executed over our bodies. Are we ready for the *robotization* of humans and the total elimination of privacy, including freedom of thought? Covert neurological communication systems are in place to counteract independent thinking and to control social and political activity on behalf of self-serving private and military interests.

One reason this technology has remained a secret is the widespread prestige of the Diagnostic Statistical Manual IV produced by the U.S. American Psychiatric Association (APA). Psychiatrists working for U.S. intelligence agencies no doubt participated in writing and revising this manual. This psychiatric 'bible' covers up the secret development of MC technologies by labeling some of their effects as symptoms of paranoid schizophrenia.

Victims of mind control experimentation are thus routinely diagnosed, knee-jerk fashion, as mentally ill by doctors who learned the DSM 'symptoms' list in medical school. Physicians have not been schooled that patients may be telling the truth when they report being targeted against their will or being used as guinea pigs for electronic, chemical and bacteriological forms of psychological warfare!

ELEVEN

4) They are control freaks.
In total violation of the Law of Allowance the masses are driven like cattle by herders who don't even need to use whips anymore as we willingly let them decide how we are to live and die. Letting go or the joy of accepting differences is a no man's land for them in their attempts to have the upper hand in every little thing we do because 'they know better than we do'.

A good example I describe in the following situation in which a SSS ex-wife obsessively ruined her former husband's innocent supper with me, a female friend she did not want him to have:

THE STUDENT'S EX WIFE
When I taught a self-help program for adults in Hollywood, CA, a hotbed for control freaks, one of my students invited me over for supper. He was a slow learner but his enthusiasm made up for speed in his desire to learn as much as possible at the age of sixty. While we enjoyed our supper together, he confided in me that he had lost all of his possessions in an ugly divorce proceeding to his ex-wife. OK, I thought, nothing new here in the human drama. Women want money, men want sex, and if they make it legal for those reasons, sooner or later the attraction is gone for him and she cashes in. Who is to blame?

We enjoyed a couple of glasses of Chardonnay when the phone rang. I watched him deflate spiritually as I heard him say that he had a guest. Raising my eyebrows, curious as to who might have such a hold over him, he sighed, "she calls almost every day to see what I am doing." The alarm bells in my head went off. If this man got divorced ten years ago, financially ruined by a woman who had also managed to take his dignity away, one could be assured that there would be a glassy-eyed intruder on the other side of the line. The phone rang again: now she wanted to give him the seal of (dis)approval regarding the company he kept. Yes, yes, he nodded. For me, still in a phase of working myself out of the matrix, it was exasperating to endure.

"Be a man, and tell her to be gone," my anger began to well up, knowing that any chance of a quiet evening was no longer an option. I didn't say that to him, but got a better idea of why he learned slowly: he was continually pre-occupied with thoughts of her that interfered with his ability to be present in the Here and Now. She trapped his attention, letting him know daily she was there watching him. The third time the phone rang I picked it up and answered. A moment of silence got quickly bridged by the noise of a lengthy explanation of what kind of man my student happened to be and what kind of husband I could expect in the future.

She did not hear my assurances that I was just a visitor, and not interested in taking her ex-husband away from her. That in itself was a contradiction in terms: an ex is no longer a partner and ***one person cannot own another***. I told her not to bother us again so we could have a moment of peace.

In her mind, however, her prey and my student were not one and the same person. She considered him one of her possessions and 'nobody but nobody would have the audacity to cut the dark vibrational leash around his neck, steal his attention from her for a moment'. For her to entertain a nobler thought was virtually impossible as I suspected that her handlers had eliminated 'noble thoughts' from their software programs. Any soul indoctrinated as well as trapped in the regime of a One World Government planet regarded personal freedom and individualism as a threat to the system.

Ring! Ring! Ring! The doorbell went. "She is coming over," he gasped. "What?" The audacity was mind-boggling. No signs of civilized behavior, manners or self-control present in this woman. "Lock the door, and don't answer the doorbell," I instructed him, after he told me not wanting to see her. He lived in an apartment complex, secured by an electronic gate and stone wall. Half an hour passed.

She used a typical trick of attention manipulation: impossible to get her off of his mind while waiting for her to show or not show up! The relaxed atmosphere could not be retrieved. The phone stopped ringing. Was she on her way or did she give up? The doorbell rang once, twice, and three times. "That's her," he said, recognizing an agreed upon code between them. She stood in front of the door. How did she get through the gate?

Our questions got answered soon enough. Within minutes she bolted through the window with a triumphant howl, holding a bottle of wine held high in her right hand. Surprise! Surprise! Eyes glittering, she parked herself on the couch, directly across from my chair and told my student to open the bottle. Well, well, well, I thought, let's bring out a toast.

He filled our glasses as if we were the most compatible, amicable threesome in the world. Plainly, he went into shock listening to his ex-wife tell me the story of his sinful deeds for the umpteenth time. "The only thing necessary for the triumph of evil is for good men to do nothing" flashed through my head, thanks to Edmund Burke's observation. "Tell her to go or shut up" followed right behind that one.

And oh, how she had suffered at his hands. No words could describe the mental anguish and physical threats she had endured, no, honestly. "If I were you, she looked at me with a significant glance, I would think twice about marrying him." She kept repeating it as a mantra, apparently threatened in an illusory way, regardless of my own intentions of assisting a man with his spiritual progression.

Tired of her presence and 'stuck record' phrases I stood up, stuck my face into hers, and said as threateningly as I was capable of: you are going to get out of here in five minutes, or else…Again, it worked (to my surprise, a Sun Libra is not a natural at standing up for her rights.) She waited half a minute before she got up to be escorted by her gopher: her ex-husband, my student.

I marveled about the simplicity of getting rid of such a tormentor; saying no, acting fearlessly and a refusal to get intimidated did the trick. Of course, the wine helped in the self-confidence department as I was far from being fearless at that time. Now I could clearly envision, after this confrontation, if people believed themselves to be strong and connected they could create a world into a place where one could be...free to BE.

__What people criticize in somebody else is usually a personal flaw within themselves__. They will tell you what their problems are by pointing out those of others. This does not work, however, for the control freakish SSS who, according to the software program they run on, are perfect in their own minds. It took a long time on my journey before my inner strength increased to a point where they no longer bothered me and faded into the fog, so to speak.

TWELVE

THE WINE MERCHANT'S EX-WIFE

A red-haired dynamo (SSS) married a wealthy self-made man. With a small business loan he started a publishing business in the Los Angeles area, printing his own dog magazine which became almost an overnight success among dog owners interested in breeding animals for shows. He invested his profits in a store selling fine wines, mostly imported from France and Italy, giving him the opportunity to increase his knowledge of wine-making. One thing led to another and, after hiring a manager to run his magazine, he dedicated himself full-time to the business of growing grapes for his own wine label in a vineyard near Rutherford, a small town in the Napa Valley district of California. The two red-haired children they produced, a boy and a girl, made this picture of happiness and success complete. Except that fairy-tales marriages are usually just that: old wives' tales.

That picture had almost totally faded when I met him a few years later. His private lawyer hired me on a create-your-own-job-basis after several other solutions to his current situation had gone awry. According to the latter, under the influence of cocaine, he had crashed his sports car into a station wagon, killing the female driver. In the back seat of his car, his two children were asleep to miraculously survive the wreck without a scratch.

Mangled, their father's head got fused in a lengthy operation where a metal plate held the pieces of his brain together. People called him a living miracle, considering the injuries he sustained. They also noticed, after he finished physical therapy that his personality had drastically changed. Had he been arrogant and aloof before, now he acted like a gentler, kinder man. There is a phenomenon known as the 'walk-in' when another spirit takes over the body when the inhabiting spirit wants to leave, but that was guess work here. I had not known him before the accident.

General consensus among his friends and acquaintances attributed his survival to him being an avid marathon runner in his spare time. But he sported several defects; a period of five years' amnesia in which the accident occurred, among them. When he got dismissed from the hospital he found to his dismay that his wife was living with another, younger man.

His now ex-wife, hailing from a low class background, had started divorce proceedings while the iron was hot. She had free run of the estate that adjoined the vineyard, including a mansion, guesthouse, swimming pool, tennis court and horse stable. For a tidy sum obtained from the divorce she bought herself a house, about three miles down the road so she could keep an eye on the estate while taking what she wanted and needed. Her entrepreneur ex-husband found himself at the age of 32 metamorphosed into a handicapped man with a metal plate in his head, atrophy in his right arm, diminished eyesight, a fairly severe speech impediment, and a singular status.

Five women preceded me as his companion, housekeeper or nurse, all of them failing to make the grade to pull him up by his bootstraps so he would become healthier and more productive again. My success consisted of tough love, not backing away when he acted like a spoiled brat. It came to a clash when I poured an expensive bottle of 1972 Chateau de Lafitte Rothschild down the drain. In the ensuing fistfight I won so it made an impression, not just to the eye that turned black and blue after a left hook.

On my first errand in St. Helena, CA I found out that there were purchases made for which the merchant had to pay. Calling his lawyer, it turned out that the ex-wife had used and was using his credit cards to buy herself some items in addition to the settlement of the estate during the divorce which had resulted in her ownership of the dog magazine, alimony, child support, BMW, and an outstanding lump sum of about a quarter of a million dollars.

His lawyer, apparently afraid of her, appeased her with additional money when he told her that the credit cards would be canceled. Not soon thereafter, in a huff, she pulled up in her ultimate driving machine to help herself to a couple of coffee table size books. Ignoring me while kissing her ex, she finally came around to me to say: "…and you must be…the companion?" I nodded yes. "I am his wife," she added to which I responded: "As far as my information is correct, you are the ex-wife. And I'd appreciate it if you could call me before you come to visit us the next time," I added for good measure.

She turned her back to me and sotto voce, in a voice not loud enough for me to hear, instructed her ex on some matter related to their children. I was allowed to take care of them over the weekend if I picked them up and returned them by car. Naturally, I complied so he could spend some time being a father.

His wine consumption on their first visit was excessive. I had retreated for a couple of hours but, when I returned, found him fast asleep in his bedroom.

When the 11-year-old boy requested to see a movie that was playing in the theater, I found that a splendid idea. Little did I know that as soon as his mother found out about it, she would verbally attack me with a holier-than-thou attitude: "From now on you are going to let me know what you are going to do with my children, where you are taking them, what you are feeding them, what you are telling them."

She was not kidding. They were her children but I was not employed by her, thus when the boy started calling her every two hours to report our activities, I decided that to have a control freak supervising us would be an untenable situation. I eventually changed it into a reversal of visits: instead of picking up the kids, I dropped their father off to spend the weekend with them at her place. I had been hired to take care of him while it had been left up to me to decide what I wanted to do with him as long as I got results.

Right before Christmas, after I had written to my parents how well I was doing, I received a letter from my mother stating that she suffered from cancer. According to her, the prognosis would see her dead within a few, short months. Knowing her to be envious of me when I did well in my life, the timing seemed too coincidental. In a large package of presents I prepared for my parents, I included one for a friend who I wanted to go there to check on my mother to determine how gravely ill she might be.

To be on the safe side, I mentioned to the merchant's lawyer that the possibility existed I had to return to Europe in case of her pending death. Why don't you take him with you, he said, "but before you do, you need to call his ex-wife to get her permission to take him out of the country." "What?" I thought I had not heard him correctly, unaware of an existing clause in the law that could make someone, relative or friend, a Conservator of one's Body, meaning that the person took the responsibility for the body and its whereabouts of someone else. Talk about a trap or a prison within a prison situation!

"I am sorry about your mother, but if he can afford to go to Europe, then he can certainly pay me the money he owes me," she informed me when I called her on the phone. Ad verbatim, I repeated her answer to the lawyer who cursed under his breath. "I'll handle it," he said, promising to take her to court to get her to renounce the conservatorship, on promise of additional payments to her already substantial income.

To her, it was a declaration of war. Nobody messed or interfered with her business, regardless whether it constituted rip-offs and pure theft. Her point of view narrowed matters to the simple fact that she deserved to be supported with financial and worshipful contributions. Even her children filled their time spent with their father to beg for more money because their mother had such a difficult time to make ends meet, reinforcing their already strong *victim consciousness.*

The holidays rolled around. The bank, through authorization of his lawyer, allotted us a fair amount of money to spend on presents. When I inquired what he wanted to get his ex-wife, he gleefully shook his head, like a boy who giggled at anticipated naughtiness. In the meantime, I had been busy getting to know him and his idiosyncrasies so I could guide him in a direction both playful and beneficial. His demeanor struck me as that of a pre-teen boy, a very intelligent one, who would not allow a moment to elapse without trying out one of his hatful of tricks to get my attention or annoy me.

For instance, a speech-therapist came over to the guest house. He asked me for a hamburger right before the man arrived, taking the opportunity to slowly chew on his meat while eyeing me surreptitiously, taking half of the hour's lesson to finish it. I smiled in return, didn't say a word, but called the therapist to inform him that from now on, I would accompany him for a lesson to his office and would he, please, be so kind to tape the lesson so I could practice with him at home?

One day he wanted a slide projector so I went out to get him one, only to watch him ditch it in the trashcan when a slide got stuck. Instead of opting to fix it, he wouldn't look at it again. After I did an inventory of his private wine collection in the cellar, I arrived at a huge figure, enabling him to drink a bottle of wine a day for the rest of his life if he so chose. We shared one bottle a day with dinner rather than the bottles he chug-a-lugged all day long when I first met him. It would be preposterous to make a guy whose pleasures came in fermented liquids, his genie in the bottle, abstain completely. My quest to free my spirit meant for him something different: to free the spirits that came in a bottle to soothe his pain.

    Financially he was not doing well anymore due to his lack of production. With all of his varied incomes, his lawyer told him that his expenditures put him further in the red. There didn't seem to be an immediate solution other than selling the property to cover his debts. Considering the situation, we thought it would be prudent to move to a more populated area where I could introduce him to shopping, restaurants, a gym to exercise his limbs, and other places where he could re-learn how to speak. A beautiful, small house with a glass façade overlooking San Francisco Bay in Marin County beckoned, so we moved.

    A luncheon invitation by his mother brought us to her house south of San Francisco. The merchant's personality changed visibly from an up-beat guy to that of a recalcitrant boy in his mother's presence. He asked for a specific bottle of wine that one of her servants opened to pour for him to create a false sense of courage. Another bottle followed. I didn't object to him surpassing his allotment, sensing the whirlpool of agitation swirling around him. He was agonizingly afraid of his mother, the queen control-freak in the family.

One of her maids, a beautiful woman from Brazil, confided in me that she belonged to a high class family in her own country. To be treated like an ordinary maid who had to bring dishes to the luncheon table at the ring of a bell, she resented. She spit into the sink to emphasize the disdain she felt for her employer.

This was unknown territory for me, the world of the wealthy, a world that I could never enter as an equal; a world I had no interest in becoming a part of. But it was also a world where policies were discussed and made by people looked upon and thought of as Glitterati—a world where almost everything/everybody functioned to cater to the tastes of the body. This world where the merchant's mother told me that "money is the root of all evil"; a woman who had disowned seven brothers and whose four children struggled to find a glimpse of personal worth they never learned how to find. Was she talking about herself?

She was amused that I had clipped the wings of her ex-daughter-in-law. I was just another servant who took care of a nuisance for her. Besides castrating males mentally and spiritually, a diversion of SSS women is to either bring their rivals to their knees or make life distinctly more unpleasant for them. Of course, control by withholding money is one of the most popular and effective methods since most people believed that they needed it to be able to function. The mother represented the lower end of the sign Scorpio, whose sting was felt in a large sphere of influence.

She admired the present her son had bought me on the insistence of his only sister, despite my own protestations: a heavy set of solid gold necklace with matching bracelet which, according to his lawyer, he could not really afford to buy. But the sister, an unhappy woman with four failed marriages to her credit, no interests other than lambasting her mother and drinking alcohol, had insisted. Under the influence of a false self-confidence, craving attention, she displayed the control freakish behavior of her mother, not realizing that she would always remain a superficial duplicate of her.

In a strange twist of circumstances, she did get an opportunity to redeem herself by donating a kidney to the second brother, a successful Super-Realist painter in Santa Barbara whose life ebbed away at the dialysis machine. The eldest brother made a living as a sportswriter for the New York Times, most of his money spent on his gambling addiction.

Disaster struck when we visited his ex-wife, her boyfriend and children on Christmas. The load of presents we dropped off for the kids could not hide the fact that he had omitted to get her one. To add injury to insult, he pointed at my jewelry and then indicated with a finger pointing to his chest, saying "Me" which translated into "I bought that for her."

An invisible firecracker went off around her head, highlighting the red shade of her hair. Several weeks later I received a summons to have my deposition taken in preparation for a battle in court because the ex-wife wanted to receive more money. Guess who got to be the lucky one to take the stand in court?

Royally annoyed to be dragged into a case where the accuser was already overpaid, I demanded a raise because that event was above and beyond the duties I had been hired to perform. A specialized lawyer was added to the team. He briefed me on how to lie which I found rather telling of the (in)justice system: the oath of telling the truth and nothing but…constructed a lie in itself as it promoted losing a case, something no participant would be willing to risk. I had nothing to hide so I communicated what I felt had to be said. The young lawyer quit the business after trying our case to embark on a new career in Germany with his sanity intact.

One day before my appearance in court, a panic overtook me. Whatever I did to appease myself was to no avail so I had to contact a hypno-therapist to give me a session very early in the morning to find out what caused it. It turned out that the fear was connected to an incarnation in England where a doctor had been sentenced to death in a court-room. Inner calm returning, at least I could answer the questions without looking like a fool or the guilty party in the ordeal.

Hoping to find me uncomfortable while taking the stand, the ex-wife sat down in the front row with her sleazy lawyer, transfixing me. The mind games came in full swing during the court's recess when she deliberately avoided me as the underling while she herself had been extracted from the gutter through her marriage! I won the case for him. She would no longer be allowed to demand additional money in any court cases. Of course, directly asking him would be a different matter. Then my friend's letter arrived to reveal that my mother's cancer had gone in remission. In effect, I had scored a spiritual victory over three SSS women in one fell swoop.

    My stay with the merchant ended when I got him to the point where he could function on his own again, under supervision of a private nurse and her husband. His mother called me over to discuss the possibility of a marriage of convenience in the company of two of her lawyers. The offer was tempting: how often does one get handsomely paid for living a posh lifestyle for three years, fattening a bank account while playing the role of wife to an obedient husband? There was just one thing that made me reject her offer: my integrity. Without it, I don't know where I would have ended up. With it, I do know. That realization assisted me in overcoming my own contra-survival DNA commands in order to perceive them in others, one of my life's tasks in order to gain inner freedom!

THIRTEEN

5) They are master manipulators

Looking back on my experiences, it strikes me as nothing short of amazement that anything gets done, judging by the caliber of person that runs large operations. Their major contribution to influencing the lives of others negatively is to play musical chairs in midstream.

Usually, an 'approved' dumb enough specimen, if it is a human gullible enough to be controlled by the aliens in charge (there are many factions operating on our planet) will do the left-over work at the top of the pyramid scheme that is so often used. That type of work entails switching managers with expertise in one area and put them in a department where they know little. It is a recipe for creating chaos and confusion and so simple. I've seen it happen in many places where I either worked or entered as a client.

For instance, there was the sudden switch from the founder of Scientology who, among his flaws, still had the intent of assisting people to become free beings, to a nasty, incompetent, unimaginative, intimidating low-level patsy for the reptilians. He had been installed to destroy the organization by ruining its reputation, changing the texts that were designed with particular wording to render them ineffective past an initial bit of success.

The introduction of Women's Liberation, promising freedom, success, financial independence to women who now felt stuck in their families, 'housewives', by their sponsors the Rockefeller Foundation. In an interview with Aaron Russo, whose life came to an abrupt end after he went public to point out that 'the powers that were' had two reasons for doing it. Quoting Aaron: 'one, they could not tax half the population and two, now they could get the kids in school at an early age so they could indoctrinate kids how to think'. That way, families were broken up and teachers or the State would be regarded as the parents. According to Gloria Steinem, the CIA funded Ms. Magazine for similar reasons.

The chaos and destabilization that ensued, the friction created between men and women was clear to those who lived through it. The only point that I agreed with, as I was already working and being underpaid, was equal payment for those who performed in the same job, regardless of gender. Naturally, that never happened (with a few exceptions.)

FOURTEEN

6) They hint. This way the other person will think he/she does something voluntarily.
The psychopath or Simultaneous Spirit Suppressor can be very convincing. One who is on a path of 'service to others' is more than willing to accommodate others (the unbalanced Light sider way): I'll give you what you want if you give me something I want in return. It leads to harsh lessons if one cannot give without expecting something in return or is yet immature enough to believe a sob story told by many.

A good example of this is portrayed in episode 19 of Season I of the series Lost. John Locke, a middle-aged man, runs 'accidentally' into his biological mother (the gopher) who came to visit him in the store where he worked as a sales person.

When he sees her after work in the parking lot he runs after her to find out who she is and why she is so interested in him. Over a cup of coffee she confides in him that he has no father because his was an immaculate conception.

Not believing her, he sets out to find out the name of his father whom he then pays a visit. The man pretends to be surprised, fixes him a whiskey and invites him for a hunting experience. When he shows up for the date, he finds his father on a dialysis machine because he can't find a donor to replace one of his kidneys. The scenes after that show John in the hospital bed ready to give his father what he needs while the latter disappears when he is recovering from his kidney operation.

When he goes to visit him at his house he is no longer welcome while his mother, the perfect gopher, apologizes to him like it was nothing: I needed the money. Left without parents once more, he continues life on one kidney and a bad memory.

Basically, no matter how duped we are by others, the resilience of the human spirit combined with a stubborn naivete, disbelief in the fact that there are creatures living side by side us that are completely devoid from remorse, guilt, compassion or love enables the occurrence and continuance of the human drama.

Most of us give others the benefit of the doubt in our ignorance or unwillingness to accept the idea of unmitigated cruelty to our well-being. Throw in a dose of laziness and the recipe to create a failed soufflé of strong leaderships is one for the books.

FIFTEEN

Sex and money and to a lesser extent religions, are control mechanisms to keep people in line. According to the SSS hive mind, we came to Earth to please them. Here are two personal experiences I describe in being offered jobs by a man, a sexual predator, who wanted to get free sex, followed by a woman who wanted money:

THE LAWYER

In the early eighties, I decided to look for a job in the Los Angeles area. Instead of going through the Want Ads, I put in an advertisement myself, describing my own wishes and background, to find a position as a traveling secretary.

Two of the respondents sounded interesting. The first one was the president of a company in San Diego who wanted to pay for my flight to visit him, and the other was a lawyer for a handful of wealthy clients, requiring him to make investments for them while traveling to New Zealand, Hawaii, Alaska and California. As he lived temporarily in the Holiday Inn in Burbank, a town close to Glendale where I lived, I decided to give him the first shot.

Looking more like an absent-minded professor, wearing disheveled clothes, he took me to a bank to open a safety-box where he kept documents for his clients. I found him a bit odd but gave him the benefit of the doubt when he offered me the job. After all, he played on my feelings of trust when showing me the documents and it worked. Little did I know he used that technique to impress any female he hooked onto to supply him with free sex.

    As I had been searching for a traveling professional, it didn't immediately strike me as uncommon to see somebody living in a hotel suite. Being only marginally acquainted with the legal profession, he could have told me a pack of lies without me having any recourse to discovering them. For someone who does the same thing over and over again, a predator eying a prey's telltale signs of fears before he closes the trap, he knew exactly how to present himself as a legitimate lawyer while leading me astray with a fictionalized story. For one week he actually had me work for him, doing regular secretarial work such as steno, making phone calls, filing, and typing out documents. Then came payday!

    He had promised to rent a second suite in the hotel for me so I had given notice at my apartment in Hollywood where I paid rent on a weekly basis. Suddenly, the night before I was supposed to move, he dropped in saying that he needed to go to New Zealand on a special request of one of his clients, alone. "Where does that leave me?" I asked, alarmed, recognizing that sinking feeling in the pit of my stomach. "I've got a week's pay right here in my pocket." He dipped his hand in his pocket to draw out a small envelope, as if that was the answer to my new predicament. The other opportunity in San Diego I had called off, thinking I had landed a job. "But before I can give it to you," he went on, "you shall have to sexually release me."

At this stage of my spiritual development I had yet to control my anger and sense of revenge. Something snapped inside to unleash a blind anger at this insult directed by a person who wanted to reduce me to a mere sex toy rather than compensate me for my expertise. Coward that he was, he got to his feet to storm out of the door without paying me, leaving me in a quandary.

Two years later, the second time I ran an ad in the hope to land a different type of job, he called again. He recognized my voice and made the mistake of telling me so he alerted me to the fact that he played that particular game of answering ads with other women/men as well. True to the interplay between Light- and Darksiders, the two polarities in the Game, now I felt like the predator as my voice turned icy calm to inquire if he stayed at the Holiday Inn in Burbank again? His confirmation was all that I needed to stand in front of his door at 6:00 a.m., expecting him to be present. He opened the door to let me in while saying that he knew I would come. Did I step into a trap? Albert Einstein said that 'insanity is doing the same thing over and over again, expecting different results'. Wonder if the NWO crowd will ever 'get it'!

It took several hours before I managed to get a check from him in the amount he owed me for the work I performed two years earlier. Claiming not to have the cash, it was all I could do to even the score and "get my revenge." In hindsight, I should have charged him more for the mental anguish, loss of another job and extenuating circumstances but it never occurred to me as money had little importance in my life.

Looking at it from my point of view now, thirty some years later, I would have never gone into the revenge mode but, then again, I would never have met him. In my natal chart with Mars in Scorpio square Pluto in Leo, I had chosen to learn the lesson of revenge, dealing with it as well as letting it go no matter how hard it would be. Over the years, I adopted the phrase *the process is always perfect* because there is a time and place for everything. The world may be imperfect but the process **IS**!

When I worked for him, he had told me a heartbreaking story about how his handicapped son was a big strain on his family and his financial resources....it was just another fictitious person invented to sap the juices of sympathy from a gullible listener. I cut him short when he brought that up again, saying that this attempt to elicit my sympathy, would lead nowhere. Within a relatively short span of time I had learned not to belief in any of those SSS stories.

Once more it occurred to me that if more people had the mental courage and integrity to stand up for their rights, even in seemingly trivial matters, we would and could have been spared the nauseating experience of being ruled by the present day aristocracy (the immoral, the ambitious, and the cruel). However, **with the process perfect,** it could not have gone any other way.

--

Below I describe an occurrence with a female SSS client who sexually intimidated the man I worked with in Los Angeles selling solar heating systems:

THE CROTCH

During the Reagan Administration a rebate was offered to people who wanted to install a solar water heating system in their homes in California. In my thirties, I took a male partner in his fifties to sell the units in Los Angeles as the rebate would make it a good deal for customers. From a sales point of view, we should cover a good age average, gaining the trust from a crowd between 25 and 60 years.

My partner would explain its technical side while I took the finances to close the deal as my area of expertise. On one of our calls we visited a woman who had just returned with her two pre-teen children from a gym. As the husband was nowhere in sight, considered a necessity in closing the deal, we suggested returning at a later hour. She wouldn't accept our protestations and took control, directing us to a couple of chairs at the table in the dining room after having shown my partner where the system would be installed: the indoor swimming pool area. I knew our possible sale was toast because as a salesperson one cannot give the reins to the customer.

Dressed in a leotard, a black net pantyhose and sneakers, her plump figure beneath a face and a hairdo that could have adorned the head of a judge in an old British courtroom, she bulged out her female wares in strategic places. Jumping on a chair, she sat down with her legs open directly in front of my partner and made steady eye contact (transfixing) with him as he attempted to do his presentation. His uneasiness expressed itself in fidgeting and blushing while she pinned him like a deer caught in headlights, before the kill.

She had delegated her children to their respective rooms. Now the question arose as to how to proceed with a customer who defied all forms of etiquette. My partner kept talking, stuttering a bit, clicking his pen audibly during awkward moments of silence. Witnessing the scene, almost like an outsider, I felt the tension emanate from my partner. Apparently, he could not bring himself to utter the words appropriate to the situation: would you mind getting dressed?

Or, breaking the spell, offer to return at another day when her husband would be present. So I butted in with" let's continue this chat on another day", to which the predator in the leotard responded with "oh no, this is interesting, not allowing her gaze to wander in my direction for a nano-second." Her gaze shot out from two charcoal-rimmed eyes, Babylon whore fashion, that reflected the superficial light from an overhanging lamp. At any time, my imagination working overtime, I expected to see a couple of miniature hunters walk down the beam to shoot my partner.

Dismayed at being shut out of the scene, frustration at not being able to spare my partner this type of sexual harassment that seldom gets highlighted or discussed when initiated by females, amazement at the brutality of treating us like some toys to play with, and a reluctant sense of awe, I watched. What power was it that allowed this woman, who sat perched on top of her chair like a black spider checking the catch of the day in her web before devouring it, total control over this man?

"This is not the only work you do, I hope?" she asked us sweetly, with an undertone of disdain, dismissing us like a fly in her ointment. With a sense of defeat and having witnessed an ugly scene I refrained from answering her question before she, victory complete, showed us the door.

It would take years of inner work, thereby gaining inner strength to withstand the SSS type, raising my frequency to a level where they could not be physically comfortable around me any longer.

SIXTEEN

8) They surprise you at inopportune moments.
I solicited the assistance of an agency for domestic help in Palm Springs, CA, in the same time period as the lawyer, described above under number five (5):

THE MEDIATOR
In the early eighties, during the Reagan administration I looked for a job as a domestic in the Palm Springs area. I registered as an available cook, maid and/or companion at an agency that served wealthy clientele. Looking at my resume the owner immediately decided that I would qualify to enter the staff of the Annenberg Estate, owners of the TV-Guide, where the Reagans visited on specific dates. Years later, when rumors of Bohemian Grove where human strays were sacrificed in rituals, I wondered if I could have ended up there?

In those days, prior to Sonny Bono's stint as mayor, there was no middle class in Palm Springs, just the rich and celebrated and the people who served them. Bob Hope and Frank Sinatra were two of the better known movie stars who had a street named after them. Three years earlier I had worked as a massage therapist in the Palm Springs Spa Hotel, so I knew the area.

Finding accommodations in a low-priced establishment for single women, I waited for the mediator to make arrangements for an interview with the overseer, a gate keeper installed outside of the stone wall surrounding the estate. When she arrived, eyes glittering, she questioned me about my past to determine if I had ever done anything I felt ashamed of, such as being arrested by the police. Oddly enough, when I had filled out the papers at her agency, that question had not been posed. She told me that I was going to be the right candidate for the job and winked. However, the requirement to enter the estate or start working there as an employee, was the passing of a security check.

    Everything seemed to be in order except for the gnawing feeling that something was not kosher with these employers. From hard-learned experience I knew that ignoring my gut instinct usually got me into foolhardy situations I could have avoided had I paid attention. On the way over, she suddenly stopped at a huge house right behind the estate. Surprise! Surprise!

    Without any explanation, she walked toward the front door, beckoning me to follow her. A character that could have walked out of the movie "Night of the Living Dead," eyes expressionless, clothes black, opened the door. A few feet behind him stood his matron flashing a smile as genuine as her false teeth, the make-up mask perfectly in place, hands outstretched to welcome the mediator who kissed the space next to her cheeks.

    Before we hit the road, she had given me instructions on how to dress with success in my attempt to land this coveted job, where I got to do domestic labor all day long under supervision of a German-born house mother who, if I performed adequately, would allow me to set the table for the guests who included the President and First Lady of the United States on New Year's Eve. Again, that uneasy feeling near my solar plexus chakra surfaced when she told me not to put on make-up, while she tied my shoulder-length hair in a knot; I wore a simple blouse, skirt, and apron on request.

The mediator exchanged knowing glances with her client, and then turned around to give her full attention to the Philippine houseboy whose face she pressed into her ample bosom, knowing well that his orientation was homo sexual. She grabbed him by the buttocks to press his body against her own in a concerted effort to further demean and disgust him. Instead of complaining, he laughed uneasily to accommodate his tormentor.

Before I had time to analyze the situation she summoned me to follow her to her car. Minutes later, I took a seat in front of an uncouth looking man in his sixties while the mediator introduced me as follows: she is here for a security check. She lives in a room in the Women's House…wink, wink….isn't that nice? Peering into his dark eyes, hearing the venom in her tone of voice, the hairs in my neck stood up. The ambiance could not have been eerier!

The interview was a hoax. It had obviously been decided beforehand—a lone, poor, attractive girl without family ties-that I would not pose a problem. Thus, I would be perfect for the role of slave inside a prison I willingly entered to make a living. After the SS mediator left the room, he asked me one question before he announced the good news to welcome me aboard.

"How did it go?" she asked enthusiastically, driving away. "I got the job," I said demurely. Watching her pull up in front of the same house, I wondered when I was going to get some lunch. She ushered me directly to the kitchen where the houseboy eyed me viciously. Feminine in his demeanor, I recognized the hostile anger of the suppressed soul whose loyalties to a despised, older female were forced upon his male body; he was looking for a less intimidating target to unleash his discontent upon. I was a timely victim to him!

He will tell you where to find everything, I heard the mediator say, as from a distance. "My client will pay you $6.00/hour to do the laundry. "What?" Now I understood the reason for the servant's uniform I had to wear. "I am hungry; could I get something to eat?" It was the only response that came to mind. "Fix her a sandwich!" She ordered him, giving me a venomous look, wagging a finger to make him move. I felt like being the food in a lion's lair. She left.

Taking my time to chew on a cheese sandwich, I wondered how to get out of this predicament. Way out of town, it would be a long walk back. Never mind, I finished my lunch. He showed me how to run the washing machine and put in the first load. Then I waited for him to disappear before I took off.

The next day I went to see her around lunch time. "I don't want the job," I stated with a smile, watching her mask of self-confidence crack to reveal the hidden fear. "Just don't want it," I refused to elaborate on my decision. "I heard that you walked away without doing the laundry," she offered. "Yes, and now I want you to order me lunch," I retorted. It was a first for me to actually order one of the SSS-ers around and, surprised, watch her do it. I mentally filed this away for further use. I specified a favorite sandwich of mine. She gave me money to get it (and hers, too.) so I still ended up running the errand. But I learned something significant: *if you give them a direct order to perform a task, they will execute it!*

SEVENTEEN

THE LIMOUSINE OWNER

In the late eighties I returned to Honolulu, Hawaii, where I had lived and worked before as a massage-therapist. I could not get my former job back so I scanned through the ads to see what was available. One ad asking for a dispatcher for limousines, offering a condo to live in as one of the added benefits, attracted my attention:

Another ad answered, not run, led to an encounter with another SSS man in Honolulu, Hawaii. He asked for a female dispatcher to live in his condominium, conducting business in the tourist transportation trade. I went for an interview. The two-bedroom condo looked nice and he led me to believe, without actually saying so, that I could move in there to live alone. He would just drop in to take care of business matters.

As part of his qualifying demands for the job, he asked me to drive a van to the airport while picking up passengers along the way. I did well, he said, then suggested for me to pick up my possessions on the way over, so I could move in immediately. Great, I stayed in a hotel which was rather pricey.

An hour after I put my bags in one of the bedrooms, surprise, surprise, a young woman entered the apartment. She lay down on the couch in the living room, making herself comfortable. No explanation as to who she was or what she was doing there was offered. Not long thereafter, another woman with an

English accent appeared. He made himself comfortable in the other bedroom, putting on a Playboy tape to get himself and his partner in the mood...with one girl on the couch and the other one in the other bedroom-not on your life, I thought.

This is the second time I am applying for a job that involved providing sexual favors without a sign of payment in the near future, and I wasn't going to stand for it. I asked the English girl what was going on and watched the other woman (the gopher) disappear into his room to bring out report about my questioning activities. Immediately he stormed into the living room with the question

"What are you doing?"

"Finding out about what your deal consists of, as you've painted a different picture when you hired me. If you think I am going to sleep with you as part of the employment agreement, I suggest you do a double take."

"Get out of my place immediately, and take the English broad along with you," he yelled, infuriated. "You can pay for her, can't you?" he added, making a non sequitur statement.

"I am calling the cops," I countered bravely, forgetting about my resolution to always take care of my own affairs.

"I'll do it for you," he said, picking up the phone.

Naively thinking I would be on the right side of the law as a victim of false advertising, I got an unpleasant lesson. The two cops that arrived explained to me that since he owned the condo, no matter what went on under his roof, regardless of his lying cheating behavior, rape or murder, I had to leave. I had no legal leg to stand on.

Back to the hotel, driven by the English woman, who took off on her own, I could not believe that anybody could have the gall to treat me so unfairly while the law was on his side due to a piece of paper with his name on it. What happened to criminal intent?

It occurred to me once again how divisive and unhealthy the whole set-up of so called civilized society functioned: as soon as the door closes of the house owned by anyone who is a victimizer, the law is automatically on his or her side. Even if you were falsely lured, kidnapped, or otherwise molested, it would be a humdinger to prove your innocence.

What could I do to erase the negative emotions I felt toward the man who had lured me into sex under the guise of offering me a job? Theoretically, he had done me no harm; his method had been to get me in the mood to offer it voluntarily, leaving him in the clear. How many of those people were advertising? Apparently, society as a whole didn't look too closely at what was being said or offered as long as the money covered it. What a barbaric motivation of existence. The advice I got, when I mentioned it to anyone was to "forget about it, be glad you came out alive."

From an energetic point of view, however, we engaged in a battle: he had tried to trick me into doing something I refused to do, infuriating me. The advice to forget about it I was incapable of heeding at this point. He stuck in my conscience as a sore thumb igniting my desire to avenge myself. I could not walk away without holding a mirror up, even though I knew it would be a waste of time. Simultaneous Spirit suppressors do the same thing over and over and over again, leaving no room for flexibility or change. I thought I could make him think twice before victimizing anyone else, a total fallacy. I did not regard that as a responsibility toward society at large, but more as a personal need.

    The irony was that fantasizing on how to avenge myself put me on a similar level as my opponent. I caught myself doing it but it was very difficult to distance myself from that course of action; eventually, I succeeded. The neo cortex of the left brain thinks about logical possibilities while the limbic or right brain offers creative solutions to the problem such as throwing a pot of orange paint over his beloved motorcycle. Carefully considering my options, I settled upon writing a letter to the committee overseeing the group of condominiums he belonged to, shedding some light on his covert activities. The only success I scored was the withdrawal of his ads in the newspapers after my complaint.

EIGHTEEN

9) They are gossip mongers.
OBSERVATIONS BY A FRIEND
The *Simultaneous Spirit Suppressor's* programmed behaviors are easily observed when groups of women come together and they are readily seen in the increasing "superior" attitude of many women toward men. Another observational arena became clear to me recently while listening to a radio talk show. This one had to do with the treatment of sons by mothers. At first, the discussion seemed innocent enough to me, but when I went into my own observant mode, the controlling, superior, belittling and manipulative behaviors shouted out: *alien commands*!

The setting was a women's talk show (Dr. R) interviewing a woman guest (M) who was a bit of a celebrity, although I had never heard of her. Here's a paraphrasing of the relevant parts of the interview. Please note that both of the women were engaged in annoying amounts of giggling and cackling. Listen for the belittling and demeaning language of M toward her grown son (W) and M's "superiority, all in context of how "cute and funny" it was. "Hear" as you read this the constant cackling in the background.

Dr. R: So, I hear your son just returned from China.

M: Yeah, he was studying abroad for six weeks. He's still having jet lag, he had the energy to go to a movie, but not to clean his room (Dr. R cackling).

Notice how M turns the attention away from her son (who had done something that most mothers would be proud of (studies abroad)) and toward herself (I cleaned his room). Notice also the belittling style that is supposed to be funny. But, she continued, he's a nice boy (BOY? – another derogatory term—he was 21.)

Dr. R: How is it, having him back at home? Does he have a girlfriend yet? (cackle, cackle)

M: No, and I'm trying to teach him some things that will help him learn to treat women right, to make them happy.

Dr. R: Yeah? Like what?

M: Well, for instance, I got a new dress and asked him what he thought—did he like it? He looked at me and said, is it for something special? No, not really, I said, but how does it look on me? He said, okay, it's very grey (both of the women now are cackling because they both know "what fools men are". So, I tell him, it's not grey, it's khaki! Look, W, I said, if you're ever going to please a woman, you have to know how to compliment them (cackle, cackle, hiss).

M continues: I read on a web site the other day how more and more men are using women's cosmetic products. So, if you find your moisturizer missing, better check with your husband (dual cackling). Yeah, take, for instance, men's feet. I've been trying to get W to go get a pedicure, explaining how women hate gnarly, scaly feet in men (cackle, cackle).

He would never do it because other guys might see him and he would die of embarrassment. I finally broke him down (take note of this term) and he had his first pedicure when we were out of town, so no one would see him (giggle, giggle, teehee). Now, he gets them regularly—you just have to stay on them and they eventually come around (tee hee)—translation: yeah, we women know how we have to manipulate men so they'll behave like we want them to.

THE REPTILIAN HEALER
By another friend
  In a training workshop with an internationally known healer, I volunteered for a demonstration of past life healing. I realized as I walked forward that I did not want to volunteer, did not trust the situation, yet I continued. During the demonstration my neck retained a painful crimp that persisted for weeks. So I phoned him to ask that he take care of the neck problem and he invited me to his office. I removed my jewelry prior to the treatment and placed it visibly on the coffee table.
  While there, I sat in a chair and after a meditation, he fixed the neck problem, and then embarked upon a guided journey in which several figures passed through my field of vision, among them a black caped hooded figure that I did not recognize. I stopped him at this point and said I did not want to continue. When I got up he said that, by the way, he had attuned me to his own healing symbol. At this I became alarmed and wanted to get out of there fast.
  I thanked him and was about to leave, but instead I sat on a couch with him and talked for a half hour. Seemingly without any conscious control, I started telling him about the mystery teachings from a very

ancient place on Earth where I had astral traveled. It was at this moment that a more eerie sensation came over me, and I finally realized that he was drawing me into his sphere for other purposes. I felt a hypnotic pull coming from his eyes, and at this moment his face changed: his eyes became yellow, there was a cold, intrusive and evil feeling coming from him, and his head became smaller with small scales all over it of an iridescent greenish brownish color.

When I left I realized that I did not have my jewelry. I immediately went back and we looked—the ring was not on the table. I had some trouble sleeping after this, very unusual for me, and a persistent feeling of him in my system somehow. I resolved to get out from under his influence by returning to an evening workshop he was holding some months later. I cloaked myself in golden light and with the protection of my guides, I went to a workshop. When I entered the room, filled with a large audience, he was near the stage talking with some people with his back turned. He rotated slowly, looked at me, and mouthed "you've come back", words I heard inside my mind. He had a genuinely surprised expression on his face. I was calm and serene, secure of my safety and my purpose. I telepathically said, "You have no power over me, I reject you and whatever you have placed into my energy field entirely, I am completely protected" and sat down. I stayed through the workshop and beamed golden light the whole time.

Afterward, I felt completely cleared from his effects.

It is noteworthy that his healing method was extremely effective. Right after doing his training, I gave a healing to a man who had a frozen shoulder for several years. Within a few minutes, the man reported he felt ice cold energy pouring out from his shoulder down his arm, and then he could lift his arm over his head with no impingement or pain. He is a colleague I speak to regularly, who has had full use of his arm ever since. This demonstrates the seductive aspect of the reptilian and the way in which he can appear helpful to spiritually sophisticated Earthers. (I am purposefully not using the term Earthling here because it is a derogatory term the aliens use to arrogantly indicate our inferiority to them which is untrue!)

NINETEEN

Life begins at forty
Right before I turned forty in 1988, I got fired from my editing job on a French textbook for high schools because I advised the manager not to hire an Algerian woman who I perceived to be a Simultaneous Spirit Suppressor. Hiding inside the hologram of a beautiful woman, somewhat reminiscent of the actress Angelina Jolie, I perceived the scaly body of a snake-type reptilian.

There was one month left on a lease I had signed for an apartment in the University district of Austin, TX. When I asked the owner if I could go because I wouldn't be able to find another job in town, she told me that it would be OK with her if somebody else would fulfill my obligation. Ten minutes later I ran into a man who wanted to take my apartment the following day, an indication I made the right decision.

I felt sad about losing a job I liked. That night I watched a movie that portrayed a woman who had to make a similar moral choice. It convinced me that I had made the right choice though it came attached with a pretty high price tag.

On the road to Los Angeles I lamented the fact that I could not celebrate my fortieth birthday. On my last day I had printed out several invitations for fellow female workers with whom I wanted to enjoy a gourmet meal in a cabin I had wanted to rent for the weekend. What was going on?

The answer did not come at once. Soul searching, I went over my previous years during which time I had atoned for people I had wronged in my own opinion. Mentally, I checked off each person and I knew that I had not missed anyone. I wanted to be a thoroughly good person who would attract solidly good people (see Law of Attraction). I had done a meticulous job in contacting them all to offer my assistance, reimbursement, apologies, etc. As far as I knew I looked back at a clean slate but spirit had some surprises for me in store. That I was about to enter a new phase, a doorway to a higher consciousness, did not occur to me then.
--

A radical shift in my perception of the world in general occurred during the drive from Austin, Texas to Seattle, Washington.

Up until then, during my adult years, I had followed a path that lead from one University to another. Opportunities to obtain a formal education had been offered but I preferred to study on my own. The professors I did experience in a formal setting had to teach according to governmental guidelines and textbook material. Those sources hampered spontaneous discussion and original ideas in my opinion. But I studied. Oh, how I studied. For years I crammed my head full of "factual" tidbits offered in books, slide-shows then videos, films and lectures. My mind worked overtime absorbing new developments, technologies, and inventions to keep me up to date. The goal was to open a publishing house that would cater to writers with views alternative to the status quo. It never came to pass because, even though I had a bank president in the family, nobody wanted to give me a loan to get started.

Excellence in work performance was a given. Innately, I responded to a need to be the best I could be in whatever I chose to do. And in the various fields I had lent my expertise I knew I had made a difference. I had not been totally successful in getting control over my mind, making me realize that an outside force or power somehow managed to invade my inner mental computer. Unwanted thoughts still invaded my personal territory and, sometimes, caused a physical reaction.

T en years earlier I had picked up a technique from a local author in Palm Springs where I worked seasonally as a massage-therapist for the rich and famous. He had written a booklet entitled CYT, short for Controlling Your Thoughts, describing a method on how to start breaking the continuous chattering inside one's head. I found it fascinating and began working with it on a daily basis: Empty your mind for one second, find that opening and you'll find you can't do it (with some exceptions). Round and round they go those pictures, ideas, thoughts, etc. Counting seconds is not a breakthrough, you're still thinking.

I also needed to answer the following questions: from whence originated the invasion of thoughts that interfered with my own thought pattern? Were there aliens involved? Sometimes the thoughts were related to sexual perversities that I abhorred so I set out to find out how I could get rid of them. Easy to get brainwashed, very difficult to stop it and fix the damage done.

"You think, therefore you are", the philosopher Rene Descartes told us. He was right if one believes oneself to be a body with all of its paraphernalia, devoid of a spirit to give it Life. Seeking to free my spirit from the knells of my body, I wanted to decide what entered my head to use my brain cells to conjure up my own thoughts.

With tears streaming down my face, I headed for Joshua Tree National Park near Palm Springs. A thunderstorm unleashed pouring rain that ran in rivulets down the windowpanes. Going out of my body to take a peek, I compared the tear-streaked face with the wet window and started laughing. What a pathetic image!

In the solitude of the desert, a Light engulfed me in the dark of the night. It had happened before; I did not regard it as anything special but its embrace filled me with optimism, strength and self-confidence. Most of all, it let me know I was not alone.

Something else happened that caught my attention. Ten years earlier I had briefly studied the communication technology of Scientology by L. Ron Hubbard, and then I stumbled upon a book that vilified his intentions, his work and his life to which I *reacted* with anger. As long as one *re-acts* emotionally to written words, scenes, gestures made by people, TV programs, stories, etc. the DNA-programmed body controls the spirit. An inner struggle is present within us, whether people are aware of it or not, for the body or the spirit to get the upper hand. *We are not born in sin, we are born in conflict.*

The word speaks for itself: re (again) action- something one does (again). Thus, at this point in my development, I reacted to somebody's opinion about the work of another person that I considered to be of value. The anger that welled up inside was directly related to my interpretation: I took the attack personally.

It is very difficult to reach a level (disregarding the catatonic state) where you can sit in total relaxation, without physically reacting to anything. Just try to remain motionless when someone suddenly sticks his fist in your face and stops one inch from your nose. Is your nose still going to be there or did you duck out of self-defense?

TWENTY

My experiences in and understanding of Scientology
In 1974 a recruiter attempted to get me to take a personality test to which I rather enthusiastically responded, only to be slapped away by my girlfriend who regarded it as a 'bad thing to do.' OK, I succumbed to that peer pressure but my interest got piqued. Six years later I took the test, signed up for an introductory communication course, and asked for my money back because I had to move to Palm Springs, CA where I got hired as a massage-therapist. They refused and I vowed to never deal with them again.

About one year later, I picked up a hitchhiker who flashed the sign Holland, the country where I was born, on my way to San Francisco. It occurred to me later that I would have never stopped to offer him a ride if he had flashed a sign with another word written on it. It squarely put me on the course of paying added attention to the silent language of the spirit, labeled synchronicity by Carl Jung. The hitchhiker turned out to be rather vehement about the subject of Scientology to which he referred as a philosophy. I shrugged it off, relating my experience of paying for a course I never got. Before he left my car he shook his head indicating his disapproval of my failure to get my money back. He had a point.

So I set out to contact the local franchise about the issue. They checked it out, assured me I had the right to take the course as they did not adhere to a policy of refund, and I got to do a number of drills that would lead me to a projected end result of being comfortable in any situation under any circumstances. Of course, it would take more than an introduction to get to that stage, and lots of hours of doing the drills before using them into everyday situations.

L. Ron Hubbard is the first one in my life who alluded to being in a Game rather than living an existence that seemed to offer neither rhyme nor reason. That made sense, I took that as a truism I could work with. It appealed to my sleuth instinct to solve enigmas and puzzles; this one pointed me in the direction of my own life's purpose.

Once again, I've never been anywhere where perfection is expressed by one of the two polarities of this universe: Lightsider and Darksider. People who embrace either polarity are subjects that want to control others as dictated by the energies of the dual universe we are trapped in. The exposure to and immersion in both polarities will bring forth experiences that are necessary to arrive at an understanding that will lead to blending both Light and Dark energies to express yin yang balance, a state I achieved during my present life.

Consider the source before you add someone's philosophy to your belief system, Hubbard advised. I took this advice to heart which has served me well in finding my own blend of truth in my life. Ironically, research done on Hubbard himself and his shenanigans with Alistair Crowley did not create an unshakeable faith in his abilities!

The state of Clear is a goal to be aimed for in Scientology; one that I discovered to have attained when I read the definition in the Technological Dictionary before I signed up for the course. Many times in my life I've gotten a confirmation or piece of information from my Higher Self that I needed at that particular moment in order to enter a new doorway that led to a higher consciousness.

A counselor who used a truth detector they referred to as an E(lectropsycho) meter did not seem to be too happy about that because he had worked for many years to get there and here I was… fresh meat flashing a sunny smile while attesting to what he wanted. The immediate effect of his sneering acknowledgment was a sense of invalidation so I refused to continue with another course I had signed up for. I liked a couple of people there but moved on to my job with the wine merchant.

Months later I ran into a new acquaintance, one who referred me to a counselor who worked in her own house. I agreed to talk to her about a possible course of action that would lead to more freedom for my spirit. For several months I embarked on word clearing, a program that would isolate words in one's vocabulary that had a ring of mystery around them as indicated by a wrong definition or other form of misunderstanding. It involved a lot of searching in dictionaries to clear words that would lead to better or other understandings of concepts obscured by faulty reasoning.

My most remarkable achievement became the clearing of the word *power* that, once I understood that its root meant *to be able*, created a significant shift from my body's control into that of spirit control. It also alerted me to one of my other incarnations, a short reign as the Emperor of Persia, who had exerted an undue vibrational influence over many other lifetimes, including my present one. Once I understood, the veil that was removed felt more like a wall that imploded, so strong had been the hold of the misconception of (external) power over the centuries.

Another concept that is tainted by fear and misunderstanding is that of taking responsibility for one's own actions. Someone who has never had the mental courage to look inside at the Dark energies (fears) present, is incapable of obtaining AHA moments that lead to new understandings. When you become more comfortable with accepting your own role in co-creating the reality, downplaying a fear of punishment, you're on your way to a healthier existence.

However, if you apply the ethics conditions of Scientology inside the organization, one gets caught in the vicious cycle of being to blame for everything which amounts to introversion, a lethal method with the opposite effect of trapping the spirit more inside the body. Do you look inside of your own accord or is somebody else telling you to do so? It makes a huge difference to do something voluntarily or being forced into. Of course, with the subtle yet commanding spell-casting the SSS-ers are capable of, it will be impossible for people on lower levels of awareness to tell whether they are doing something voluntarily or not!

The skills of my counselor were such that her expertise in steering me through vital inner pitfalls inspired me to want to learn similar techniques. What could be a nobler goal than assisting another spirit into achieving more freedom? Here the seed was planted that would blossom later on, an unselfish desire to assist others, an important facet of my life's purpose. The impetus to do this put me squarely on my individual path although I was then only vaguely aware of this fact.

After finishing my job with the wine merchant I moved to the Hollywood Hills to look into the available training programs for auditing. The high priced courses were now out of reach for me so I decided to work my way through it by joining the Sea Organization in Clearwater, FL. Big mistake! I turned around, packed my bags and left.

I had heard stories about how difficult it was for some people to break up with the organization. That was not one of my problems: I refused to hang around to get some signatures on a form that would give me authorized permission to leave so I got declared as an undesirable. It entailed a total ban for anyone associated with the organization to have any contact with me whatsoever under threat of punishment and a similar fate. It provided me with a clean get away! I thought about it and regarded it as an opportunity to go my own way and look inside myself to determine why I needed this experience on my way of gaining freedom.

About six months later, after a visit to Europe, I returned to Los Angeles where I happened to talk to a high placed Sea Organization member who, accompanied by her husband, was 'on a mission'. Regardless of my ban, she offered me what I had wanted in Clearwater, a place on the Technical Training Corps leading toward a position as an auditor. I perceived her to be a reptilian and therefore knew in advance that she would, somewhere along the line, sabotage my intentions. Reptilians never give you what you want without the future surprise element of screwing things up for you. Amused, I didn't care.

So I got trained, having a fun time listening to tapes by Hubbard who had a great sense of humor. Then, right before I could function as an auditor (one who computes and listens) the reptilian, who was very popular among the students due to her 'appearing to be busy and committed to the cause', came over to tell me that I had to go because….here the SSS-er told me I was a suppressive person, reversing the role but I took the hint gladly. I pretended to be upset and I objected while laughing inwardly, glad to be on my own again. She managed to sabotage the organization by 'firing me' and expected me to be in tears. Of course, I had simply enjoyed the opportunity to study without going broke!

PART II

ONE

Adventures of a Psychic
Life began truly at my fortieth birthday.
Leaning against the wheel of the Chrysler I steered across country to Joshua National Tree in California, I had no idea what to do with the rest of my life so I mumbled 'Happy fucking birthday" beneath my breath. A beam of light hit me filled with comfort molecules but my personality wrapped itself in the dense jacket of pouting and fears.

As I mentioned before, I had just managed to get myself fired by telling the leader of a French High School book project we were working on, not to hire a beautiful female from Argentina, because I knew that her human hologram hid a scaly extra-terrestrial with vertical irises in her eyes. I only did it for the good of the group, I murmured *Lightsider-style*, punishing some innocent pebbles by kicking them.

Looking back upon my life, I had the feeling there was no rhyme or reason to it on the surface. Of course, the golden circular line that appeared before my mind's eye whenever there was a completion to a cycle, a period of time spent for a specific reason, could hardly be called co-incidental because coincidences do not exist other than in some narrow minds.

So far, I had lived on two continents, Europe and the United States in many different places where I had to bring a task to completion, a task that had been chosen for me by my Higher Self. Amsterdam was my place of birth; in Apeldoorn I worked a stint as an air-traffic controller in the Dutch Air Force. The two lessons I learned during my military days were discipline and the notion that I did not want to kill after I accidentally wheezed a bullet past the shooting instructor's ear. Amsterdam became my place of reference, a yardstick to measure my spiritual growth, where I returned to face my humble beginnings, periodically.

In the United States, I studied Creative Writing and Art-History at UMass Boston before moving to Honolulu, HI where I became a licensed massage-therapist, Palm Springs, CA, then a manager/companion of a vineyard in the Napa Valley, CA, a driver/cook/companion for a one-eyed Professor in Oceanography while writing a novel, then the editor on the French book.

Of course, my psychic resume was far more exciting and real to me than any of the jobs I held, but since nobody was interested in reading or hearing about it, I clamped my motor mouth shut. As a child I learned soon enough that my parents were primarily interested in survival instead of living, after their narrow escape from death by hunger during the five years of occupation by German neighbor forces. Instead of them guiding me, they expected me to guide them, not an optimal situation for a child.

Other people would just brush me off as having a wild imagination or their eyes would glaze over, letting me know that there would be nobody home if I pursued telling them my stories about my escapades on the astral or how grandfather, the first and only funeral I ever attended in my life, stood above his grave smiling at me. An illiterate man who had sailed more than the seven seas for more than seventy years, he thought I found it funny if he pumped up his cheeks, then hit them with his fist to send a make-believe apple into space. 'Opa is making apples', I yelled to the gathered family members who stared silently at the gawking hole in the earth where his coffin was going to be placed. They found me eerie while I cringed at their blindness.

    The first DNA command I found inside that influenced my actions was the phrase *"I have to get out of here."* Putting it in perspective over the years during all of my traveling I used it as a personal guideline to determine if I left a scene or place because I was subconsciously obeying a command or whether I had finished my purpose and/or tasks before moving on. This self-questioning eventually led to the discovery of my purpose after my third eye opened, and I got a stronger connection with my Higher Self.

TWO

A new direction
On my way to Seattle I experienced several incidences that served as arrows for future events. Attempts to 'settle down' failed altogether. I knew my way around in that city as I had house-sat a place on the Puget Sound for several months. Within a week I got a job in a law office and rented a room in a stark, unimaginative place in the University District with a middle-aged guy who had gone prematurely grey. Soon I felt trapped. Making money to pay bills seemed to be a dead-end street; it created a void inside that no luxury could satisfy.

I decided to return to Amsterdam for the holidays. To be able to pay for the trip, I wanted to sell my car. The buyer showed up two hours before the deadline to get the ticket. I marveled at the magical timing: *the process was always perfect*! Although I let my car go for a lot less money than I asked for, it provided me with enough money for the ticket and to obtain lodgings in Amsterdam as my own estranged family would not put out the welcome mat. For the first time I experienced the city without the straight-jacket of my biological family who criticized my every move as I did not conform to their standards of living. There are many such proverbial black sheep, I was one of them.

Synchronicity increased to the point that I began to feel like I had more control over my destiny. The people I met were the ones I wanted to meet, I found the things I wanted, and I immediately got another temporary job as a secretary. After staying in a Youth hostel for several weeks, I found a room bordering on Vondel park, located in a gorgeous part of the city.

Then the idea to return to Seattle presented itself. Shaking my head, not sure whether I should do that, I checked with a travel agency. There are no flights open this summer, the clerk told me. OK then, I turned to leave the room but got as far as the door when I heard her say: "A cancellation on a plane that flies in three days just got in. Do you want it?" Yes. By this time I had learned not to ignore such well-timed changes. *There are no coincidences,* I heard my cousin say in my head. It is the one piece of wisdom she clung to during her generally unconsciously lived life.

Once back in Seattle, three female SSS-ers had me in their clutches. They did not know I could perceive them as such but did see me as a threat that needed to be eliminated. Doing my 'research' about their behavior and wondering why they were living among us, I computed the following:

The first one owned the house I had taken care of two years earlier while she went on a vacation to the Hawaiian island of Kauai with her husband and children.

1) Her 11-year-old daughter was the kindred spirit who told her mother to hire me. (If something went awry the mother would not be the one to blame-perfect in her own mind!) The mother was born under the astrological sign of Libra like me, providing me with additional material to make comparisons in regard to

intent. I got instantly sick when she physically approached me (at this point in time when I was more 'dense' I needed additional clues to analyze, draw conclusions and learn the behavior pattern of the SSS.)
2) As soon as she left on a short trip the next day, my health fully returned. This alerted me fully to her suppressive presence.
3) The couple had worked for a sales team benefiting a local TV station only to retire in their thirties. Naturally, she used the lure of 'starting a family' as the emotional trigger for him to give up his career as an executive so he could become a house daddy. Isolated from co-workers, drinking and hunting buddies, forced into volunteering jobs such as taking care of abused children while managing their finances and real-estate possessions, he became an unwilling prisoner in his own house. His anger came out sideways to unleash itself on his two daughters (one of them a toddler) and, occasionally, myself. The trophy wife was naturally not to blame for his misery.
4) Her routine consisted of looking very busy without actually accomplishing much, being the life of the party, perfectly fitting into an upper middleclass lifestyle, community-oriented, and totally in charge. Super mom! Her intent revealed itself, to me, in the uncertain, angry, fearful attitudes of her children and husband who she continuously needled with offbeat remarks and barbs to promote a broken spirit. My presence assisted her daughter's spirit to perceive comparisons between her mother and myself. Her name was Erica which means 'strong woman.'

5) After I left, I learned in our correspondence that the girl became so fearful in expressing her unique self that she became a bed wetter.

THREE

Other (Past) life connections
I met a man who introduced himself as an eternal student. I recognized his spirit as one I had interactions with in another incarnation. Questions directed to my Higher Self as to who he might have been and why I met him got answered as we went along. The other life I narrowed down to either Switzerland or England. *There had been a promise made that was about to be fulfilled.* As a student in philosophy he lived in an attic room with a roof that had a triangular shape. Bookshelves held hundreds of books on European philosophy written by Kant, Nietzsche, Sartre, Kierkegaard, and Teilhard de Chardin, etc. Soon I decided he was the Swiss contact, after I got more clues:

As a woman of means he worked for me as a gardener in 1835. We carried on a clandestine love affair. I wanted him to kill my wealthy husband so I could enjoy the latter's money without his intimidating presence. The gardener loved me so he did what I asked of him but I was not capable of loving him either. I let him be hanged for the deed after making the promise "to meet him in another life." And here he was, offering me work in his personal yard-cleaning business.

"We will be lovers in the next life," said the programmed wife of the young lawyer in whose house I found temporary lodgings. She referred to the philosophy student who was one of her gophers (see list). The phrase also triggered details of our shared other life in my memory. Ah, that's how I piece my other lives together to determine how to disentangle my spirit from the Matrix: how I tie loose ends to prepare for departure from this density.

"Could you explain that to me?" I asked her. Her human image was beautiful, long, blond hair with blue eyes, delicate nose and full lips, nicely proportioned body.

"Well, we love each other but I am married and I don't want to leave my husband," she said. I wondered if she planned on eliminating her husband the way I did in the Swiss scenario. It turned out that behind the sweetness beat a fearful heart. She used her daughter, her husband's step daughter, to lash out at me and him. I ignored the girl, knowing she had no idea what she was doing under the influence of her mother. Years later I learned she had tried to slash her wrists after I left.

During a conversation the mother had told me about a friend who had special abilities and who had reached a high level in Scientology that purported to assist to free people spiritually. I nodded. Yes, I am familiar with that program and know all about it, I stated. This information shook her up badly as she saw her control slipping. A sharp inhalation of breath indicating an upset followed when her gaze failed to hypnotize me.

My refusal to participate in her gossip upset her. One night I found her drunk when I arrived home. I talked to her for a few minutes, not immediately understanding the significance of this moment until her husband approached me with the question: do you know what is going on with her, she never drinks? I shook my head. After I left, the fear of exposure factor hit me. Her intent was to control her family and other people and keep them from finding out *who they really were* and here I was, telling her how committed I was to my spiritual progress. It was awesome to see how the alien controlled slaves were not afraid but petrified of being exposed. I almost felt sorry for her.

I worked in the front yard of the third SSS -an elderly widow who had enjoyed the status of top seller in her field of cemetery plots sales. Upsets galore after I met this woman!

On the first day my co-worker drove off in an angry huff caused by her and abandoned me. Waiting in vain for him, she approached me with the 'milk and cookies' approach that is so soothing to people who are despondent. I was still looking for the good in everybody using the unbalanced Lightsider approach which is based on "doing things for the good of others" while the Darksider is motivated by the premise "me, myself and I."

After a shock event staged by this woman, I discovered how naïve and unduly optimistic I was about my surroundings, people, and the world at large.
1)   I survived her attempt to kill me in a car accident.

2) The moment before the other car hit ours I didn't see my life flash in front of my eyes making me wonder if that was a lie altogether or if I would just survive.
3) The realization that the aliens would not hesitate to kill me hit me as a new piece of information, toughening me up immediately.
4) I observed how the female SSS manipulated several people (all males) including the driver of the other car, her lawyer, the rep at the insurance company, eye witnesses, and myself. Frantically looking for a reason to make herself appear as the innocent party even though she deliberately caused the accident, she nailed him on an out-of-state license/no insurance. At her place she put the phone in my hand, instructing me to tell the party on the other side that I got out of the car unharmed. Later on, when I refused to budge on the fact that she caused the accident, pointing out that I could have been killed (the wheel axle broke, the door bent inward so far that it almost touched me) she asked me if I wanted money. It was a question, not an offer, but it threw me off as I had to deal with a new observation that refuted my existing knowledge of them: they were indeed dangerous. Giving money is not something they did unless there were strings attached. That type of person would not hesitate to kill me.
The philosophy student kissed me farewell after the promise had been kept: we met in this life and our roles had been reversed. I was his gardener! Consciously he did not know about it but there was an air of finalizing our encounter. We both felt it.
--

FOUR

My last two jobs
 I left for an island off the coast of Seattle where I had been hired to be the live-in assistant of a guy who claimed to be the owner of a consulting business for cancer patients over the Internet. I wanted to do some writing and figured I would live in a nice place with free time to do my work.
 Unfortunately, things had a strange way of keeping me mobile. Within a couple of days I pegged him as a crook, a liar and a pervert. He kept me busy all day long with trivial errands so I decided to take a closer look at the man. During the lunches I prepared he answered my questions about his work, his education, and purpose in life. Candidly, he admitted to a fee of $500 for a few written pieces of paper in which he 'advised' dying cancer patients to go to the doctor most likely to extend their stay on Earth for a couple of weeks. He thought this to be hilarious because he would get their money right before their unavoidable deaths.
 It became clear how he had attained his riches as displayed in his beautiful, shorefront home in which he had an indoor swimming pool and Jacuzzi. When I went around cleaning the place I found a few drawers filled with sex toys. They did not fit the image he had painted of himself. He told me that a French woman liked them, the one that planned on visiting him for the

approaching holidays. Ah, I thought, and I can be the maid, cook and errand girl?

He told me that women usually did not stay with him very long! I did not wonder why. His secretary, a young woman who came in five days a week, to assist him with his business, was an immature person who believed in his self-promoting importance…that is, until I pointed out that he overcharged people while he did not offer them a cure or information remotely in balance with the money he charged. I also pointed out that in his resume he mentioned that he had attended Yale University without graduation. For all we knew, he may have been there for one course during one semester.

On the fifth day I told him that the position was not working out for me. He had told me that day to pick up the phone if the secretary did not get it and I simply refused to function at his every beck and call.

When one travels spontaneously, acting on an (spirit directed) impulse to go somewhere without making reservations, unpleasant experiences can be the result. Those experiences can and often will serve as lessons for the seeker.

Staying briefly at a Youth hostel on the Strip in Las Vegas, I met a man who offered lower priced trips in his car to Lake Mead than the travel companies. As I had just gotten a job as an editor on geological reports for a company that had been contracted by the DOE, he suggested sharing a hotel suite with him to lower the costs of living; it never occurred to me that his gimmick was to fraud single, naïve women. As soon as I got my first paycheck he picked me up at my work location, and insisted upon driving me to the bank to get my check cashed. The gnawing feeling of a pending disaster alerted me but I had little choice but to comply.

On Monday, looking through my wallet, I missed several bills. My shocked face alerted my co-workers. One of them offered her mobile home as temporary lodgings for me to retreat to. I accepted, and then called the man who left his Bible with underlined passages lying open next to my bed to remind me of his religious fervor and noble intentions. He offered no apology when I asked him about the money he had taken, just ordered me to forgive him. His arrogance infuriated me and I let him have it before the supervisor gestured for me to keep it down. Upset as I was, the latter allowed me to go to pick up my belongings so I could return calmer to do my work.

When I got there, the guy explained that he was in "a similar position as me" and, therefore, he had taken my money. Two days later, after my refusal to forgive him, he dropped off an envelope which contained half of the money he had stolen from me.

I found a great apartment in a new complex with sauna, swimming pool and Jacuzzi while I engaged upon a whistle blowing activity that would cause obstacles for me:

Problem was that I found geological reports about the Yucca Mountain Range in Nevada that I should not have seen. The company I worked for, using the most sophisticated computer programs to delegate reports to attorneys and scientists in the United States, sent their edited scientific reports across country to all interested parties. The government wanted to dump their nuclear waste into the Yucca Mountain region regardless of volcanic activity on its bottom.

The whole business of safety investigation turned out to be a hoax. The government owned the land, the scientists were given insufficient funds to do a thorough investigation, and the decision had already been made to dump the rods, safe transportation or not. The manager who had put the project together got fired in midstream only to be replaced by a woman who knew next to nothing about the project. The intention to cover up illegal activities came across loud and clear. The choice to protect people's lives and make this information public knowledge I found easy to make. To be sure, I alerted Bush, Sr. to my actions in a personal letter in which I compared his leading abilities to those of Mickey Mouse, in fact non-existent.

When the untrained woman took over the reins I quit. My test to tempt fate resulted in an emotional letdown. I needed that job to pay for my bills. Without it, I was on the verge of depleting my resources altogether. Somehow I refused to believe that my morally inspired actions of whistle-blowing to 'save' others would lead to homelessness, one of my greatest fears, but my Higher Self gave me a shove to make a reluctant leap of faith, the start of my quest!

There are two concepts at play here that took years for me to fully grasp:

1)   I still looked at the situation from the point of view of ' I am doing it for the good of others' although nobody had asked me to do so. In the back of my mind I expected to be rewarded for my actions which put a condition on it: I wanted something in return.

2)   I expected to be saved by an outside force like the Powerful Being who judged our actions once we depart for *turquoise, azure or emerald* pastures. This reflected a victim consciousness that creates complacency and fear. Religions (group directed belief systems) will tell one without fail that salvation is to be found outside of oneself in a Higher Being that remains invisible. Even the popular X-FILES TV series used the slogan 'the truth is out there', doing us a disservice. Trusting in one's own Higher Self is not the advice offered because it prompts you to ***not give*** your ***power away***.

FIVE

Hitting the Road
    Although I was aware of the disincarnate entities that hovered around me, I could not see why I kept losing or quitting jobs I actually liked. Walking away from the last mess, after sending a letter to Bush, Sr. to tell him what I thought about his corrupt methods, I had no longer any interest in doing work just to pay bills so my solution to the problem was to hitchhike out of Las Vegas. If someone would have explained to me that I had started on a quest, I would have given them a rather flowery speech to the contrary.
    According to my understanding, a quest was something a fictional character like Frodo in The Lord of the Rings would embark upon to save the hobbits by destroying the ring that held them in bondage but I felt like an outcast, alone, a female to boot, something I had been keenly aware of since I breathed life into my body. It had been an oft repeated familial anecdote how I had torn the wall paper down in fury at the age of two when my little brother arrived to complete the family: I wanted his body, the male body I had gotten used to in prior lives.
    The esoteric knowledge I had acquired so far came first from the Bible, then courses in Astrology, books that independent people had written addressing a certain problem like stilling the mind, a number of tapes and books by L. Ron Hubbard, the founder of Scientology and Carlos Castaneda's books. I found the

description of their experiences and adventures hilarious because I could easily put myself in their shoes or in the shoes of those who became their enthusiastic students.

It took a few months before I became aware of my spiritual guide, one whose delightful sense of humor and point of view I could not possibly share for years because it was so vastly different from my own. Just when I thought that all the books I read and situations I had handled had given me an outlook on life that I regarded as superior to most others, a far more powerful spirit tapped me on the crown chakra to remind me that the next phase consisted of application of gathered knowledge: *walk your talk, seeker*.

It shocked me to the core. My spirit had reached a level of maturity where most thoughts transferred themselves into manifestation. In other words, if I wanted something I pictured it in my mind and waited for it to be created on the earth plane. One got the feeling that there was such a thing as control over one's destiny. One got also the sense that the summit had been reached in spiritual maturity. However, it is a false summit!

I was going past the point where arrogance and a superiority complex prevent us from doing the real work. How irritating to hear people proclaim how the world is their oyster and to hear them give advice like "all you have to do is......you can fill in the blank as to what that may be according to their belief system."

To find yourself out in the streets with no place to go and nobody to lend you a helping hand, and your thoughts do not conjure up a winning lottery ticket or castle to roller-skate in (one of my fantasies), we can safely say that the reality check works like a cold shower on a wintry day.

I found out soon enough that despite all of my knowledge I could be looked upon as a babe in the woods who did not know what plants were poisonous and which ones were edible. Did I know the intent of people or entities on the astral, could I read it? And if I could, what would I do when duped or uplifted by it?

My guide steered me according to the book knowledge I had chosen prior to its application on a quest. One of my influences was the book *The Teachings of Don Juan, by Carlos Castaneda*. In one chapter, I recognized the arrogance of Carlos when meeting Don Juan for the first time, totally underestimating his power. Simultaneously, I got the bemusement of Juan as well as the intellectual ferocity of Carlos and found it hilarious. Since I was not a lucid dreamer, the area I had to concentrate on was stalking of which the basis is controlled folly. In order to practice controlled folly, as it is not a way to fool or chastise people or feel superior to them, one has to be capable of laughing at oneself.

"The first principle of the art of stalking is that warriors choose their battleground". *"A warrior never goes into battle without knowing what the surroundings are"*. Since I had surrendered to an advanced guide I had little say in the matter of choosing any environment, but I did learn fast how to measure whatever arena I was thrown into.

SIX

Freedom from Sex
The underlying dynamic of sex is power and not sex. When one is out of control with their power center, the addiction occurs and cannot be satisfied by sex. It is an experience of powerlessness. In random sex one soul desires to prey upon a soul more shattered than one's own. It is the central core of negativity within our species.

I hitchhiked out of Las Vegas. Soon I got a ride to Colorado in a big truck. The driver explained the mechanics of driving a semi, and that sounded inspiring enough for me to get my license in Louisiana. That done, I spent two years on the road to make me aware of an addiction that my soul had to let go of in order to heal.

It showed up in my astrological natal chart, a *tool par excellence,* as Mars in Scorpio in the 5th house while Pluto in Leo made a hard aspect to it. Marina Macario from www.darkstarastrology.com interprets it as follows: " Mars square Pluto is the classic predator aspect, they will quietly stalk their desires skillfully, in very much a "softly, softly, catchy monkey" manner.(…) Mars square Pluto's stamina is unrivalled, these folk are the phoenixes who rise from the ashes time and time again. The square really gives them the edge for it seems that every accident or emotional wound just makes Mars square Pluto even stronger, like some sort of hydra. You really don't want to attempt to cut off their heads"!

A couple of rides with different drivers resulted in $60 paid for sexual services. Momentarily I got confused into thinking that, perhaps, this is what I should be doing to make money? Let down by the universal indifference to my holy inspired actions (self-pity in action) I looked at other venues to keep on surviving in a hostile world.

The second one dropped me off in Boulder, Colorado where I met a woman who invited me over to her house. My spontaneously created "white lie du jour" consisted of saying that I was on a mission to tell the truth about what was really going on in the world. All I accomplished was them thinking I was a crazy woman who should be sent on her way as soon as possible. I could not blame them but felt like an actress on the world stage, flubbing her lines: I had to attend a few more rehearsals before I could become more convincing.

Some intense experiences followed. Not knowing what else to do, I aimlessly continued to hitchhike until I ran into a fellow thumber! A younger, street-smart guy, a type I had never encountered before, talked me into taking a temporary job as a detailer of sports cars in Houston, Texas. The outstanding memory of that week's employment involved a Chow dog. The business owner had a female Chow who got all excited when a woman dropped off a male Chow.

Problem was that the male Chow displayed no interest whatsoever in the female but got excited when I approached with his food. It didn't take us long to surmise why she had to get rid of the dog: the woman had engaged in sex with the animal who had developed a taste for human females. We tested this when he reacted the same way when the owner's wife and some other females got near him. The poor dog's unnatural sex life came to a halt in the pound.

    The guy with whom I shared a room in the garage wanted to go to Florida where we, he assured me, could stay with friends until we could get our own place. Reluctantly, I agreed. As a woman who used to have her pick of brilliant, wealthy and handsome males without getting overly interested in or attached to any one of them, the notion of hitchhiking across country to share a pad with a street-smart guy in Florida made me shudder. However, the alternative of detailing cars for little money was a novelty experience and not a life's dream.

    We bid the owner goodbye before we walked down with our bags to the highway. A bottle got hurled by a driver in our direction which nearly hit me on the head. Had I gone so far down the drain that I became a target for disdainful drivers who wanted to hurt me? Being non-violent myself, I couldn't believe that anybody would do such a thing. However, it was my companion's energy that attracted that type of action.

    After a couple of uneventful rides we arrived at a house that was located in a black neighborhood in St. Petersburg. A Caucasian couple, house half-way empty, lived in their bedroom while four neglected children ran around in the place. We put our bags in a small room before heading towards one of the two couches in the living room. Fifteen minutes later, the police arrived.

Non-comprehending, having had practically no interaction with representatives of the law, I listened to their accusation/investigation of the eldest boy who had stolen an expensive golden diamond ring. The kid lived in a foster home but had arrived to solicit his mother's help. Fierce denials led to their departure before I wondered what kind of place I had landed in. I spent five horror filled days there.

There were a 13-year-old girl followed by two boys of 11 and 10 respectively and a girl of 8. The kids walked around without underwear and barefooted, something I considered an affront. However, I wasn't invited to air my opinion about how things should be done as the couple avoided me like the plague most of the time. With good reason because I would have caused problems for them had I known what was really going on there.

My companion left every day to do labor work. I assumed he saved his money but it turned out that he handed his entire paycheck to the woman for our accommodations. In a rare moment of companionship she showed me her family albums, explaining that she had been married three times to murderers who were in prison. The guy she lived with was out on parole after he had killed four people in a barroom brawl. Oops! I had to swallow hard as I heard this news and froze when she pointed at her own baby picture with the comment: nice pussy, eh?

I had seen the 8 year old girl masturbating on the floor with the result that her face turned beet-red. In my confusion I asked her to go to her room because I did not enjoy the sight. How could you explain to that child whose mother encouraged her to do this that others frowned upon such actions? For the first time in my life I was surrounded by people who used children for sex and who taught them how to seduce adults for money. Pedophilia had been a huge peeve of mine. If I would have had the chance I would have become a lawyer prosecuting pedophiles who I considered to be a virus in society. Now here I was offered a peek into the other side of this seedy proposition: children who were used as bait by their parents to solicit just such sick behavior in humans in exchange for money that supported their habits!

The mother was on welfare but worked a part-time job in a restaurant as a waitress. An hour after she left for work, one of the children would visit her to get some tip money to buy food for their supper. When I decided to cook spaghetti the kids wanted to help me and learn how to do it. This request was frowned upon by the huge guy who lived there. Ignoring him, I did it anyway. These kids were starved for attention and still curious enough to want to learn something useful. It broke my heart to know that such desperate lives existed in American society!

When the mother, in her late thirties, heard about my cooking lesson she told her kids sarcastically that I wanted to adopt them. Unbelievable to me, she didn't care one way or the other what would happen to them.

Her kids had to provide for her. Even when we walked together on a Sunday afternoon to the beach, the barefooted kids engaged in begging people for food and money.

On another occasion I saw the mother kiss her oldest daughter, the only affection she measured out to any of her kids while I was there. But she did it as a way to advocate violence because the daughter had just won a fist fight with another girl.

The topper, aside from the sexual perversities, came in the shape of a pair of cowboy boots purchased with the monthly welfare check. There were four birthdays in that one week, the husband's, the two younger boys' and my own. The husband got the cowboy boots, the kids got nothing and she wished me a happy, fucking birthday. Emotionally, I got hit with feelings I did not even know existed. Fury, consternation, panic, disbelief, vulnerability all fought for my attention.

That day I announced my departure to my companion. I could not take it anymore. He refused to say goodbye which is what I wanted to do while giving her a piece of my mind, so we sneaked out of the house in the middle of the night. That family stayed mentally with me for a long time to come even though I was kept busy with all kinds of new situations I had to handle.

SEVEN

Hitchhiking

Back on the road I noticed my companion smoked marijuana. He had told me he didn't and something about people not being able to tell me honestly what their habits were, did not sit well. He wanted us to go across country again to Oregon where his mother lived but he told me she could not host us. So I wasn't sure why we were headed there in the first place. When a truck driver offered me an extended stay I accepted, telling my companion to go ahead alone.

The new random sex partner gave me a jar filled with coins that amounted to about $65. Of course, after he had been serviced sexually he dropped me like a hot potato causing me to consider my own actions. Why did I get upset if I had done the same thing to another person only a few days earlier? To be rejected is one thing but to flit from one person to another without being able to change it, began to take a toll on me. I'd been in situations where others were dominating me but now I felt as if I had no control whatsoever.

Armed with my jar I went into a restaurant to eat. Hunger had little to do with it, I was upset and I subconsciously tried to fill an empty feeling with food. Sexual activity without reverence actually exacerbated that empty feeling. Then I went back to the road to continue my traveling escapades until, months later, tired of moving around without getting anywhere, I made the conscious decision to settle down in Missoula, Montana.

The price of riding along on the big trucks was contained in the popular phrase "ass, grass, or cash." There were few exceptions. Charity on the road did not exist. What comes around goes around was one of the credos most of them lived with. Of course, this translated into conditional giving: there were strings attached.

There are pivotal points in our lives when we hit a fork in the road and we have to decide which direction to go into. The major changes for me came about at the ages of 22, (transiting Uranus square my natal one, semi-sextile my Sun), my beloved left me. This meant saying goodbye to a cushy future with a highly intelligent, compassionate, wonderful man and possibly a great family in favor of the freedom of an uncertain future in the United States.

The second one loomed at the age of 31 with Uranus quincunx my natal one when I walked away from a marriage of convenience that offered financial security in exchange for my service, time and loyalty, to a low-paid job in a B&B in the Hollywood Hills where I met fascinating people and began to get an idea about my abilities.

The third one arrived ten years later when Uranus was opposite my natal one, when it was a matter of choosing the red or blue pill a la Neo in The Matrix. The 'pills' consisted of two trucks, one a high-end, state-of-the-art condo on wheels with a young, bright-looking driver while the other one was a rickety old flatbed with cramped quarters, a young hefty girl who had just finished trucking school and a middle-aged man with a back problem. Naturally, I chose the underdog, I was getting good at it.

In all fairness, I ended up on the flatbed after I saw the intent in the eyes of the driver peering at me from over the floorboard of the truck. His gaze directed itself like a laser beam in which every wave of light precisely reinforces every other. I did not feel transfixed like a moth drawn to a light bulb or a deer caught in the headlights of a car. This was different. Within this gaze shone a powerful and effective intention directed by its spirit-controlled integrated personality.

Over the years I had learned how to gauge the strength and maturity of a spirit and here was one I could not fully perceive. *A spirit on a lower level of awareness cannot 'see' the more evolved one but the latter can fully perceive the other!*

Impressed as I was with the driver's presence, sharing a cabin with him and his obese younger driving partner did not entice me. She sat behind me in the cabin; I took place in the passenger seat while he sat in the driver's seat both literally as well as figuratively. He managed to capture my attention in novel ways. I tried to listen to him speak over the CB radio but could not capture one word of his soft-spoken sentences which frustrated me. He asked me the date of my birthday and looked baffled when it turned out to be the same as that of his ex-wife. I squinted. What's wrong with that day? I wondered, not grasping that the odds of meeting a kindred soul whose wife had been born on the same day were phenomenal.

I had told him a few white lies when suddenly it occurred to me that this guy may be the exalted soul mate I had been looking for. Often I had heard that I was the type of woman every guy was looking for; if that was true, what was I doing hitchhiking around? Sometimes my life did not make one bit of sense. Gasping, I thought I had made an error, that the chances of starting off on the right foot, were diminished. How are you going to convince a stranger (kindred spirit) of being honest after telling him a few lies? Oh no.

When that thought cruised through my head I started to pay better attention. Was he or wasn't he? Again I got the full blast of his directed gaze that made a powerful connection before he left to drive an accompanying truck. The young woman climbed behind the steering wheel and made the truck hiccup before she engaged the right gear to make it move.

Are you afraid? she asked. I shook my head. She had abandoned a driver who had taken her on as a trainee fresh out of school, now she was on her way back home. This driver had offered me the chance to learn how to drive a truck but now my interest was piqued in a different way. I did accept his offer, however.

I went to sleep and was impressed when he got back on the truck to drive some more without getting any rest. I had never been able to comfortably skip a restful sleep of seven to eight hours without feeling its draining effect on my energy level the following day.

He asked me whether I wanted to go to his home in Spokane where he lived with his two children and his ex-wife or spent the weekend in Missoula before I joined him on a haul across country.

The notion of having to deal with an (ex) wife and two children did not appeal to me so I chose the latter. I got out to pay for a room, and then couldn't find the truck because he had moved. After a few seconds of confusion, I looked to the right and spotted him driving towards me. Surprised, I noticed the number of the truck matched the room number key in my hand: 23!

While contemplating my future in solitude, I could not conclude whether I had met an exalted soul mate, a driver's instructor or a *Don Juan.*

EIGHT

Re-connections
On Monday morning, after having spent an enjoyable time in Missoula, I had to hitchhike to get to Spokane. A car sped by me only to stop right on top of the ON ramp to reverse its gears and back up to where I was standing. Wow! A young mulatto businessman, out to have a diversion while doing his job, picked me up. He hesitated when he had to tank up in Idaho because of its reputation for White Supremacy fanatics. A bit fearful he entered the store where, to his surprise, a Caucasian man did him the courtesy of opening the door for him. Smiling, I enjoyed seeing that positive gesture!

Spirit in action, although I did not yet recognize it fully! When he invited me to spend the night in the fanciest hotel of the city, I accepted gladly. This would be more fun than bunking on the couch of the driver and his family. The latter told me he would call me around 9 in the morning to set a time for picking me up. Little did I know that he was a more powerful and mature aspect of my Self, staging scenes for years to come to disentangle me from the matrix.

When the phone rang in the morning I picked it up. A woman's voice answered asking for the guy who had paid for the room. The damage was done. Expecting the driver to call me to let me know when he was coming down to pick me up, it turned out to be the guy's wife. "This is serious," the guy looked worried.

"You should have told me, how would I know? I expected a call too," I said in my own defense.

After I got the right call I descended to the lobby where somebody wearing a cap picked up my suitcase. He came out of nowhere, giving me a similar feeling I experienced when I did not see the truck in the same spot when I left it to check into the motel. His beautiful son with whom I had an instant rapport waited in his pickup truck. When I wanted to talk about the incident in the hotel room, he beat me to it by saying: you answered the phone, and got his wife on the line. Now how would I know that?

How indeed? That people had abilities that would cross dimensional boundaries I knew about, having read hundreds of books that unraveled mysteries and offered solutions to unexplained phenomena and problems. To meet somebody who actually used his abilities to make it happen in front of my eyes rendered me speechless, a near miracle in those days!

Vaguely uneasy, I put it on the mental backburner to see what developed here. When I met his 13-year-old daughter, 13 being one of my guidance numbers that usually indicated a necessity for me to be in a certain area, I got a vision that led back to a lifetime shared on the Greek island of Karo as botanists.

The striking red-haired (ex) wife of the driver greeted me. Since I had dyed my hair red and shared the same birthday with her, I felt duplicated. The circle with the two figures standing on the bottom came back to mind. We were two similar-looking women to the eye, but one had to journey the entire circle while the

other one was almost done. We operated spiritually on the opposite ends of the spectrum. Our meeting had a significance of which I became only fully aware after one of my awakenings which occurred shortly after I left trucking for good:
1) She was a SSS-er behind the attractive human façade. In her case I could not perceive that; I got blocked by her (ex) husband whose spirit was far stronger than my own, a totally new experience.
2) Her intention (function) was to introvert people to trap their spirits, incorporate them into the hive mentality of the future New World Order, the opposite of my goals.
3) She made me aware of how they always do the same routine, in her case carrying a basket with laundry through the living room to the stairs leading to the basement where the washer and dryer stood. She did this when she wanted to interrupt a conversation in an attempt to attract attention towards herself.
4) It was the first time I met one of them who was controlled by a spirit far stronger than the alien group that had her spirit in its grip. That was a revelation connected to the new realization that spirit ruled, regardless of how many governments claimed they ruled!

NINE

Unknowingly recruited

Back on the truck, the driver told me several stories about women who had not minded waiting for him. Knowing perhaps that I didn't like to wait for people I wondered why he was giving me that piece of information. One night he went into a truck stop while I fell asleep in the truck. It took several hours before he returned. According to him, he had been playing the poker machines but he did not always tell me what he was really doing. Why should he? So far he had not allowed me to take the steering wheel, saying he didn't want to let me crash. Within three days he threw me off his truck in Omaha, Nebraska.

Sitting in the restaurant of the truck stop enjoying breakfast I thought I must be wrong about this guy if he is so uncouth to drop me in the middle of nowhere. Sighing, I decided to return to Missoula where I had wanted to get settled down in the first place.

I got a ride from a guy who was in love. What an odd phenomenon! He could not concentrate on anything thanks to his yearning for his beloved. He stopped frequently to call her just to hear her voice and didn't get much done. Was I supposed to fall in love or was this just some cosmic joke? Did I miss something in life if I was not in love with somebody? No answers came but when I woke up in the morning *the face of the avatar trucker popped up above my head like a stamp on an envelope.*

Along the way it struck me to return to his house to find out what had prompted him to ditch me like that. I didn't like not understanding something, a question mark that would hover in my mind forever! I encountered several obstacles that made me grit my teeth and made me more determined to return there: I got bitten by a dog when I wanted to use the bathroom in a house where the driver visited some friends. The bite and loss of blood made me feel close to fainting and I ended up sleeping the night away in their daughter's bedroom.

Getting back to his house became a chore, and when I arrived there, I learned he wasn't due back for a couple of days. When he returned, he murmured he was busy when he passed me, and then left again without talking to me. I felt totally ignored but determined to find out what was going on.

Inner questions to be answered:
1)   Confused about whether this driver was the soul mate I had been looking for, I wanted to find out, but he remained mum.
2)   The mystery of why he lived with his ex-wife who had the same birthday glued me to it.
3)   If he still had the better looking wife why would he be interested in me?
4)   Why couldn't I get him out of my head?
5)   Why did he tell me the stories about other women waiting for him?

6) Being ignored without knowing why resulted in anger and a morbid fascination with the enigmatic driver, acting like the ultimate high level Scorpio.

TEN

Instructions

Round and round the questions went inside my head as I returned to the road to resume my life as a hitchhiker. During my next ride I got a guy freshly out of trucking school, one who loved every bump in the road and did his best to hit them. He repeated over and over again how he loved doing that. (*In hindsight it reflected the sense of humor of my guide who amused himself dearly in setting up situations, teaching me not to be too serious about my life.*) His advice to me was that I should never refuse an offered meal. I waited in vain for him to do so but when another driver offered to pay for a buffet I thanked him gladly for the food. It also became clear that I would get verbal messages directly through a companion so I would know what to do!

There were other questions that I could not answer. Was there a mad plan behind this hitchhiking? Initially, I thought it quite interesting to land in a world I had no knowledge of but the novelty wore off quickly. My fears had subsided somewhat as I didn't seem to be standing alongside the road for too long very often. Every time some driver picked me up I learned something new and sometimes stayed with the same driver for several days. I sometimes functioned as a sex fairy working her magic to service the sturdy men in motion!

ELEVEN

Temptation is a thought form that is designed to draw possible negativity from the human energy system without harming others. The soul understands that. (Gary Zukov)

For a while I got into the full swing of acting on sexual temptations. Without feeling too much guilt, I could not shake the driver out of my head who had ditched me in Omaha. What if he was the One? Wasn't I supposed to be loyal and faithful to him? That was irrational. He didn't need my body for his own satisfaction. His ex-wife could do the same job or a better one while he did not seem to have a lack of interested females. Is that why he told me those stories? Round and round the thoughts looped through my head!

For some inexplicable reason my flow of menstruation had stopped. No menopause, no children, no family, a woman without a mission who found herself now in perpetual motion. *I was my own Home.*

Occasionally, when a feeling of despair began to develop, I would get a break from the road. My current point of view he would perfectly match with people who needed my input in their lives. In return, I got some human contact, a bath and shelter for a few days.

For instance, while waiting for a ride near Superior, a small town not too far from Missoula, I got invited for a cup of coffee by a woman who lived alone with her two children. I felt like a member of her family, exploring the town, joining in their meals, talking about life on the road. I told her I had my truck driver's license but moved around hitchhiking. To her, it didn't matter. I found out later that she smoked marijuana joints all day long to forget her troubles.

Her low self-esteem showed in how she conducted herself and the boyfriends she chose. As soon as she got money she blew it on buying people drinks in the local bar. It appeared as if she abhorred the feel of it, compulsively getting rid of it as soon as she had it in her hands. This did not stop her from complaining about her lack of funds and hitting her father for financial support. She also had sued a doctor who, according to her, had performed a poor operation on her procreative organs.

She told me how her younger brother had perished in a car accident. Her eldest brother had been the driver. A lot of insurance money had been paid out which had disappeared in the pockets of the surviving brother. For me, it did not take too much imagination to surmise what kind of a person the brother would turn out to be.

When the control freak showed up, we instantly disliked each other. He didn't want his sister to get any ideas about getting money or help in her life while he controlled her and his elderly father's every move. Fuming, I tried to explain to her that this brother had killed the other brother deliberately, (I saw it in a vision) but she misunderstood the words I spoke to mean that this brother had suffered because of the other's death. Yes, he did change after the accident, she conceded. I gave up.

He wanted to drive me, his elderly father and his sister and her children to a restaurant. Oh joy, I thought. I knew he wouldn't show up on the agreed upon time so I fixed a steak for myself. One hour later he arrived thinking we would be starving. Her little daughter was about to point out we already ate but I stopped her from volunteering that information. Rightly so! In the restaurant he insisted that his sister and I should share a club sandwich because 'he was short in funds'. The only act of rebellion I could muster was to order a turkey club instead of one with chicken as he proposed. It didn't matter anyhow, I was no longer hungry.

On the way back, when I mentioned my desire to see a moose from up close, he stopped to supposedly accommodate me. Running down a slope he gestured for me to follow him. I hesitated, felt my attention directed from within to look ahead and, by golly, a huge moose darted forth from the bushes. What a magnificent animal! I clapped my hands in delight. Of course, I also applauded the spiritual victory over the dictatorial attitude of the brother who was not amused.

He returned to drive the car and decided to drop off his family at his father's house. Then he took me back to his sister's house while stepping on the gas plank. In that instant I knew for certain he had been his brother's killer. He looked aside to see whether he scared me as I could sense his intent to slaughter me as well if it would have been lucrative. The vicious glee shone on his face when he mentioned obliquely how his father suffered from the loss of one son while he was about to get all of his money so he could 'invest' it for him.

When she did win her court case she confided in me that the money would go to that brother so he could invest it for her as well. "Blood is thicker than water," is the cliché she used to justify her action. My lesson was not to interfere in people's lives. I had not convinced her that this brother would steal her money, leaving her in the financial ditch for the rest of her life if she insisted upon escaping from reality. At best, I had provided her with friendship.

TWELVE

Earning my keep

Not long after my departure from Superior, Montana, I climbed aboard the driver-owned truck of an Oklahoman man who hauled electronic equipment for shows and expositions. He wanted to hire me as his driving partner. I accepted before finding out he was going through a divorce in which the SSS wife, finagled her way into getting her hand on everything he owned. Prior experiences with these situations made me immediately think of the legal aspects so I convinced him to register my presence on the truck the same day. Luckily he did, because only hours later she had phoned the company about the mystery woman on his truck.

This driver was a nice man trying too much to please others in an attempt to find harmony and balance in his life, one of the negative traits of the sign Libra. Before I knew it, I got entangled with his problems and the people who were like vultures preying on his possessions. A flashback showed my elderly friend Bill, who was a retired rigger, in Hawaii. When he got cancer of the throat and had only months left to live, all of the people that came into his life were vultures that snooped around for pickings, including his own son. The latter, a big wheel embroiled in politics of Washington, D.C., came to visit before his father passed on, so he could get his name on the deed of the valuable condominium his father owned.

Recognizing the SSS-almost ex-wife to be way of doing things, I urged him to make it legal for me to be on his truck. Rule-bound, the SSS-er does not have the courage, or imagination for that matter, to do something spontaneously. But they 'catch' any simultaneous spirit who is ignorant of the law to put major obstacles on their paths. Guess who make up the prison population? Speaking for myself, it takes years before a seeker can actually appreciate the challenge of the obstacles once they are overcome and dealt with!

After he separated from his wife, he had rented a house in a small town of Oklahoma that was owned by a couple that lived only a few miles away. It turned out that they did not hesitate to use that house whenever they felt like it. We had been introduced on another occasion when she showed me her cellar stocked with edible supplies in case of an emergency. The unmistakable air of haughtiness, her superiority flanked by his gopher-status, permeated their attitudes.

An obese female in her mid-forties, wearing black trousers to hide her muffin-top with wide blouses, and her pussy-whipped husband of small, skinny stature, she wanted to know where I had met the driver, where I came from, how long I was going to stay, the whole shebang. I gave her minimal information but did mention how I had met him as a hitchhiker. Knowing glances were exchanged at that revelation!

Living my life using brutal honesty, thanks to the biblical command 'thou shalt not lie' I had to learn what to say and how to say it to whom. A passage from the book The Hiding Place by Corrie Ten Boom fascinated me so much I had made it my own, testing it out wherever I went, because it meant living on faith. When the Nazis came knocking on this watchmaker's family door to recruit the son who was hiding in the basement, a table put on the carpet that hid the access stairs, Corrie's sister Betsie faced inner turmoil as a deeply religious woman. She did not want to lie but she also did not want to betray her brother. 'Where is your brother?" the Nazis demanded. Giggling, very nervously twiddling her thumbs, she stated: he is under the table. 'Where is your brother?" the Nazis demanded. The Nazis thought her crazy and moved on.

    This remarkable family assisted many Jewish people escape to England during the Nazi Holocaust before a neighbor ratted on their work so the sisters ended up in the Ravensbruck camp for women and children in Germany. Betsie died there while Corrie, the first female licensed clocksmith in The Netherlands, was released due to 'a clerical error' so she could tell her story to the world.

    Shortly after my interrogation by the simultaneous spirit suppressor, she came to visit the driver's home when I was there alone. With her husband in tow, she passed by me, she glanced over her shoulder to her husband and remarked "how she hoped that someone else would accommodate him" while she was going to take a nap in the heart-shaped bed where the driver and I slept. Excuse me? I had to swallow twice not to react to this superbly played out insult to my dignity, but I managed. Then I noticed that the wimp started to get out of his clothes and the picture was complete. Of course, the manoeuver intended to show me how lowly a person they considered me to be!

She obliquely inferred for me to have sex with her husband because
1) I was by my own admission (the hitchhiking) slut and she was a properly married wife who 'allowed' her husband to fulfill his needs with others; when he did she could control him with guilt.
2) The fact that she disappeared into the bedroom into the spot where I slept indicated total control. She owned the house and she had permission of her renter to use the house as she saw fit. There was nothing I could do about it.
3) If I had consented I had merely proven myself to be the slut and hurt the feelings of the driver who needed to have a friend to stand by him in his stressful separation from his wife.
4) The ugliness of the situation almost made me puke, a physical reaction I had to get under control. Such parasites, such suppressive, misguided and immature souls!

THIRTEEN

Another battle
Immediately I got up and went for a walk, doing breathing exercises to calm myself down.

Back on the road, when his divorce proceedings smoothed out to the point where he could keep his truck to make a living, I left. I noticed the tears in his eyes but I knew he did not cry about losing me. He cried because he was lonesome and felt sorry for himself. It didn't take him long to find a mate.

When I came through his town a few months later I met her. This woman was a mess. After a couple of days she moved into his place with an 11-year-old daughter who controlled her mother completely. Well, I thought, if you have adult control freaks why shouldn't you have children who were like that? The only time I teach another person's child a lesson is when they personally affront me without the parent correcting it.

I recognized the girl as another simultaneous spirit suppressing creature and, therefore, not open to any suggestions to learn anything new. It was a waste of time for anyone to even attempt to teach her manners. When I cooked a nice meal for them, she refused to do dishes and made some derogatory remarks about my cooking to which her mother responded with a smile.

She did not like the room she had to sleep in so I told her she could sleep in the hallway. She exhibited behavior that defied my presence, that mocked me and wanted to boss me around like she did her mother. The driver watched while I showed him what a piece of misery he would haul into his house if this girl would be living there.

She was not the girlfriend's only daughter. Apparently, she had four more children who were living with foster families due to her alcoholism, the socially accepted people destroyer. Three days into the stay she went out by herself (I found out the next morning) and totaled her car under the influence of too many whiskeys. Her parents had left her with six Greyhound dogs that had been bred for races. Those were taken away from her to cover debts she had incurred to feed her drug and alcohol addictions. Good luck! I wished the driver before I left; pointing out that being alone is sometimes preferable to a mate with a heap of problems in your home.

Cruising through the area, one year later, I wanted to check out how he was doing. I met him in the bar of a town where he played billiards with the same couple. Playfully, thinking that perhaps the wimp, whose wife had given him permission to use my body while she rested in my bed, could muster up the grace to welcome me, I playfully grabbed his cue stick from behind. He froze.

The bitch did manage to insult me again. It is a hard and tedious road to get to a state of not taking anything that is being said or done personally, the way of the spirit, but there are no short cuts so I had to keep handling situations in the human drama until I got there!

Ayla's Quest

I sat down at the table where she had positioned herself next to my friend while his new mate sat next to me on the other side. After listening to her derogatory remarks about my life as a hitchhiker, I noticed her subtle control over the woman next to me who laughed on cue. The latter was a bit concerned about my presence as a former girlfriend but I reassured her that her man had been more of a working partner than a romantic one. I had hit upon the phase of not liking to have sex with random partners any longer, healing myself in the process. That information made her relax a bit.

After I returned from the bathroom a man had taken my seat. Out of the corner of my eye I noticed her making gestures just to see how I would handle the inconvenience. To deal with a situation in which you know you are being insulted on purpose and not succumb to anger is hard to do. The energies of my Mars in Scorpio used to have a field day with an occasion like that but here I was, getting the opportunity to show myself to be the better person (gnashing teeth included.) Of course, one can always walk away but I knew that there was an underlying spiritual impulse for me to have those experiences.

I stated that he was sitting in my seat and I wanted it back. Slowly arising, it took a couple of minutes before I could sit down. Inside fuming, I decided not to say goodbye to her. I ignored her. A strange thing happened then. She seemed to fall apart at the seams and shriveled up. I marveled at this revelation. After all the insults I had endured, *a simple action of ignoring the victimizer made me no longer a victim!*

FOURTEEN

More drivers

Back on the road I got a few rides that were fascinating for different reasons. I learned both Light and Dark inspired points of view. Always the lessons were infused with the spiritual banter that set it apart from more mundane attitudes:

One driver hauled a load of parts from the East Coast to UCLA Medical Center in California. What kind of parts? He didn't know but assumed them to be auto parts. Before crossing the border of Texas, the guard opened the trailer only to drop backwards in a faint. Curious as to what caused this unusual reaction we peeked to find human body parts hanging on hooks like frozen animal meat for consumption. Just the sight and knowledge of the contents of the trailer changed our entire atmosphere on the way over from that point on.

Body reaction!

On another occasion, I listened to hear a Caucasian driver vent his racial outrage against African-Americans. Nearing the center of Chicago on the freeway, he suddenly noticed that his tank got close to running on empty. This never failed to baffle me. As a professional driver, isn't that one of the first things to check? He had to park, then yelled some more about the frustration of getting stranded. Another truck stopped next to his. The driver asked over the CB if he was in need of assistance. Yes, he wanted to siphon of diesel fuel so he could make it to the nearest truck stop.

Spirit-determined, the 'savior' was a dark-skinned man! He 'got' the irony of the situation, and stopped talking about his racially motivated hatred!

The only Vietnam veteran I met who actually enjoyed killing people came ironically in the person of a toilet paper hauler. When we got stuck in a white-out in Cheyenne, Wyoming, road and sky forming one seamless snow white blanket covering the land, he delighted in telling me how he would join any army just to participate in a war. Killing was his only motivation, nothing else. Therefore, as the psychiatrists stamped Unfit on his evaluation paper, he set out to create his own killing field. (Isn't that insanity? Isn't killing exactly what a soldier is supposed to be doing or be killed?)

He related to me how he had killed the woman before me on his truck. Why? I asked, instantly on my guard while using a technique to detach myself emotionally from the situation, knowing he would look for signs of fear in my face or body. "I got her a job with a friend who took her in," he said, slyly observing me. "Yes, and," I said patiently, waiting for her 'sin' to be revealed, what did she do? "She stole money from him and then thought she could get away with it." "Ah, and you wouldn't let her, of course?" "I stalked her until I found her, then took her back on the truck where I strangled her during sex. Ah, a sexual snuff experience. Well, it seemed ludicrous to me to have a sexual experience where the blissful waves of orgasm would blend with the throes of death in the last sigh.

"What did you do with the body?" I asked before realizing that I did not need that piece of information to remain safe. Glad he had an opportunity to share his handiwork with anyone, he proudly announced that he had stuffed her body in a cement sewer. I did not ask where, mind you; shit happens, as the truckers say and this guy was full of it. Guess that's why he hauled toilet paper! Was he full of crap or did he relate a real story here? We separated on the note that he couldn't wait for the next war to participate in.

The pain of frozen fingertips being infused with feeling is one I found nearly unbearable. It felt like they were stuck in a pot with boiling water. It made me weep like a little kid. I managed to create this experience in a truck that broke down near a tiny town in the south eastern part of South Dakota. We were caught in a snow storm and the temperatures were far below freezing. For a few hours we found some respite from the cold in the local bar, where no farmer was willing to drive his tractor to attempt to pull us out of the snow bank, where one side of the truck had become stuck. One farmer promised to do so in the early morning.

In the meantime we were left to our own devices. After the bar closed we spent some time outside which made my fingertips freeze. They caused me unexpected misery. The fire inside of them when the sensitivity returned warped the few minutes into an infernal spot of eternity. Or, that's how I experienced it.

Soon thereafter, I got on a local truck with a guy whose life had been ruined by a false accusation of pedophilia. It reminded me of the horror family I had spent some time with in St. Pete. Perceiving his aura, looking into his soul, and noting his handicapped body, there was not a shimmer of a chance this guy would have raped a child. My preconceived notion about the crime of child-rape shifted some more. Horrible to find out that innocent men were victimized by mothers who used their children as bait to make money.

His story centered on his decision to marry a woman with a 9 year old daughter to help her raise her child. Most men were taught to bring home the bacon for their families before the Women's Liberation Movement. This guy, being on the road long days and nights, was no exception. When one partner is too compliant, the other is tempted to take advantage of that. In such situations there are two at fault simply through actions of omission. *If you allow somebody to victimize you rather than defending yourself, isn't that an open invitation for a victimizer?*

So he allowed himself to be used for most of the work, including washing the back of his naked step-daughter in the bathtub on instigation of her mother. Showing her daughter some tapes on sexuality she began asking her questions about her step-father touching her in certain places with the result that the daughter started to say things her mother wanted her to. This indoctrination led to a complaint she filed at the police station; this, in turn, led to a three year' stint behind bars in a cold prison.

I met his mother who looked wearily at me, knowing her son's naivety with women. My attempts to reassure her were not successful. Having no intention to start a relationship with him, I wished them both farewell and moved on.

A chicken hauler from Georgia entered my life. Here was a guy who proclaimed to have an open marriage. This meant that both partners engage in having sex with other partners other than the mate but that is not what it turned out to be. It meant that he was the one who enjoyed extramarital sex while his wife consented (probably did not have a choice but I mulled this over!)

He had only one eye so his depth perception was imbalanced. It did not appear to hinder him in his driving maneuvers. A strange, irrational fear lingered inside when he told me about that. The body is so loaded with fears that you sometimes don't know what you are afraid of until it gets triggered in a new type of situation. The idea that I rode in a semi driven by a guy who had one glass eye caused me discomfort. Of course, since I liked to test everything for myself, I sat around closing my eye to see what the exact effect it could have on his driving. This did not reassure me in the least but I recalled my days as a coordinator for social workers who worked with visually handicapped people. I had learned how to walk outside using a cane in a sweeping motion just to gain understanding of a blind person's situation. Prejudice has a sly way of creeping into one's mind as I had learned from the people without eyesight. My attitude towards them, when they hired me, carried a false note of sympathy and disdain: I considered myself superior. And boy, did they sense that. *When they called me on it, I felt ashamed and the one who was truly blind.* From that moment on, our relationship could develop into a healthy one.

I gave him a chance. Then he reciprocated, but not quite in the way I had anticipated it. He let me drive but only on the long stretches which is rather boring. I wanted to shift gears and go over mountains but that got halted by his fear of my inexperience. So here we were, I was afraid of his driving and he did not trust mine. My Higher Self decided to let me do it however and, one night, his uptight self notwithstanding, he fell asleep and I could tackle the mountains in Tennessee. It wasn't that difficult because I had watched other drivers do it, I just had to be more careful shifting the gears while lowering the speed considerably when going downhill. The driver broke out in cold sweat when he woke up to realize that his truck was parked on the foot of the mountain!

When I asked to meet with his wife, curious to know how she dealt with him, the opportunity did not seem to present itself once during the months we worked in tandem. I was still fascinated about finding out who controlled whom in different settings and if my theory of the identical behavior pattern of the SSS-ers had any merit to it. When he talked about his relationship with his two children, I knew instantly that the son was the programmed human slave and guardian for the aliens. This knowledge confirmed my suspicions.

The regularity of having sex with different partners did nothing for spiritual satisfaction. There actually was something to the verse of that song that The Rolling Stones made popular: "I can't get no satisfaction" although I assume that Jagger meant he was insatiable! The more I went after a spiritual union with another soul, the farther away I felt from it. My inner emptiness increased rather than diminished. I did not understand that power and not sex itself was the underlying motivator. I began to get restless and bored with the physical side of sex.

But sometimes the best remedy is to saturate an addiction with an overload of supply. I began to wake up to the fact that, although my self-esteem was not that low and I had lived a life in which my physical needs had always been met, the drivers generally regarded me as an opportunist and footloose female, to be used as they saw fit to meet their own needs. The unmarried ones wanted to make a partner out of me but that did not seem to fit my itinerary on my personal path. Whenever the temporary partner became serious about keeping me aboard, something would interfere. He would lose his job, his truck or another troublesome situation would demand his attention.

Besides, although I enjoyed my new life which had opened up a whole new spectrum, I knew it would not hold my fascination for a long time to come. All the years of study that had preceded this phase called for further investigation in various fields. Truck driving is a man's world where I circulated as a female who did not quite fit in. I had one foot in, one foot out. It was like being in limbo, I did not want to commit and I did not want to run away.

During this time I also became a puzzle fanatic on the sly. Waiting around in noisy truck stops and terminals to pick up or deliver loads, presented lots of idle time. Reading a book was possible but usually the hustle and bustle around me kept me from being able to concentrate. The perfect solution for my need to be mentally active consisted out of solving logics and crosswords; it was a form of meditation for me.

The most interesting parts of the truck driving endeavor were arguments I got into with drivers who behaved as boors. Not because I enjoyed arguing that much but because of a new awareness that began to shine through. I started to notice how people's actions, just simple ones like stepping in front of somebody, involved manipulations to control. I am not referring here to someone who accidentally steps in front of you. The haughtiness of "I am better than you", mostly unconsciously conducted, is rampant. Turning off the television set or changing the channels while several people are watching was a favorite in the recreation areas. Not too many people objected but I did. On a higher level of awareness getting into arguments is a sure way *to give your power away* but here I was learning how to stand up for my rights, a necessary act on which the higher levels are based.

I always asked for another viewer's agreement when I wanted to change the channel, so the saying popular among truckers "what goes around, comes around", did not apply to civilized behavior. When somebody's control is challenged, the verbal fight that ensues can be quite ugly and accompanied by loud screams. For somebody like me, who had been brought up with the notion that girls 'have to be good' along with the quote by W.C. Fields that ' children should neither be seen nor heard from' it became a rather exhilarating pastime for a while, just to break that DNA command.

Besides the television etiquette, there were other annoying habits like men asking if it would be alright to join me while they're sitting down without waiting for my answer. There is no excuse for somebody to start taking up my time and attention without my permission. Out of necessity *my self-esteem, which is connected to my spirit, not to be confused with pride that caresses one's ego, got a boost.*

A prime example comes to mind when a guy sat down next to me to hit me with a negative blast about Al Pacino getting an Academy Award for his portrayal of a blind, retired general in the film Scent of A Woman. I get great results, with a penetrating gaze like a laser, I drill into somebody who intends to harass me. I allowed him to ponder this gaze for a while before **I told him that**

1) I had not given him permission to sit down at my table
2) I was busy doing log books
3) I did not agree with his moronic opinion, as Pacino deserved to get the Oscar for this role and

4) He was a personal friend of mine. (I did meet the actor when he rehearsed with the Boston Repertory Theater for the role of Richard III by Shakespeare, a play he was obsessed with and for which he gave me tickets. At the time I wrote poetry in a room next to the acting company.)

With his tail between his legs he got up and called me a bitch loudly as he passed by. That is Ms. Superbitch to you, I yelled after him, proud I could finally express my repressed anger at appropriate moments.

FIFTEEN

LOUSIANA

In the early nineties the Bush, Sr. administration made it mandatory for truckers to get a Commercial Drivers' License which translated into a return to school to learn the 'new' system. Computers were installed on the trucks presumably so truckers would always be found in case of an accident. It is so easy to take people's rights and freedom away under the pretense of being concerned about their well-being.

I enrolled in a school. What a disaster that turned out to be. During the six week' program I shared a room with a woman who immediately wanted to use me as her secretary/errand girl. As soon as the telephone rang, she expected me to pick it up. After the first buzz I told her that I didn't expect any calls so it was up to her to answer or not. Of course, recognizing the type of person she was, the programmed SSS whom I was still fighting rather than enduring or ignoring, we were immediately embroiled in a battle of wills. Judging by the number of calls that came in, she had already established herself as the most popular girl in class.

Imitating her modus operandus, I asked a guy to call me just so she could answer the phone for me. Knowing she could not manipulate me, the gossip started and troubles ensued with her newly acquired gopher friends: weak-willed, dense humans who would confront me about anything I did during the day. At night I warned her not to mess with me and that if anything happened to me, I would hold her responsible. The harassment halted immediately. It is helpful to know what to say to whom, knowing who you are dealing with, how to play the Game with awareness!

There was a swimming pool and a Jacuzzi. One day I wanted to sit in the hot spa but the temperature of the water was so high that my leg felt like it burned when I put it into the water. Withdrawing it, I saw the redness of my skin and felt the heat course through the limb. My roommate watched me and decided to challenge a big guy to jump into the Jacuzzi. I warned him not to but in vain. Her hypnotizing power over him made the hapless man splash into the water, stay in there while burning up while she laughed at his body turning beet red.

I did not learn much as the curriculum consisted of a 'teacher' who read aloud from a book most of the day. It was so boring that after a week I decided to call it quits. When I asked the owner if I could stay another night in the room, he refused, telling me that I owed him money for the program and that I should hitchhike if I did not have the money to take the bus. That good ol' money control! In a quick rich scheme he opened a 'school' for which he reserved subsidies for every student he taught without caring one whit about the quality of the program. He changed his tune when I retorted in no uncertain terms that I would sue his school if he refused to accommodate me. His final response was that 'I did not owe him a penny'.

One of the negative traits of the Sun in Libra in a horoscope is that the individual likes peace at all costs and avoids confrontations. Here I was given chances to rectify that. With the Sun in its fall, it is hard enough to actualize the real Self, but that is part of the astrological curriculum. Reaching a higher level of awareness, I realized, however, that the Sun/Moon and Neptune in Libra were there to steer me towards the state of yin yang balance, one real goal in my life!

That night, another woman stood in front of the door with her possessions, ready to move in. My roommate had already invited her to take my place, glad to have a more cooperative and willing errand girl. I laughed.

About a year later, I ran into a student in a truck-stop who had finished the course successfully. I found out that my roommate had started an affair with the married instructor, thereby wrecking his marriage and life before moving on to the next one. Her popularity had diminished drastically after I left. Initially, people can be fooled but after a while they catch on to who they are dealing with!

Around that time, I enrolled in a trucking school in Eugene, Oregon. Being freshly without a home base, confronting the greatest fear of my life, I dragged all of my clothes along; it turned out that I had no practical clothing to do the work necessary on trucks. Dresses may be worn in an office but they had no function in hooking a trailer onto a semi. The immediate lesson was to match my 'costume' with the role I had to play in the world theater. This time I had a roommate who was already an experienced trucker. The problem with her was that she kept telling me what to do while inviting other students into our room from early in the morning until late at night, regardless of what I was doing. Quarreling, she decided to move into another room and started gossiping about me. However, she told others that I was the gossip!

Over time I learned that what people gripe about most is their own worst problem since they can only perceive themselves if their spirit is unawakened.

    Revengeful, (the way I used to be) she organized people to teach me a lesson. She selected another roommate (without my knowledge) who presented another type of challenge. She turned out to be a local woman, married to a guy who came to see how she was doing. I met him and wondered about their story. Why would his wife be trained to go on the road away from him and their children? Soon enough I woke up in the middle of the night to her moans emanating from her heated passion with the guy who lived in the room next doors. Now I had a woman with a cuckolded husband and a lover who shared our room. I got up silently, and went to the local bar to ask the barmaid what she would do in my situation. Give her fair warning, she advised me, which I took to heart. However, it was no longer necessary as the two lovers had fled the room.

    Needless to say that most of the people on welfare who wanted to get out of the system to learn a profession also paid for by the government, were not too serious about the program. They were not there to learn how to drive but to party while fulfilling an obligation to be rehabilitated so the checks would keep coming in the mail. I decided to move into a room with one of the guys, so I would not have to deal with the women and their cohorts. Also a bad move as this guy drank vodka all day long, oblivious of others.

After three weeks of extremely boring paperwork in class we got assigned to teams of four people to learn how to drive some old, dilapidated trucks. A woman who had taken it upon herself to befriend me so she could report to my revengeful (the Law of Attraction at work here) ex-roommate what I was up to, and who also detested the fact that I now lived with the man she wanted to have an affair with, came over to announce the names of my future three co-drivers, released by the teacher.

When I heard their names, I sighed. They were all recruits for her posse, determined to punish me for refusing to go along with her agenda. So I took a leave of absence for a few weeks to circumvent that problem. The vodka swilling student got dismissed one week before Graduation and started working in a convenience store, I learned later. Weeks later I did return to stay in the motel for one night, only to learn that the scene was not much different from the class I had entered.

New Insights
1)   The most obvious mistake I made here was to bring everything I did not need to perform the tasks at hand. I had to learn to let go of material things, identify my authentic needs, as opposed to just collecting things.

Easier said than done, at this point I felt panicky about losing everything I owned.

2) Gossip. I noticed my need to discuss incidences to blow off steam but my audience here turned against me so it was a signal for me to exercise silence. Aside from having to deal with a new-found homelessness or home freedom as I later labeled it, here I was forced to confront my unconsciously driven negative habits.

3) I could not return to an ordinary existence. As soon as I endeavored to get a job, in this case truck-driver, so I could pay bills, something happened to get me off course.

4) There were many instances where I could have been hurt or even killed. For instance, passing by a chemical spill by a derailed train with windows closed. Other people who inhaled the chemicals got very sick. Getting into accidents and walking out of them unharmed happened a lot.

SIXTEEN

A Crash Course

Earlier, my life as a truck driver came to a screeching halt when I ran into the mysterious driver who had a wife with the same birthday had preoccupied me in moments of solitude. Although this happened before I ever attended the two trucking schools, I did not catch on until I failed finishing the school's program for a second time.

The man, who really was the highest aspect of my Higher Self, also referred to as the Awakened Final incarnation (a term borrowed from The Author of the Matrix V volume I), had a great way of avoiding issues; at times I was convinced he messed with my head because suddenly I would not recall the matter I was going to want to discuss with him. This did not happen to me before we met. I also ended up doing things I had never considered doing for anybody else like cleaning his entire house. At my present level, that of being convinced that I was the creator of my own destiny, doing menial work like a janitor did not fit into the picture. Apparently, humility was the first thing I needed to embrace.

Years later, it dawned upon me that getting into arguments is a way of giving your power away. His silence steered me more effectively than any words could ever do. Time and space non-existent, the oneness of spirit communicates clearly. Unlike the 'we are all one' in body which is a total lie.

New Insights
1)   The presence of his (ex) wife served to teach me that 'appearances could deceive'. For the first time I saw the golden circle, gold being the color of Balance that put two women on the bottom; spiritually: one has done the journey around while the other has yet to get started. No doubt she was the better-looking one but my beauty began to shine from the inside.
2)   Compared to her, having reached a much higher level of spiritual maturity after much work and living, our roles should be reversed: she should be doing the cleaning while I could rest on my laurels. However, touching surface areas in a house does have a healing effect. It puts one more in present time while it also grounds someone. Naturally, I only became cognizant of this after I removed mouse droppings and cleaned other messy areas.
3)   The menial work led to an insight that pointed to my function as a spiritual janitor. Later I noticed energetically that I tied loose, vibratory ends for my other incarnations.
4)   His daughter was my maternal grandmother incarnated (she was not aware of that.) Doing some psychic inquiry, I recalled the two of us in several lifetimes where we were friends or colleagues. The most vivid one was the situation on the Greek island Karo where we both worked as botanists.
5)   He showed me my flaws, to be dealt with one by one after I got kicked out once again.

6) He showed me samples of how people controlled and policed each other which I recognized in many situations on the road.
7) He showed me how to take care of myself, to be independent.
8) He showed me how to protect myself against psychic attacks from unbalanced people and astral entities.
9) He showed me how to circumvent control mechanisms used by others without them knowing it.
10) He showed me how to confront, deal with and get rid of my fears.
11) He guided me on my path to inner freedom.
12) He served as ***the role model for the type of guide I wanted to become and learned how to be***.

SEVENTEEN

Spiritual Guidance
Not long after I finished the cleaning, (still not aware I was being launched into a quest) I embarked once again on settling down, getting a job, doing volunteer jobs, and being a productive member of the community; basically, a continuance of the lifestyle I had lived so far: habits are hard to break.

This did not last long as I got embroiled in another power issue with another glassy-eyed woman in the real estate office where I worked. A temporary job agency had sent me over there to expedite backed-up work. Typing documents for closed real estate deals took up most of the day. It involved paying attention to a lot of details but there was one woman who had been assigned to instruct me so she checked my work.

Two days of producing a lot of work prompted the SSS-er to come over to give me instructions contrary to the ones I had gotten from my supervisor so I refused to follow them. That same afternoon there was a meeting I had to attend. It turned out that the gossip monger had prompted the wimpy male supervisor to stop me from producing results. (Amazing that anything gets done in offices with those characters constantly interfering). Of course, it should be clear that *'they are perfect so it is always the other who is to blame, a major reason why they never spiritually progress.'*

They attacked me obliquely, without mentioning my name. Before I got fired that same day, I witnessed an interesting scenario. The instigator had been told to assist with work from another department which she could not handle. Every ten minutes her new supervisor returned to point out the many mistakes she had made to which she responded with one of the generalities the hive mind-connected individual use: *everybody* makes mistakes.

A few hours later, the supervisor informed me that he had to let me go. Another temp got sacked as well, aware of the same female SSS-er who had instigated the move. Even though there was some satisfaction to be gotten from observing the lack of flexibility of the adversary, I was getting royally peeved at this constant interference in my life by those mediocre characters. *What did I need to learn to get rid of them?*

Within one day I lost my apartment, job, friends, and volunteer jobs. Not knowing what else to do, I headed with my possessions to a motel where, after a few days, I gave my clothes and books to the maid who, in turn, offered me lodgings in her modest house.

Soon enough I recognized the SSS pattern in the family again. The woman was married to a trucker who called her at the same time every night to tell her he loved her. One overweight son idled at home, unsure about his future and trying out different careers just to make some money, not feeling any passion for what he was doing. My inner sleuth, looking for clues, usually asked the question: who is the simultaneous spirit suppressor? She made a comment about how he was constantly on the road, away from home, to which I honestly responded that I thought that love meant you wanted to be sharing a lot of time with someone. She turned her head away for some reason but the subtle move told me she was the one who controlled the two men: *people around these control-freaks are never doing well!*

Walking
Since nobody would believe my truth of an invisible spiritual guide/teacher who had turned my life upside down in one day, I thought of a modified version in case somebody would ask me what I was doing. (When the mind/personality is in control of the spirit, it looks for reasons and/or explanations for events) "I lost my job and decided to walk around Lake Coeur d'Alene" I offered to the woman who stopped to give me a lift. She invited me to her home, the first one of many where I played a role in raising the awareness level of the contact person while learning how to increase and enhance my connection to my true Self.

Her dilemma involved two men. She was married to a parasitic type of man who kept her in a prison of guilt about her past and present actions. She loved the man with whom she had an affair. When she mentioned that I could spend only one night at her place, I knew that my presence had already made an impact. Unpopular measures were always relayed by the gopher as her Master/slave (perfect in his own mind) had to maintain an image of benevolence, false or not. Of course, ***fear of being found out*** played also a role.

Her lover turned out to be a rookie cop who came over to check me out. After questioning me, he decided his girlfriend would be OK. Of course, he failed to comprehend that the real damage would be caused by his own actions and her husband who knew about the affair! She told me that she had spent time in prison which he used against her to create a guilt complex, an effective control mechanism that most religions use.

I knew she filed the new information in her mind to ponder about later on. She looked surprised when I told her that her husband knew about the affair because she considered it to be a well-kept secret: the latter waited like a serpent for the right moment to poison his prey, take all of her money and possessions while getting ready to play the role of the cuckolded husband. When she drove me back to the spot where she had picked me up she apologized for not being able to offer me a longer stay but the seed of change had been planted. There was no reason for a prolonged stay as seen from a spiritual point of view. What she needed to know had been communicated.

Observations
1) Thoughts are forms of energy. This woman had asked for answers to questions she could not find within so I responded to that energy, appeared to explain it to her. This happened without fail along the way.
2) I focused on my own knowledge. Having observed the behavior of aliens and the people they

control mentally, I immediately recognized one when I met him or her. So for a while I naturally taught that subject to the 'students who were ready to meet a Teacher.'

3)   A guilt complex, aside from being a control mechanism, can serve as a motivator to clean up one's act and atone for intentionally causing problems for others.

EIGHTEEN

Homeless

Several days later, I went to a shelter for women and children where I used to work as a volunteer, to find temporary lodgings. There was no room. I kept walking, wondering where to go next.

Western society frowns on poor people. One can only learn how hard it really is to try to have any kind of life, not to mention lifestyle, when one is destitute and has to deal with churches run by people who never missed a meal in their life, but who usually advocate a life without wants and/or needs. I pondered that concept a lot. How can one not need basic necessities such as food, medical care if injured, a roof over one's head, and friendly companions? How can one not want to have a life rich with opportunities to enjoy supreme performers in arts, ballet and other cultural events, books that offer various points of view, travel to foreign countries and so forth? If one could not manifest needed items instantly, what are one's survival chances in the concrete jungle of modern society?

With a fat bank account a person does not set out to explore the world by proxy. One buys a car and isolates him/herself driving alone. One meets people primarily from their own social class because a barrier exists that's almost impossible to overcome when that line is crossed. The wealthy one looks down on the poor one, and in return the poor one is intimidated by the rich one while wishing to have his riches. Often the rich ones are crooks who got their money through thievery, oblivious or disdainful of ethical methods of doing business, just to sample the illusionary power that fills their empty Selves. Money in itself is worthless, paper or plastic, but the agreed upon idea among people that it lends power to live a more active and interesting life, is prevalent.

The greedy poor who want it for themselves are locked out of the wealthy circles where members often use gestures as well as specific handshakes to identify themselves to one another. It is a vicious circle. Dealing with the middle-class one encounters a whole set of values connected to money that is linked to 'earning your own keep'. If one has no income or recognizable status in society, the welcome mat is usually missing.

To illustrate this with an example I recall the following situation my invisible spirit guide created: rain set in when I walked outside. I passed by houses surrounded by property in a posh section of town. Again, I had to do something I would have never considered when I was employed: I rang the doorbell of a house to ask if they could provide temporary shelter until the rain passed. The man scanned my appearance before he opened the door gesturing reluctantly for me to enter. He pointed to a couch and proceeded to read, ignoring me. After a while I ventured the question if other strangers who were stranded had approached his house. Usually they have a car, he snarled. Ah, I thought, feeling anger well up because the personality takes things personally although my true Self enjoyed its high self-esteem. His prejudice pulsed in the air creating an imaginary wall that could not be tackled.

Not to be outdone, I struggled with the arrogance of my own personality combined with the energies of a very active Mars in Scorpio. There was no written law that obliged him to be friendly to me or make me feel comfortable because he did not know me, a stranger, my mind reasoned. I wanted to be physically out of the rain and he met that need. When the uneasy silence began to feel oppressive, I started to get up in order to depart when the door opened. His wife and eight-year-old daughter entered the room with a friendliness that took the chill right out of the place. After a short chat, she invited me to join them for supper which I accepted, ignoring the furious dark cloud emanating from her husband. The friendly wife even supplied me with an umbrella.

On another occasion when I walked outside, somewhere north from San Francisco, I got soaked in a shower. In one of my weaker moments, when I began to feel deprived of kind human contact or nutritious sustenance, I cried. Hunger set in, I felt chilled to the bone, had no money and did not know what I was doing or why. With my intelligence, abilities and skills I found it ridiculous to have to live without money. It made no sense to me then.

As soon as I stopped crying, a pickup truck stopped and the driver hailed me. Climbing in the warmth of his cab, he offered me a peanut butter sandwich, my least favorite, but it would keep me going. His kindness tasted great.

--

Near New Orleans I had another memorable experience involving a Mexican driver and rain. He represented the transition into a phase of meeting with men without having sex with them. The friendly guy offered me the opportunity to share a hotel room with him and his younger brother. I actually stayed with him in a bed just to get a good night's sleep. Before they left in the morning to get to their work, they had impressed upon me not to touch anything in the room when I left. I consented.

However, I got caught in a downpour and got soaked to the bone again. Since this became my third experience of getting soaked, I grimaced indifferently. You can get used to (almost) anything! Actually, to be more exact, I felt rather exhilarated. Looking like a drowned cat, I was sure nobody would want to offer me a ride but I proved myself wrong. Within a couple of minutes a guy stopped who helped me out with dry clothes and a ride to New Orleans. He dropped me off at a Denny's to have breakfast on him but he left to check in with his sales boss.

Wondering if he would return to pay for the meal, fear kept me from ordering what I wanted to eat so I stayed within my own budget of a few dollars to satisfy my hunger. He did return, however, to pay for the meal.

On another occasion in Spokane, bumbling along while learning how to adapt to new situations, rain became a factor in going home with a guy I met at a convenience store at night. Before I moved to walk along with him, the store clerk called me aside to confide in me that the guy was known as a psychopath. I acknowledged her concern but reassured her that I knew what I was doing. What I refer to as 'someone pointed out to me' is the notion that my Higher Self only sent people my way that I needed to have some interaction with. So I went along on faith, only to hear him say that "I had reached the end of the line." Eight words that put me on edge, adrenaline going, fear setting in, pit in the stomach talking, you get my drift.

There was another guy at the house who spoke with a gravelly voice. Their conversation centered on getting money to buy more beer and cigarettes. Not really interested I asked if I could lie down to get some sleep. When I did, I overheard him talking about how his mother had forced him to have sex with her when he was a mere 12-year-old kid. Ugh!

I couldn't sleep due to the noise. Then he entered the room to demand what I was doing in his bed. Not understanding what he meant exactly, I reminded him of the fact that he had invited me to join him. He repeated this same question several times before I sensed danger and got up to get dressed again. That's when he grabbed me by the throat in a way similar to my father's when I was a teenager. Feeling quite detached from the scene, in a matter of speaking, I offered him my other cheek, the way it is described in the Bible, instead of fighting or resisting him. For me, rather than lashing out or trying to wriggle free, it felt like I had entered a new, less fearful, phase.

The non-resistance stance took away his momentum; he ended up giving me the money he wanted to use to buy more beer. Unheard of for someone like him to do so I recognized that as a miracle! His gruff comment masked the residue of goodness in him: "you are just another liar down the road." Grasping the significance of the moment, I felt exhilarated and looked utterly amazed at the dollars in my hand.

New Insights
1) The notion of an unending quest kept popping up. My thoughts centered on linear concepts such as...where there is a beginning, there will be an end, mostly to pacify myself. Whenever I felt a slide down to sadness, rescue would be near; like the man with the sandwich when I got soaked. I would get what my body needed not what it desired so trust in my Higher Self increased.
2) It would take a much longer time to learn how money controlled our lives and the various attitudes people had toward it. If I decided to go someplace or do something I'd do it whether I could afford it or not.
3) Rolfing had released stored memories of my father's intent to strangle me but a Reiki master years later still had to remove lingering sadness hiding in the area. Their combined work actually made me feel I passed the test of being non-violent as I did not feel threatened in any way and did not feel like attacking the man who grabbed me by the throat.

NINETEEN

A second set of parents

Passing by an odd looking private church, I knocked on the door. An elderly, angry sounding man opened it to tell me to go to the shelter for women and children that had refused to take me in. I mentioned this and he went off in a huff to phone them to see whether I spoke the truth. He let me stand outside. Then he came out to tell me that he planned on getting me a hotel room downtown. It was close to midnight!

OK. Thank you, I said. Another night with a roof over my head; the appreciation factor for being physically sheltered went up dramatically after losing my home base. What most of us in western societies take for granted becomes an ordeal when it is taken away. Going voluntarily on a trip tenting in the mountains with the knowledge that warm shelter awaits when it is over, would possibly not be as enjoyable when the warm shelter is 'not there'.

I listened to how he pointed out to the clerk that I (wink, wink!) was in need of a room, thereby projecting himself as the do-gooder and I as the victim. To me, who had never been in need of assistance, and had been often the provider for the under privileged, it was another lip-biting moment.

Two new realizations presented themselves for closer examination:

1) When one *did not give voluntarily and unconditionally*, the gift became more of a burden than an enhancement for both parties involved.
2) I resented having to accept this type of help.

The elderly couple took me in. They had their own church and brand of religion and gave me some chores to do while they tried to figure out why their God had chosen me to cross their path. To them, I was a middle-aged female, slightly bewildered at the turn of events in her life, without family or a decent explanation of her situation. The human mind looks for a reason why when something out of the box happens in its environment: "everything has a reason" is a cliché many people believe in. It is not a Truth.

Their belief system included helping down-and-outers especially females, according to the minister's wife. Thus, I met their qualifications! The assistance they wanted to provide consisted of the middle-class notion of getting me back on my feet; in other words, an apartment and a job to pay for the rent. She introduced me to a Bible class with four elderly females but, as soon as one of them responded to me as an equal, she immediately made a gesture to indicate that I belonged to the lower category of needy people. The woman's stance instantly adjusted itself from friendly to haughty.

Looking at the situation, I knew that my past desire to have a different set of parents now manifested itself. *Thoughts have form and energy.* Immediately, I grasped the necessity to stop wanting and/or needing things/people. The saying *"be careful what you ask for, you may get it"*, floated in front of my mind's eye.

The second set of 'parents' were kindred spirits. However, they had taken on so many characteristics from my list of simultaneous spirit suppressors or New Age World accepted behavior, that they kept me guessing for a while before I noted that they had managed to escape total enslavement. Their days were filled with routine, chores that were done at certain times, Bible study at set hours, and a sermon given by the husband on Sundays to the same people with the same ending: a description of the *'crucifiction'* of Christ. *"All you have to do is believe in the Lord Jesus Christ"* was a mantra that rang false to me because I had to earn every prism of enlightenment that entered my Being the hard way.

At night, invariably, they would sit side by side in two armchairs to either study the Bible or watch television. That was my clue to retreat to my own room in the basement as the designated underling.

I recorded the following shocks/lessons in the time I spent with them:
1) The wife, meticulously braiding her long hair to wrap around her head, did the chore of washing dishes. I offered to dry them. As she prepared the setup like a ritual, I decided to sit down for a few minutes. The clean dishtowel rested on my lap. When she saw that, she burst out in an irrational fury, stomped over to me and yanked the towel off my lap, murmuring under her breath. Breaking her armchair routine she descended

from her pedestal to talk to me as an equal. She did wonder about the validity of her own actions then, as taught by her mother, cracking the veneer that kept her spirit chained down. It was an important AHA moment for her.

2) The minister made a pass at me, ogling me, making some remarks about my physique. I did not respond but recorded it mentally because he presented himself as the righteous, superior man of the cloth. It triggered flashbacks of my Bible teacher in high school who harassed me by brushing his hand against my breast when he pretended to grab me by the arm. "You have to read the Bible in the spiritual sense," the minister told me after I communicated my lack of interest in the book. After several occasions discussing passages, I concluded that the man could verbalize his intellectual comprehension but his own spiritual understanding lacked considerably. This observation reinforced my conviction that listening to what people were **not** saying provided me with more clues about them than what they themselves thought they were all about. *"You hear (with your ears) but you do not listen,"* I told him.

3) They wanted me to get a job. I obliged and got a temporary job working for a lawyer who needed to have several legal documents flawlessly typed and executed. Three days into the project I got frustrated because I made some mistakes that were not easily solvable. To my surprise, the following day the documents printed out perfect in the computer. When I proudly handed them to him, he told me I was no longer needed but had

to fulfill the four hours minimum for which he had to pay the agency with answering the phone. Message: my excellent work got rewarded with a punishment of less money because I finished two days ahead of schedule. How did the miracle happen? *A powerful, disencumbered spirit can hack at will into the matrix across space/time.*

4) The aged couple had two adult sons. After the short job their minds figured I must be destined to become the wife of one of her sons. Attempting to hook me onto the eldest failed when he confided in me that he was gay but still in the closet. Relieved, I congratulated him. The younger one, in his forties, with two teenage sons, had lost his wife to cancer. He looked for a housekeeper/sex partner. I recognized him as one of THEM and knew he would not attack me as he saw himself as "perfect". His tricks to get me to offer myself out of my free will I deflated by not responding. His attempts to hypnotize me failed also.

5) Interested in finding out about a future husband and children, I questioned my Higher Self. Opening the Bible at random, it fell on a page where I read: *the barren woman has another purpose in life or words to that effect.* A bit disappointed at this answer I vouched to do it again later on. I let a week pass and repeated the cycle. Astoundingly, not to be ignored, the book fell open at the exact same page where my eye fell on the same words!!!

6) When an opportunity came along to sell a product that was supposed to make people lose weight, they invested a large amount of money in it so I could spend

my days knocking on doors selling it to people. They presented it to me as "helping me with a job" but I sensed their underlying greed. Without consulting me, they had decided to "set me up" with an outfit that was a pyramid money-making scheme in which only the very top would greatly benefit. When I listened a couple of times to the guy who had launched it, telling the same sob story about his mama, I decided I was not going to support his riches by doing a lot of work for little money. I refused to do it, leaving them to the task of selling the products themselves.

7) An important lesson for me came through a phone call. Several weeks earlier I had written a note to John, the truck driver, about offering him my full support because I knew how hard it is for anyone to get to a state of being almost fully operational as a spirit; **I recognized it!** Apparently, he accepted it as my consent to embark on a quest, of which I was still unaware. *In hindsight, he probably made me write it.*

During a game of Scrabble with a church woman with whom I endured an uneasy relationship due to her prejudices, the phone rang. It turned out to be his upset teenage daughter, my former maternal grandmother. She had opened the note, misunderstood its contents and called me to let me know what a piece of scum I was. I got upset, thinking I had harmed somebody and left for my room. The minister's wife went after me while I broke out in sobs. Thinking mistakenly I had gotten into a fight with the church woman she tried to console me.

I pointed out that it had nothing to do with her but with another girl. Then she proceeded to cuss the girl's father out, showing even more misunderstanding. I had mentioned meeting him, being impressed with his abilities so she pointed out that 'he was not honest' in an attempt to blemish my admiration for him. The vibrational ripples in the universal pond caused by a simple action, that of a teenager opening a note that was addressed to one of her parents, were palpable in two homes. Not long thereafter, when I was no longer regarded as a future mate for their sons, I hit the road once more to start another truck driving cycle.

Several years later I knocked on their door, dressed in expensive clothes, to see how they were doing. They just eyed me wearily, never asking how I was doing but welcoming me in their church. They had aged considerably. The same people listened to the same sermon with one exception: this time the minister mentioned the folly of those who adhered to the New Age religion, making eye contact with me. I didn't bother telling him that I followed my own path without the need of living as a flock member of any religious practice.

TWENTY

Walking again

Setting one foot in front of the other is a simple motion most people do not think about. It is something you do automatically to get from point A to point B.

When walking becomes a repetitive motion done over weeks filled with long days, without a specific destination, wholly learning to surrender to my Higher Self, the story changes.

Early winter in the eastern part of the State of Washington in 1995, heading north from Spokane, I braved light snowfall during my first night. I felt horrified. Glaring lights emanating from passing cars hit me squarely in the face, as I walked alongside a highway. I carried a bag that seemed to increase in weight as the hours passed. I had no money, food or anything to drink and attempts to sit down anywhere on the wet road failed entirely. I wondered what I was supposed to be doing, how long it was going to take, why I was doing it.

At dawn, getting very tired, I spotted a house with a porch where I wanted to sit down and rest. As soon as I neared the place, someone shoved the drapes aside to look at me angrily. Shocked, depressed, I turned to move on. Just when I decided not to be able to keep moving, a driver in a van across the street gestured for me to come over. (I learned that if I *really* was tired, assistance would come but if I whined about it, nothing happened. One cannot fool one's Higher Self!)

Gratefully, I sat down in the passenger seat. He offered me $5 which I accepted with the explanation that "I was on a mission somewhat like Brother Joseph, a Dutch minister who had written the book God's Smuggler. I am not allowed to ask for money but can accept it when offered," I said, more to convince myself to accept help than to accommodate him. One of the chapters in that book describes his experiences of reading the Bible aloud on a street corner, having to rely on donations to provide him with nourishment. "I don't envy you guys" the man said sympathetically, dropping me off at a gas station where I purchased a cup of tea and a muffin.

An inner impulse spurred me on to keep moving. I tried to lie down in a shed I passed but the cold was too much. Shivering, I heard the words 'get into the cold.' Yeah, right, and how do I accomplish this, I asked, filing the information in my head. I got up to walk some more. My feet began to ache, the muscles in my legs vibrated like finely tuned violin strings.

When I passed a diner I spent the rest of my money on a bag of French fries, my comfort food. Then I headed in the direction of Priest Lake where I got a bit of sleep in an abandoned shack. I woke up to a breathtaking view of the lake engulfed in a light fog that lent it a supernatural glow. The silence underscored an eeriness that made me fantasize about the uprising of a monster from the deep.

On I went, another day of walking, fantasies drowning out the pain in my blistered feet: I pictured myself walking into a fancy hotel where the desk clerk handed me the key to room number 23. Unlocking the door I stepped into the candle-lit ambiance where an elegantly set table with an iced champagne bottle in a bucket, awaited me. The piece de resistance faced me: my idealized lover, the exalted soul mate I had been searching for all my life, dressed in a tuxedo.

A siren brought me back to the reality of passing cars that sometimes honked at me. I began to cry from the lack of physical comfort, hunger, thirst, and, worst of all, no understanding of what I was doing. Then I noticed a car turning around, speeding passed me, turning again, and parking ahead of me. A dark haired woman hailed me and I walked over to her. "Can I do anything for you?" she asked. The words 'a hot bath' rolled off my tongue with a life of their own. "Get in, please," she said kindly.

Her contributions to my journey consisted of a back pack filled with snacks and bottles of juice, a twenty dollar bill, a Mormon Bible with underlined passages she deemed worthwhile reading and a hot bath/bed for the night. I fell asleep with Frodo of The Lord of the Rings on my mind: at least he had companions and a ring to destroy.

Before I crossed the border into Idaho, I had ditched an expired library card. Apparently, a man had picked it up, called the police and forwarded it to a woman who ran a shelter for the homeless. She told me about this when she called me by my name while I enjoyed a hot breakfast in an eatery.

The woman wanted to drive me over to her shelter to get me off the road. I said no and gave her my 'Brother Joseph' explanation about my mission on the road. She got it, saying that it was just the opposite of being a victim. Then she offered to pay for my breakfast which I gladly accepted.

Another woman who had run away from home after being abused by her husband saw the same type of victim in me walking down the road. Amazed, I listened to her and other stories.

New realizations
1)   People who came over to offer assistance did not see me, they saw themselves.
2)   I experienced anguish over my role as a down-and-outer, having been independent and on my own since I left my parental home.
3)   I had to learn to Trust My Self. I trusted my skills and know how learned along the way but this was different. It denoted surrender to an unseen force whose intent ran in reverse to my way of doing things.
4)   I became aware of a claustrophobic fear I nurtured – a feeling of wanting to get out of places. The command "I have to get out of here" still had power over me.
5)   My own charity had been motivated by a need to keep people emotionally at an arm length's distance. It had been easy for me to give things, money, and time away to needy people, but I had lived behind my own

wall of mistrust, isolated, never allowing someone else to help me with anything.

TWENTY-ONE

Other lives – incarnations

While walking I started to ask questions about other lives I had lived before. If one is open and sensitive enough, impulses from one's Higher Self are received that are like arrows pointing in the energetic direction of simultaneous lives in other time zones. A *déjà vu* moment arrives when one occupies the space where another incarnation is but in a different time zone.

My incarnation from the 12th century presented herself to me: an Apache woman in Arizona who was unwillingly married to a tribal Chief. I could not make out her Indian name so I dubbed her Annabelle. Apparently, she did not appear to have much control over what happened to her as she got abducted from her elderly home to join the Apache tribe. A life filled with physical hardships was her fate. When I got a peek at how the Chief dragged her through the mud by her long, black hair I stopped feeling sorry for myself. In the scheme of things, there were always people in worse situations than my own. Knowing about her lent me vibrations of encouragement to endure the hardship I suffered in present time.

I got a confirmation of my new awareness regarding Annabelle: a car stopped with a native woman who ironically started talking about being able to see ghosts after I accepted her offer to ride along.

The sole of my shoe let loose. There was no possibility of walking farther on it so I stopped at a cobbler's shop. The embarrassment of not having money to pay to get my shoe fixed made me break out in a cold sweat. I entered the store and told the owner a long story about being on the road and not being able to walk on my shoe. I offered to pay as soon as I got home (non-existent). He nodded laconically, pasted the sole, told me to mail him $5 if I could and sent me on my way. Why was I so reluctant to accept assistance from another human being?

Another one of my incarnations turned out to be a guy who looked like a character from a spaghetti western. Seated with his back to the wall of a saloon, he turned cards in a poker game while puffing on a stogie. When I asked about the time frame/location I got an 18th century location near Tulsa in Oklahoma where he played the role of the local sheriff, a star pinned on his jacket as proof.

As soon as I made his acquaintance the confirmation came in the form of a car with three gamblers inside on their way to a casino. I ended up staying with them for a couple of days during which time I learned that they had already lost a lot of money.

After I picked a number for one of them on the roulette which hit during the second run, I got interested in numbers. What were their vibrations and what role did they play in one's life? This question resulted in an increased awareness regarding the numerical symbols. Numbers became an important guidance mechanism during the rest of my outdoorsy part of my life's journey. Every time I absorbed a lesson and progressed spiritually with new insights, the 'guidance' numbers would change to indicate the conclusion of one cycle and the beginning of another one.

Miraculously, when night neared, I always found a spot where I could lay my weary head. When I needed to get some information it always came to me. I passed through a town, for instance, that did not offer any accommodations for me; and then somebody offered the solution of going to the police to spend the night. I learned to let go of my pride and pre-conceived ideas about lodgings to embrace the adventures that lay ahead of me. This did not include liking it or not worrying about it at this point.

When a man in a pickup truck offered me a ride I got a nagging feeling I knew him but no vision would ensue. He drove into a secluded woodsy area and my inner bullshit detector rang its alarm. After he parked, he ordered me to get out, so I did. Unmistakably, he had targeted me as the slut who could be used for a moment of sexual pleasure. Excuse me? I thought, is rape part of my spiritual enhancement program?

That instant the rain began to fall. It began to pour and had an effect of a cold shower: he decided to forego it and return to a bar to resume his drinking. He even deigned to buy me a few appetizers before he turned his back to other women. Again, it occurred to me how timely the rain had interfered with his intention to harm me.

There were many occasions along my route that were so inspirational that it left me panting for more.

Each successive level brought additional surprises, something I really enjoyed.

New realizations
1)   During the six weeks of walking through the State of Washington and Idaho I learned that no matter what happened to me, I would be taken care of and protected. That knowledge, however, did not prevent my body from experiencing anxiety in future precarious situations.
2)   The tendency to offer explanations for my situation/predicament I considered a habit I needed to overcome. It really was nobody's business what I did with or in my life and why I came to be walking around. But it would take another couple of years before I could be comfortable doing just that: no regrets, no explanations, no reactions.
3)   No husband and children were in the offing. I had to give up the idea that I would have a physical family so I embraced every new person as a member of my spiritual one: *'a stranger is a friend I have not met yet'* became the slogan to keep me going.
4)   The walking was a tour de force. Questions arose connected to my other incarnations that got confirmed. I felt the vibrations and met others, an obscure emperor of Persia, a wealthy Italian matron with eight children, a Chinese market woman selling live snakes, a baker's wife in France, a farrier in New England, a recalcitrant monk in a cloister in Switzerland, an Ethiopian priest, an African Chief, a doctor in England, a princess in

Nepal, a Roman Gladiator, and a Mongolian warrior, etc.

5) Truly nice people like the cobbler would help me on the honor of a handshake.

6) The whole issue of money was complex. I experienced for the first time the survival possibilities the "system" presented without using any paper or plastic!

TWENTY-TWO

An Awakening

Still thinking I had something to say over my own destiny despite the presence of a guide who had already proven to be more of a nuisance than a pleasure; I assumed that the walking had been a sideshow for entertainment. Issues such as getting a home base, jobs, my future, prompted me to return to Seattle where I had been successful before. An entirely different program came to light.

My body had dropped twenty pounds due to a diet based on sporadic snacks combined with the hundreds of miles I walked on the road so I looked attractive as measured by society's standards.

At the airport SeaTac, amidst the hustle and bustle of passengers getting on and off planes, I experienced an awakening somewhat reminiscent of the disconnection of the cocoon in which Neo found himself in the movie The Matrix. Instead of getting unplugged and dropping down a chute I felt like a thread spool on a sewing machine put into motion by the foot of the operator. Layers of energy went BOINK and dissolved while my eyes felt like they were popping out of my head like they are depicted in cartoons. In fact, they felt like they were slightly in front of my face instead of in it. Of course, this was another clue I was on an extraordinary journey but that fact escaped me completely.

Going against the Grain

    My first assignment consisted of taking a suitcase that belonged to a woman who was headed for a cruise. My nerves were so shattered that I yelled at a person who said something to me, not hearing the words, convinced that I looked guilty. I had no clue as to what it contained but when I opened it at a safe spot I found enough money to get a room in a modest motel and beautiful clothes in my size. An awful desk clerk checked me in and it turned out that I had to haul the huge suitcase up two flights of stairs to get to the room.

    I had no money left but got the instruction to put on one of the dresses and go sit at the bar. So I did. I ordered a glass of ice water (,) looking like a lady and became the snickering laughing stock of the customers. A woman wearing a chiffon dress who sits alone at the bar without spending a dime, in what direction would the gossip develop? I was not amused but played my part until I could leave. In this simple situation without spoken words I had a huge impact on the immediate environment through sheer presence. The very fact that I used no credit cards or dollar bills made me an outsider. The next morning I returned to the airport on a shuttle but left the suitcase in the room.

    A wealthy looking woman stood in front of me. Thinking the rest of the world saw me as a freak with eyes that projected out of her face, it just felt that way, I got an inner nudge to ask her for one dollar to cover bus fare. It triggered the memory of asking my female cousin, the accountant, for money when I really needed it. On another occasion when I designed jewelry and sold them on an individual basis, I wanted to get a small business loan from my female cousin the bank president which she refused because I had left the family for the States.

I watched her open her wallet to extract a crisp one dollar bill for the bus fare. Handing it to me, she spoiled the moment of victory by saying: "I certainly hope people will give me a dollar when I need it." I grimaced. Her clothes were expensive and she had no doubt a stash of money in her bank accounts. She made a fuss over one dollar? People, who gave something conditionally, spoiled the entire act!

The bus I got on passed by the hotel and didn't stop for several miles to come, making it impossible to return to the room. Later in the day I called to tell them to put the suitcase in a storage room but it was in vain. I never could get back to the hotel so I assumed that the suitcase with the woman's name and address on it would be returned to her!

I stepped out of the box. Deliberately I took all of my identification papers including my driver's license, green card, and passport and dumped them in a trashcan. It had a liberating effect on my soul but it created instant mental worries. How was I to survive in this harsh society without papers or money? Learning How to Trust My Self was the intensive course in the school on the Earth plane where I was enrolled as a student!

New realizations
1)   Several years after having finished doing atonement for perceived wrong doings I now embarked on another spree of actions society frowned upon. The main difference was that I did it unconsciously before and now I did it in an awakened state, fully aware of being cause rather than effect.
2)   I still suffered from low self-esteem: I did not object to being treated like a low class citizen by a nasty clerk.
3)   I yielded my personality to my Higher Self, giving the reins of control held by my personality firmly over to my spirit, and reality reversed itself.

TWENTY-THREE

Still going against the grain

Over the years I had been imbued with a strong sense of morality. Growing up in a Protestant home in the Netherlands, my spiritual guidance consisted of adherence to the Ten Commandments as put forth in the Bible until my mid-teens. My own standards of conduct were guided by "Thou shalt not steal, lie, covet others' possessions, etc." Often I refused well paying positions if I felt the management of the business was playing their customers for fools. I'd rather starve than rip off senior, illiterate and/or other potentially disadvantaged people. But this is easier to do when you are not experiencing a lack of anything in your existence.

Now I had to tear down that inner wall of restrictive thinking by 'helping myself', raising the level of self-esteem in the process. I headed for a mall in downtown Seattle and grabbed a salad off the counter of one of the franchises in the food court, having no clue as to how to feed myself without money. Indifferently, I watched the young guy with his company hat come furiously after me, taking the salad back while yelling: "you didn't pay for that salad." Right he was.

My next attempt consisted of going into a store where I grabbed some items while my knees buckled. I felt paralyzed by fear and acted as if the whole world could see my downfall. "You're not acting right," I heard a voice in my head. "Get out." I managed to secure a small sandwich under my coat to eliminate my immediate hunger. Wiping the sweat of my forehead after I noticed that nobody was after me, I proceeded to eat the swiped food. Certainly this would be over soon, I reassured myself.

Other actions were on the itinerary of breaking the inner code of moral convictions. I walked into a fancy hotel and got into the elevator. Getting out on the third floor I asked the liveried attendant to open a door for me as I had forgotten my key. He opened the door to an immaculately cleaned room. There was no sign of occupancy so I lay down, fully clothed, on the bed. Ten minutes later the door opened and a nice gentleman entered who asked me what I was doing there. "Waiting for my (non-existent) husband," I said quickly, breaking the Commandment of "Thou shalt not lie." Somewhere in the back of my mind a vision of hell and brimstones beckoned as my future home. Talk about being religiously brainwashed!

"I'll walk you downstairs," he said amiably, checking out the clothes I wore, no doubt assessing their value to determine whether I 'belonged' there or not. "Don't worry", he added, "mistakes happen, I've run a hotel myself." Another very uncomfortable feeling passed through me as I did not know how to get myself out of this dilemma.

The manager demanded to know who had opened the door for me after my temporary roommate explained the situation. I circumvented this problem by saying that my husband had made a reservation for that particular room…blah-de-blah. The words had a life of their own which made me go OOB (Out Of Body) to marvel at this figment of my imagination, putting an end to the charade by demanding to use the phone. Then I quickly exited through the back door with a wildly beating heart.

My mind assessed I had escaped a potentially dangerous situation. There was no such indication, so it was irrational, based solely on my held belief system that I would be punished if I was dishonest.

Observations
1)   It took mental courage to go against your own held belief system because the body reacts with discomfort and fears.
2)   I had no clue what I was doing but had to learn to Trust my Higher Self and if this is what it took, I was going to do it.
3)   Accepting help was very difficult for me. I used to deny others the chance to reciprocate, a form of control and imbalanced behavior.

TWENTY-FOUR

Creating shock effects
With my bad memories of being inordinately punished for taking a bikini as a teenager, I could see how my fears of stealing would dissipate if I did it again but what follows is so out of character, that it certainly took a long time before I understood the tasks I had to perform:

With my svelte figure wearing some elegant clothes, I stepped into an upscale department store downtown to do some serious shopping. Following my heart, I proceeded to go to the fourth floor where suitcases were for sale. I picked one out, and descended to the second floor where several boutiques featured imported couture by French and Italian designers such as Chanel, Yves Saint Laurent, Dolce and Gabbana and Scaasi.

I took a white Chanel dress from the hanger, folded it and put it in my new suitcase with the price tag still on it. In the next boutique I took a blue Scaasi dress, opened the suitcase to pack it and proceeded to the next one until I loosely filled it. I wondered why no salesperson attended to the boutiques but I was too busy packing to give it much thought.

I saw a mannequin wearing a red leather jacket featuring a capuchin with trimmed beaver fur so I undressed her. Her black leather pants also found a place in the suitcase. Still nobody stopped me while I continued with a few sweaters that included a canary yellow one. Sunglasses, perfume, shoes, anything I wanted I put in my suitcase. I fully expected to be arrested when I stepped out of the store but, to my surprise, nothing happened.

Carrying the filled suitcase, now with the price tag removed, I headed for the Sheraton Hotel where, in the bathroom, I put on the leather outfit I had taken off the mannequin. Dressed to kill, I sat down in the corner of a large area where a waitress served tea and other refreshments. When she came over to take my order I gave her some reason why I wasn't going to order. This somehow resulted in a chat in which I indicated to be a tourist. She fetched me a tray with a teapot, cups, cookies, sugar and milk and invited me over to stay at her house.

The waitress lived in a small suburb of Seattle in a huge house furnished with antiques she shared with her husband and teenage son. Naturally, her husband was another one of those reptilians hiding behind a human hologram. I resonated on that vibration apparently and regarded it as a cosmic assignment to find out what it all meant. In contrast to the woman with the cop as lover, the first one I met after I lost my job, this one didn't want to hear new information that would implicate her husband as a possible oddball. She claimed to be happy with him regardless of the control he exercised over her.

He was employed as the director of a retirement home for senior citizens. Matter of fact, he informed me how the home got all of the monetary savings and property of the old people who died in the home. This type of legal theft by 'people' who will never land in jail because they know exactly how to use the system, made me furious. I was a long way from the application of Allowance, letting people BE without feeding into the human drama!

The next day, the waitress barged through the door with the announcement that she had found the "granddaddy of them all". She referred to an antique chair she had located in a store. She collected antiques which she bought and sold as a hobby and to make extra income for her husband no doubt. When she saw me, she made a grand gesture for me to feel free to use anything in the house, anything at all. I did.

The next morning I picked up a new credit card that had no signature on it. The following exercise had me checking into a hotel with the credit card while proclaiming that my (non-existent) husband was parking the car. This worked quite well and the clerk handed me a plastic card key with instructions on how to use the amenities. For two days I enjoyed myself tremendously with room service, a suite, and watching the latest movies.

Then I got the impulse to go shopping again in the same department store where I had obtained the designer dresses. When I got to the elevator, a strange occurrence happened. Going down, I readied myself to get out and noticed that the entire group of people shuffled over to my right to let me pass. It triggered a memory of being inside my Higher Self that I could not place at that moment. I got the feeling that I was in charge of them and didn't know why or how.

With my blank credit card in tow, I returned to the department store dressed in the canary yellow sweater and black leather pants and picked out a pile of clothes that amounted to $5,500. The clerk, friendly at first, started to act suspiciously and I, catching her new mood, asked her what was wrong? I am happy that you are getting all those new clothes, she said, but the credit card has a $5,000 limit. Oh, well, how was I supposed to know? I had never owned a credit card, not wanting to be a part of the system or wanting to put myself into debt, so I did not pay attention to the specifics. All I knew was that I began to have fun shopping like I had seldom done before. OK then, so I can't get those clothes? No. She shook her head, waiting for me to leave. "Please return my credit card," I demanded, seeing she was about to take off with it. I turned around and left without stopping. I shrugged it off as a failed experiment.

    On the next day, having checked out of the hotel, I had to return to the store again dressed in the same loud yellow sweater. It crossed my mind that I would be easily spotted and, when I picked up a pair of sunglasses, I got surrounded by security personnel. Amazed, I let myself be led to a room behind the store where I got interviewed by a young guy whose birthday was one day after my own. Both dates formed the number 23 that would have significance for me later on in my journey.

    I asked him why he was not teaching a Little League Baseball Team instead of catching shoplifters for big corporations that ripped people off by charging exorbitant prices. It turned out that he was a baseball fan who had been thinking about doing just that. He informed me that they had been watching me on separate occasions, including the use of my host's credit card. This prompted the question why they did not stop me earlier? Because they were afraid to do so, he answered. Really?

Thinking the whole affair to be a joke, I got a reality check when the cops were called who handcuffed me before they put me in their paddy wagon. Any moment I expected to hear a voice that would say OK, that's enough, let her go. I waited in vain while I got booked in the station for shoplifting. While sitting in my cell I overheard the cops talking about my shenanigans, laughing their heads off, only regretting that they had to fill out a lot of papers itemizing the stolen goods.

Then the waitress, accompanied by one of her friends, came to identify me as the culprit. As I had stored the loot in her house, the police would return everything to the store. A minor inconvenience had a far reaching effect for many people involved, including myself. At least, that's how I looked at it. They've got all of their items returned so why make a fuss? The authorities, however, did not share my sense of humor. It turned into a nightmare when they brought me to the downtown jail where I had to sit in a waiting tank before I got fingerprinted and booked. Infuriated, I lashed out at the guards who gave conflicting orders for me to sit. I was completely dumbfounded about finding myself behind bars. I simply refused to believe it! This could not be, the joke was over. When would angels fling the door open for me?

Claustrophobic, freedom loving, I found it horrible to be kept locked up. Cooperation was a word that did not appear in my vocabulary on that day and a middle-aged guard got the brunt of my anger. I appeared in court to be arraigned, and then met with a female lawyer who had been assigned to me by the court. In the passion of my diatribe of how the "elected" officials wrote laws to cover their own crimes and harass us for minor offenses I registered to my surprise that she agreed with me. Slowing down, I pointed out that I had had fun trying to get some expensive items that amounted to approx. $15,000. Too bad I didn't get the chance to be the belle of the ball in my Scaasi dress.

Then I met an upper middle class mulatto woman who, just like myself, experienced jail for the first time. We attended a sermon together while she said that she had asked for a comforter. When we started to sing a psalm, I felt a force enter my body to lift my voice above all others in perfect pitch.
A miracle! I had always wanted to learn how to sing and now I was doing it. I loved to hear my own voice but it did not last. As soon as the song was over, I heard the woman say while nodding her head, yes, and the comforter is here, meaning me. That was an extraordinary moment, one that will stay with me forever!

After two days they let me go, warning me not to visit with the waitress or her family ever again. I had completely forgotten about her after my new escapades.

Question/Insights
1) Why did I have to do this? Silence surrounded the shopping spree.
2) I had fun doing it, by now convinced spirit ruled this world that others claim to rule.
3) I could see the effect it had on others, getting the notion that everything I did would have some impact on somebody. To my Higher Self, it obviously did not matter whether an item of clothing cost $1 or $1000.
4) Everything got returned to the store but I opened a venue at the local jail, creating further opportunities for incarceration in the near future.

TWENTY-FIVE

More shock effects

Next on the agenda of breaking taboos I found car theft.

I made no plans to do that. Dressed in my red and black leather pantsuit, I snuck into a party given for volunteers of the Muscular Dystrophy Association. Having been a mandatory volunteer while working for them as a receptionist in Honolulu, HI, I felt right at home getting roast beef sandwiches and some tapas. Taking a break after enjoying some of the hors d'oeuvres I walked into the hallway and found a small purse on one of the chairs. Besides a handkerchief it contained a set of car keys which I took out. They fit into a Lexus that was parked somewhere in the garage.

After trying the keys on four different Lexus I found the one in which they fit. I never drove one before and had some difficulties getting it started. Once I did, I spiraled down the lane towards the exit where the attendant stopped me to pay for the parking. Holy cow! I didn't have any money on me and I told him that I had attended the MDA party but could not find my change purse. Again, the white lie worked! And I took off.

For one glorious day I drove around town and then to a rustic spot. Thoughts of possible police investigation of stolen cars fleeted through my mind but I did not let them bother me. However, when I noticed how a police car stopped close me, I wanted to get the car started to flee and it didn't work. A reasonable fear mixed in with an irrational one – the one of actually being accosted in a stolen vehicle by cops who were taking a break; they didn't even look at me!

Whatever I tried, I could not get the car to start. Beaten, I fell back into my seat to ponder this dilemma when I noticed an invisible hand clicking the switches that corresponded to the window panes. Try it again, I heard a voice telepathically say. This time there was no delay in getting the motor going. Wow! Such a simple maneuver unlocked the steering wheel and ignited the motor. I had no idea.

After a few hours driving around the city the gas tank read empty and I decided to put it near a park in the downtown section. I fell asleep in the back seat only to wake up with my mouth covered by a hand and my torso in a vise grip. Fighting to get air, I tried to kick but to no avail. On whiskey breath my attacker uttered threatening words that sounded somewhat like "taking me to a secluded spot to do what he wanted with me." Struggling without getting a foothold, he dumped me in the trunk and locked it.

Yelling to let me out, I heard him turn the radio on loud enough to drown out my voice. I stopped screaming to save my breath in case things got bad. Looking around I noticed a CD-player in the darkness. For some reason, I did not think I would suffer a suffocating death as my final experience.

Then I heard him say: how do you get this car started? Dumbfounded, this struck me as idiotic. Here is a guy trying to steal the car I had stolen earlier in the day only to ask me for directions on how to do it while he locked me in the trunk? Hello, what's wrong with this picture? You've got to be kidding, I said curiously, you don't know how to drive this car away? He explained that a Lexus had not been part of his arsenal of stolen cars.

The gas tank is empty, I offered, lying. The real reason was the steering wheel lock. Then I told him that I had stolen the car with keys I had found rather than bashing the front window in as he had done. Somehow this made him decide to let me out of the trunk so I could assist him in pushing the car to the nearest gas station. After he paid for a filled tank I asked him to buy me breakfast at the nearby Denny's. It was two o'clock in the morning but I was hungry. He did.

I handed him the driver's manual so he could figure out what he had to do to get the car going. I refused to tell him and bit into a hot cheese omelet while watching him. A black, thirtyish guy who proclaimed that he was "actually a nice guy," yeah right! Was he an Adonis who threw women in the trunks of their own cars and drove them to a secluded spot where he could have their way with them? Why would he think I could not decide for myself whether he was a nice guy or not? The circumstances showed another picture. Was I the only one who had outsmarted him?

After he had figured it out, I let him drive. We ended up in some area where his cocaine befuddled buddies came out of a house to admire the Lexus he had swiped including the white moll in her leather pantsuit. Man, we were a hit! I smiled sweetly. Next he parked in the entryway of a house that he entered in the back. I sat in the car wondering what he was doing and how long I was supposed to sit there. He had taken the car keys with him so leaving was not an option.

Without saying a word, he got back and handed me a checkbook and three twenty-dollar bills; an antique item he planned to take to the pawnshop slid into his pocket. When he mentioned that he wanted to go to the bank to cash some checks drawn on the account of the woman whose house he had just broken into, he told me to write them out. Automatically, he had made me the designated accomplice. I looked at the account trying to find a way to get out of this situation.

The idea of following a spiritual path that included being an accomplice in a premeditated crime seemed incongruous. To get spontaneously involved in a situation where I find a set of keys or have to invent a lie on the spot to handle a situation was one thing, but to be a partner to a real criminal was something else. No way, I wasn't going to do it! I looked at the account, noted that small amounts were withdrawn and convinced him that it would not be prudent to withdraw a large amount suddenly to arouse suspicion.

He listened to me. Then he said that he wanted to get a motel room for the two of us. Instead of getting raped in the bushes I would now be a willing participant in a motel room? Was this guy for real? As I had had no experience in dealing with a crumb thief like him, I didn't know what made him tick. He had offered his apologies for stealing my purse and throwing it into the park but, hey, did that make him a nice guy or a powerless dope that had no control over his existence? I knew his spirit to be kindred so I could empathize with his quest to survive, but that did not give him the right to use me!

When he stopped in front of a mall to go to the pawnshop, I asked him if he could leave the car keys so I could listen to music while he did his business. He did. Patiently I sat there, waiting, until a car pulled up in front of me with guys dressed like FBI men who looked at me curiously. A chill went through me, prompting me into the action of starting the car and driving off. They were the incentive to make me move, otherwise it would not have occurred to me to do so to get rid of the guy.

Moving on, I wondered what his reaction would be once he found me and the car gone. Then it dawned upon me that I now had $60 and a full tank of gas so I could drive for a while. Guilt, another control mechanism, made me call the owner's phone number to leave a message on her answering machine, letting her know where her car had been parked. Then I found a key that fit a hotel room with the number 911 which I left in the car. The emergency number of the police, the broken front window, the guy's jacket and empty whisky bottle would create some vibrational clues to the identity of the culprit.

TWENTY-SIX

Breaking Habits

I spent an entire week going through a mall changing ownership of items from shops to indicated recipients. In fact, I played Santa Claus to learn to get more practice as a shop lifter to overcome my fear of being disobedient to the authorities, my parents and anyone else who intimidated me into it. At night, I had to sleep in bushes found near the mall.

With a new found clarity after entering another stage of my spiritual awakening, I perceived the underlying dynamic of some concept much faster than before. Going around the stores in the mall I would obtain items that I would then pass on to individuals who were in need of those items or who wanted them very much. Occasionally, when somebody would express a strong desire for something, I would go and get it. The whole exercise consisted of perceiving the reactions and appreciation factor involved when I went about being serviceable to please others.

The cycle made me aware of the flaw that I had been giving most of my possessions and money away to other people to keep them at a distance to cover up my own fear of intimacy. **In essence, I gave my power away.** I became also aware that wall had crumbled around my body, leaving me now vulnerable to the invading auras surrounding other bodies.

A pair of sunglasses and a necklace went to a woman who relayed to me her sorrow over her teenaged son who had committed suicide. My calm and open attitude has enabled many people to tell me their innermost secrets, things they would not dare discussing with anybody else. I considered it one of my special gifts. However, the expensive sunglasses and necklace were accepted without pleasure. Items could never replace the loss of her child so the better gift was to lend her a truly listening ear in the Here and Now.

A clerk who worked in a stationary store and liked a bracelet I wore which she could not afford to buy, I delighted by giving her a new one. Her whole face lit up from the inside.

There were occasions when people hardly acknowledged me or forgot to thank me for the gift but it did not matter. It became clear that some people were helped by my gifts but most were not.

I wore a beautiful new coat I had gotten to before moving on. That was part of the cycle-I never knew why I would take something as I had seldom gotten anything new in my life. As a child my mother claimed poverty while sewing all of my clothes from patterns she got from a German magazine. I could not fully appreciate her gift as other girls would show off their purchases from fancy department stores while I walked around in home-made clothes.

One day, early in the morning, I went to the train station because I wanted to "get out of here", a phrase that became a subconsciously activated command until I became aware of it. The restaurant was closed when a black woman in her thirties entered and I asked her where I could get a cup of coffee. Not a chance, she answered, then returned twenty minutes later carrying a tray with a pot of coffee, milk, sugar, and a cup. Unsolicited, she had taken the initiative to see to my comfort and well-being without expecting anything in return.

    I relished the coffee while listening to her story of having fulfilled her life's dream of buying a small house on a cook's salary. It became clear that this hardworking woman who also supported a teenaged son by herself had little money left for extras. An impulse from above made me offer her my new coat which she, hesitatingly, accepted. I knew well how hardworking, independent people, who deserved to be rewarded for their efforts, were the hardest to convince to accept a gift.

    Generally speaking, a drug-addict, alcoholic or welfare recipient takes it for granted that society owes them a living and expect people to provide them with money and basic needs without offering anything in return! In essence, they are responsible for the creation of those situations to learn needed lessons; I met many of them. As soon as they are ready to make a change, the teacher will come or they will get an 'ally' or opportunity that will suddenly catapult them out of their miserable circumstances. But, anyone who supports them with sympathy and/or money and gifts supports their victim consciousness, *for it is complicity in disguise*! Sympathy will not solve their misery, just prolong it.

    I took an item, I gave it away. It was fun. It created a new feeling inside, this fluent motion that involved no exchange of money. What freedom not to have to stand in line to hand over your cash, not to be treated like another number, not to be dependent upon the mood of the clerks who went through the motions of doing their job! Just walk in, get something and walk out. Then make somebody else happy with it. If life could only be so simple!

I began to relax more as I got used to shopping without a money exchange. The novelty of the experience felt liberating. The hustle and bustle of all the activity within stores where shoppers performed their daily tasks of stocking their cupboards happened outside of me. No longer did I feel part of it. Sometimes I could even perceive the vibration in the air when my guide protected me with invisibility!

But mentally I was not even close to freedom. Before I would take something my mind would create excuses to give to the authority in case I got arrested to justify my actions. It took a lot longer before I would arrive at the point of just doing it…..comfortably!

New realizations
1)	Breaking habits is a hard thing to do but liberating.
2)	My assistance from the invisible realms made me aware I was never really alone.

TWENTY-SEVEN

Putting a new skill to use

In a cheap motel I witnessed my watch disintegrate while I took a bath. Awestruck, I surreptitiously looked around to see if some specter would materialize but nothing out of the ordinary could be felt or presented itself. My watch simply disappeared into the void. If I had told someone it would have been shrugged off as my imagination, but it wasn't it. My guide showed me the introduction of a new cycle:

One becomes aware of a habit like reading time on a watch when it is gone. The lifting and swing of the left arm to position the watch so it could be read I performed many times before it finally clicked in my head. George Carlin, the late comedian, mentioned in his brilliant "On Our Similarities", how most of us live so unconsciously that we look at our watch over and over again before the present time even registers. So true!

It was gone. I had to determine time in a different manner if I wanted to be aware of it so I started to get proficient in reading the sun positions. Once I could do so flawlessly, the guide would create opportunities to apply the knowledge vicariously to others. When it was directly overhead, noontime, for instance, and someone asked me the time, I would point up silently.

One of the hardest fears for my body to overcome was the daily routine of wondering if I would eat that day or where I would sleep at night. Slowly but steadily they dissipated when spirit provided me with nourishments and lodgings on a daily basis. In the beginning, it would take more effort than in the later years, when I became so detached from considerations of survival that it no longer mattered whether I ate as I never felt hungry, or if I slept in- or outdoors. But, after I finished the cycle of learning what to give to whom, based on what was needed or wanted, I got to use my newly acquired skill of taking things to find accommodations for myself.

Walking along, dressed nicely, I met a teenaged girl who delighted in taking me home to meet her parents. Again, I perceived the reptilian behind the human mask of a very attractive female who was married to a gentle guy who confided in me how he had envisioned an entirely different life for himself but, instead, had done his 'duty of giving the baby a name.'

I had told them a story of being well off to match my appearance when I presented them with a few well-chosen swiped presents. In return, she presented me with a bottle of vitamins she sold at home to produce extra income accompanied by the following piece of wisdom: I think we all should share our bounty! What a marvel! It sounded so innocent, caring and socialistic. Those words usually rolled off the tongue of someone who wanted riches without having to do anything for it. Also, very much inspired by the beehive mentality of the group soul of which I was not a part.

"Yes, I agree. I buy items, use it once and give it away," I said knowing that was not what she meant. I had just finished reading a book describing choices of paths to take, such as a path of knowledge, a path of the heart, and a path of renunciation. I used some of the information that belonged to each one.

"You are crazy," offered the girl, smiling. Brought up by a mother whose personality displayed all the traits of the SSS model, the daughter had taken on many of those traits like I did in my childhood. How would she know of another way of doing things unless she opened up to perceive the differences between her mother and an individualistic person like myself? My presence, spirit-directed, may just have given her the impetus to do so. Her mom learned through doubt and fears, I learned through truth turning into wisdom.

A funny moment lightened the scene when the mother told me to watch out for slugs that were rampant in the area. Right after pointing that out to me, she stepped on a big one, crushing it. I exchanged glances with her husband who shared a chuckle with me. He was a man oblivious of the true nature of his life, content to live the illusionary life of a kept man.

She ignored it completely, no emotional reaction of any kind whatsoever. She went on like it never happened. Another sample of a barren woman who could not take responsibility for a mistake that could crack her self-image of perfection!

On my next stop I found myself in Bellingham, a small town in northwestern Washington State.

Beautifully situated on the Pacific Ocean it delighted me to inhale the salty air from the sea. Here I was invited by a guy in his mid-thirties to share the freestanding cottage he owned.

Born under the sign of Leo it was only appropriate that I would experience some creative times with him. No doubt his motivation of welcoming me in his sanctuary had been motivated by the sex and money dynamic as I still projected the image of someone who had been born with a silver spoon in her mouth.

Videos were on the menu. He had taped all of the Simpson's episodes which I had never seen. Then some bands like Pink Floyd, the Moody Blues and, naturally, Bob Dylan provided some marvelous entertainment with their taped concerts. I enjoyed myself tremendously. In return, I offered to "pay" for the stay in goods I collected at the local specialty markets where they sold succulent meats, imported cheeses and expensive wines. Remarkably, when I cooked the meals, from a grilled salmon to a tender filet mignon, it came out cooked to perfection. I knew my creative cooking to be good but not on par with a chef's so I did ascribe it to getting some "help" in this endeavor.

A difficult moment arose in the market when he entered while I was on my way out, my bag full of goodies in tow. I couldn't refuse to accompany him without good reason so I went back inside carrying a bag with unpaid for stuff. It was another exercise in acting normally without feeling guilty about taking things.

The guy was perceptive enough and at a spiritual crossroads so new, valid input was necessary to make him progress. I decided to celebrate my birthday over two evenings to show my host something new because the guests I carefully selected from the local population represented different spiritual levels. For the observer, this is noticeable in how people behave, the language they use and their points of view.

One of the perfectly cooked meals was served to a group of artists that included a woman who owned a store in which she sold her handicrafts and pots. She brought a guy (a reptilian) I had not personally invited, one who wanted to ruin my party. Arrogantly, he helped himself to the goodies, and did not wish me a happy birthday. When he offered some critique I cut him short by pointing out that it was my party and if he didn't like it....oh well, figure it out for yourself, Sherlock!

I gave the craftswoman a book that made her exclaim "Oh isn't she marvelous? We should be giving her presents." Her companion, seeing no opportunity to spoil my party, left. The Leo man took everything in not knowing what to make of it yet. Later on, he may have gotten some understanding. Sometimes it takes years to understand something that happened in the past depending on the spirit's maturity, as I was well aware of in my own life.

A female SSS appeared with her companion on the second night. For me, the fun factor ran on low as I knew her to only laugh about jokes with a double meaning. However, my single host who was looking for a partner did learn something about differently spirited women.

New realizations
1)   I was in the process of becoming a natural guide, showing others whom I got in contact with, precious information about their lives. Silent communication is so much more effective than talk.
2)   I still needed to work on emptying my mind. The habit of inventing excuses to justify my actions was still operational.

TWENTY-EIGHT

Camping

The next morning I took a bus with the money I took out of my host's wallet. I had learned the lesson that if one asks for money it would not be forthcoming, unless you ask a person *who cannot say No*, but there are not too many of those walking around. Shaking badly, still coping with guilt, that superb control mechanism, I retrieved a $20 bill out of the wallet. Then I heard a voice instruct me telepathically to do it again because the amount was not enough. I broke out in a cold sweat but did it. This turned out to be right as the bus fare amounted to $35 to head towards Wenatchee, a town located in the center of the State of Washington, known for its apple orchards.

What a marvelous change of scenery! A river ran through the town which, at one end, featured a beautiful park where I pitched a tent I had taken out of a department store across the street. Whatever I needed I had to take out of stores; I already began to wonder how long I was required to live like that. The apple and other fruit orchards impressed me with their silence. An awesome, neutral silence that spoke louder than words, permeated with the scent of fresh fruit, soothed my soul.

It also flashed me back to the pregnant silences I endured between my parents. Two people who stuck with each other to the bitter end in a loveless partnership filled with silences that were penalizing or extracting vengeance. If my father did not give his wife enough money or if he had an affair to make up for her intentional withholding of sex, they would not speak to each other for months. But the invisible daggers flew across the table where we ate our food.

On one memorable occasion a young guy on motorized water skis stopped to check me out. Immediately, a feeling of alarm rose in the pit of my stomach where the third chakra, our power center, is located. This turned out to be justified as I heard footsteps fall around my tent close to midnight. When I peeked outside, I saw the same guy standing near the water's edge with a shirt and an exposed erect penis.

Out of the corner of my eye I noticed *four* ducks on the waves, my 'guidance number' at that particular cycle. This made me feel a bit more comfortable because it indicated spirit presence, but the fear I could not control. My throat went dry as I answered his question about whether I wanted to have sex with him or rather watch the ducks with: "I'd rather watch the ducks."

Not knowing what to expect, it almost surprised me when he honored my choice as he neared to walk past my tent into the shadows of the trees. Nevertheless, it took several hours for my body to become sufficiently relaxed to be able to embrace an uneasy sleep!

Wenatchee had a fantastic bus system that got financed out of the sales tax. Thus nobody had to buy a ticket or fumble around with small change to get on the bus. Somehow they even managed to make it profitable. The buses were new, clean and the uniformed drivers serviceable and relaxed. It became a joyful meeting ground for people who would otherwise never meet one another.

That's how I got transported to the next town of Leavenworth that had been modeled after a town in Bavaria, Germany. The picturesque houses were surrounded by an Alpine forest that provided trails that could be explored for a lifetime. In one of the cafes, coffee was still served for one quarter that the customer flipped onto a saucer. The owner told us that she still made a profit on the coffee. Remarkable!

That's where I met a middle-aged man who invited me over to his trailer. Since he had parked it up north, it took a half hour drive in his pickup truck to get there. Gushingly, he had told me about a couple that took care of his trailer when he was away and I got to meet with them the next morning after he had taken off on an errand. Oh horrors, another SSS, this time in the form of an obese female, coffee cup in hand, wimpy husband in tow, pushing me aside (or trying to) as soon as I opened the door.

By this time I was in no mood to play the down-and-outer any longer as I had it experienced in the driver's house in Oklahoma. Clearly, my self-esteem had increased dramatically. ' Explain to me why you think you're better than I am and I'll listen to you. However, exercising some humility in regard to your fellow human beings is far more attractive in interactions than a superiority complex', I told her.

As soon as my host returned I relayed to him what had happened and he defended her weakly by saying that she was funny and considerate and….enough already, I'll walk back to town, I said. Thanking him for his hospitality, I took my back pack and started walking down the road. Her wimp husband followed me on his bike on the gopher errand to harass me. I ignored him. Soon a car stopped with a nice woman who had been asked by my former host to give me a lift.

    I kept running into this programmed specimen of humans. Their intent was negative, designed to stop my spiritual progress and still hard to deal with. My own mother whose intent had been very negative towards her own children had made me wonder about her sanity. She would sabotage my plans to become educated as a pediatrician, take away anything I loved and keep me busy with things I did not like to do. I would endure it without having anyone to run to besides her mother who understood but could not or would not interfere. I had to develop my own system of protection so I left my body often, watching from the corner of the room, looking down.

    When I ran into a neighbor girl I walked to school with some forty years later, she mentioned how my mother was known as the 'bubblegum' mother. She also recalled how she looked happy in the kitchen cooking meals that had a nice aroma. I only remembered having stiff fingers from folding bubblegum into packages to earn money for the summer vacation. Later on, when the skinny girl had turned into a large woman, feeling a bit more comfortable in talking to me after all those years, she offered that Mom also appeared as a Dark witch. I could identify with that image better. When my favorite cat died at the age of 12 after someone had thrown rocks at him, she put his body on the threshold of my room for me to find instead of preparing me for its demise.

As all paths return to self, there were some inner issues for me to work out before I could change the dynamic to attract other types of people. (See Law of Attraction) I did study them to conclude that these people all displayed that identical behavior pattern I listed in the beginning!

After my four days' tent adventure in a public park, I spent a few weeks wild camping in a remote area accessible by a shuttle that ran twice daily from town. There was a camping nearby but since I had to learn to survive without access to money I headed for an area where I could hide my tent in the bushes and enjoy solitude. I did make use of the showers on the campground to keep clean. Lacking the quarters to make the water hot I had to endure cold water which was reminiscent of my stint as an air-traffic controller in the Dutch Air Force when I had to participate in simulated war exercises in the field.

I learned to love being alone without feeling lonesome, but my days were still filled with anxieties from past experiences and new ones that were connected to present activities. Anything I needed to survive I had to lift from stores and the fear connected with that program spoiled the serenity of the environment. Two or three times a week I would take the shuttle back to town, a two hour drive. Then another bus to go to a supermarket where I went 'shopping' for soups and meats I could cook over a hot fire in the wild.

It could have been the perfect camping vacation if I had managed to keep my fears at bay. Looking back upon that phase in my progression, it turned out to be somewhat like a school semester for learning new skills and dealing with new fears that accompany facing the unknown. My 'assignments' became increasingly more difficult while my self-confidence in adapting to new situations proportionally increased so I could handle them with more ease.

A couple of years later, for instance, I took the shuttle to look at the area where I had spent a few months camping and got stranded when I missed the last shuttle going back into town. I ended up sleeping on ice without a tent, blankets, and a pillow with a cougar curiously eyeing me. The mode of intense living over a couple of years had brought me to a point where I could now live through it without getting overly fearful. They were spiritual rewards, AHA moments that allowed me to perceive how all the work that seemed meaningless while doing them resulted in peace of mind.

New realizations
1)   The fears combined with guilt stayed with me while I sat in my tent counting the days when I had to return to the store on the shuttle. It basically spoiled the

pleasure of eating the food. And I had no power over shutting it down yet.

2)   I was convinced that it was only a matter of time before somebody would recognize me, going into the same store all the time (no option here), and arrest me for shoplifting. That fear I could not suppress successfully because it flashed back to one occasion during my teenage years: in mid-winter a girlfriend challenged me to take a bikini from a fancy department store. I obliged, thinking it a game. A store detective called the police who took me to a cell where my Protestant mom picked me up. Her belief system branded me now as a sinner for the rest of my life. She informed the entire family of my innocent escapade which she exacerbated, never letting up over the years to remind me how I was not to be trusted. She created fears in me related to stealing and the police!

3)   I actually ate better foods than when I worked for the money because I could take whatever foods I wanted regardless of the price. Money truly was no object now but the enjoyment factor was less due to my fears of getting caught.

TWENTY-NINE

Still breaking habits
Life on the road continued. I perceived the difference between my bodily needs and those that my soul craved. An accumulation of material possessions creates a barrier to cultivating one's soul and builds up artificial power. These insights I shared with other souls that were open to those lessons.

A thief always returns to the scene of the crime. Before I moved on to another area in the country I returned to the upscale department in downtown Seattle around closing time one day. A new fear had been created after my first official arrest there so I looked around to see if anyone recognized me. I didn't really want anything, having been punished for actions I felt I was forced into. After all, it was my invisible guide who spurred me on to do them. When I later learned that guides are aspects of the Higher Self, I understood that the responsibility for my actions lay squarely on my own shoulders. In fact, growth is not possible without understanding that concept!

Looking around while getting exasperated about what to take, I asked the salesperson if the store was going to close soon. Yes, she said, while running towards the escalator, then turning around to tell me joyfully how a woman could still do a lot of damage in ten minutes flat. This sort of banter came directly from spirit, I recognized it immediately. Another 'signal' I noted was the way the other person moved for just a couple of instants. Suddenly another consciousness moved her body. After I felt his spiritual signature enter while I sang a psalm with a beautiful voice in the Seattle jail, I recognized the entity as my guide.

A jacket with an electric green color beckoned me. Feather light, warm in cold weather and vice versa, beautifully tailored, I put it under my arm and sped out of the store. The material had been used in astronaut suits by NASA. It became my favorite piece of clothing for a few weeks, on my way to the Midwest.

In another upscale mall in Oklahoma City, I took a pair of pants attached to a device that triggered an alarm on the way out. Slowly walking out, I felt panicked when I heard people running after me; I took a right into the parking area where I got stopped. There seems to be a small interrogation room in every mall for people who wanted to get away with something for nothing. The questions two officers asked me indicated to me that they were more interested in finding out what they were all about rather than me. One of them accused me of being a drug addict. He assessed the irises of my eyes and decided I was a habitual offender who fended clothes to get money for drugs. I protested that I had never even tried drugs in my life other than the Novocain the dentist injected in my mouth before he pulled a tooth.

His female partner then brought up the mystery of why I walked into the parking garage. It did not occur to them that I was out of town, visited their city for the first time in my life, and just decided to go right instead of left. Simplicity was apparently absent in the cops' training where suspicion was the main motivator for their efforts to enforce the laws that were written by the SSS authorities.

This time I ended up in a cell that had six cement bunks attached to two walls, three on each side. I obtained the last available cot. A toilet was attached to the separating wall facing the bars.

One of the most difficult things I have ever had to do in my life was to take a crap on that toilet in front of five other women. I did not consider myself to be inhibited but to do something as personal as relieving yourself in front of a crowd, became a tough task to perform. I could not rationalize it and convince myself that nobody was interested in watching me because it did not work. Constipated, I sneaked onto the pot in the middle of the night. I peeked at the other women who did not appear to be bothered by it. But the overall claustrophobic feeling inside of me connected with a compulsion to 'get out of here.' I planned on escaping the jail!

There was a dark-skinned woman who lent me a hand in exchange for my beautiful jacket. For months to come I regretted having to part with that jacket but it served to make me detach of material things more. The plan comprised a faked heart-attack that would land me in the local hospital from which I would escape in an unsupervised moment. What an experience!

I had gotten instructions on how to successfully answer questions of the paramedics before I succumbed to my heart-attack and the others called in the personnel. It worked. They came, hoisted me onto the stretcher, and brought me to the hospital. On the way over, the medic threatened to inject me with an approved drug to see if I would react, apparently there had been escape attempts before. I did not react, courtesy of some drills I had done earlier in my spiritual training.

In the hospital I wondered about the procedure of having to answer a list of questions in case you are actually dying. The two nurses snickered when I mentioned that my menstruation had voluntarily stopped without any signs of menopause discomforts. What a shame that people had to be envious of another person's health or happiness but, of course, I came out of jail. We are living in such a rush society where the slogan 'time is money' actually dictates our actions without paying attention to differentiate among people. As soon as the moment arrived when I was left alone, I got up and walked out, it was that simple.

Freezing without my comfortable jacket on, dressed in thin, blue cotton overalls, I looked around and found a thin raincoat on the seat of an unlocked car. A loose scarf I wrapped around my head. The coat did not keep the cold out but it was better than nothing. Shortly thereafter, I ran into a woman who brought me over to the house of-what else- another reptilian. It was early evening.

His idea of being a host was to let me use the shower, invite me to sleep in his bed without blankets, and fix myself a cup of instant coffee. The sympathy oozed out of him when he remarked that the instant coffee was awful but…aw shucks…he did not have anything else. When the phone rang he ordered me to be silent as one of his sex partners or gophers called; he didn't want her to get upset at my presence. The guy had no inkling that I had no intention to be used as his next sex toy but I complied (with silence, not sex).

Ignoring him, I climbed in bed only to find that the sheets did not offer enough heat to keep my shivering under control so I joined him again in the living room. After he got off the phone I told him how I had just escaped out of jail just to see what he planned to do with that piece of information. Perfect in his own mind and bound by rules, he could not call the police to have them pick me up because he would be regarded as an accomplice, he reasoned aloud.

I announced my departure. I want my sex, he protested, I love my sex. Without looking at him, I proceeded to put my thin clothes back on, hating the idea of spending another night in the cold while doling around but the alternative was worse, sharing a bed with this cold-blooded guy. When he kept on insisting about having sex I raised my voice to say NO. Immediately, he ordered me to stop screaming otherwise he would…the or else threat that works so well on children to make them do something they don't like, did not work on me. *Sotto voce,* I pointed out that he was the one who was screaming while I unlocked the front door to get out. Seeing he could not influence me, he changed his tune to saying get out of here then, yes; I think you should get out of here. Unbelievable, it is impossible for those control freaks to ***allow people to make a decision for themselves!***

The night opened to new experiences. I got the impulse to enter a neon-lit building where I found a door leading to a small area where some crackers and cookies stood waiting to be eaten. I still had difficulties picking something up that did not belong to me so I went looking around to find some people in the building. Still scared I did grab a handful of the edible wares to eliminate my hunger.

Another night of walking in unknown territory followed. On a country lane, in the pitch dark, I saw the contours of a farm house and a car. Still cold in my thin coat I walked down the entry way to the car and opened the door to reveal a thick winter coat. Again I looked guiltily around to see if there would be witnesses if I traded my raincoat for the winter coat. This struck me as ludicrous but I could not help myself: nobody in sight, the inhabitants' probably fast asleep, the place engulfed in darkness, no dogs, silence all around, and I acted as if I was the mastermind behind a heist.

I did it. Back on the road, feeling so much more comfortable, it didn't take long before a car stopped to offer me a ride. A very nice gentleman brought me to the edge of the city where he bought me a breakfast in the wee morning hours. Tired, without any sleep, I walked back to town where I got arrested again when I wanted to get some decent clothes and triggered another alarm.

In the interrogation room one prejudiced white man looked at me as if I was a piece of dirt he had just removed from the sole of his shoe. Bastard, I thought, still taking that type of insult personally. I still felt compelled to defend my behavior so my story described how I got robbed and how I got so mad that I wanted to get some new clothes. A sales woman from the store laughed at me, thinking it funny. Didn't the alarm go off? She asked when it turned out that a new coat had another device on it which I had failed to notice. Strangely enough, in that particular store it had remained inert.

The woman who had my jacket was not happy to see me. After a successfully executed escape I landed in the same cell, what were the odds of that? They had also given her an additional charge of being an accomplice to my escape. I needed a new coat, I explained to her, and I froze in the below zero temperatures so here I am again. When the judge let me go on my own recognizance to appear on a later date, the convict actually allowed me to stay in her house where her boyfriend waited. I moved on, court date or not.

In Dallas, a shopper's paradise with many malls, I played my role as a well-dressed woman after getting another suitcase filled with very expensive clothes. I met a woman who invited me to go home with her after I gave her a present. The well-tailored clothes I had gotten from one of the most expensive stores in the United States were awesome. I loved modeling them in front of a mirror in her house. One night we went out to a nightclub where I paraded around without getting a beverage because I functioned without any cash whatsoever. My entire survival mode was based on my ability to communicate. I could handle any situation with verbal communication without the need to settle disputes by means of violence, so far.

When I met a nice woman who worked in a booth selling cards for some benefit she invited me to stay at her house. I know it when I meet a good one, she said, complimenting me, but, looking at my clothes she added, my house is humble. Fine, I said happily, glad to get out of the other one's house because she kept poking me about 'sharing my riches'. Where did I hear that one before? I got my suitcase, left it with her in the booth, then proceeded to get her a present from a mall store like I did in my exercise near Seattle.

It was not to be. I got out of the store, sat down on a bench and saw the store manager accompanied by a security man rush over to me to take me to one of their interrogation rooms. The woman in the booth I never saw again. Just like in Seattle, the suitcase ended up either in the store where I had taken them from or as Christmas presents for the abused women and children she benefited with her work. Sigh! It would have been nice to wear some of those dresses but I hoped that my efforts benefited the right women.

The two cops that came to fetch me looked like a young couple. The young female cop pushed me ahead and made the sarcastic comment: Age before Beauty to the audience of proud sales personnel who had caught the shoplifter. After booking me for petty theft, they let me go. Ironically, they did not find out about the expensive clothing in the suitcase that was hidden in the booth.

I returned to the house of the first woman and paid for my stay with several bags filled to the brim with groceries I had gotten from a local supermarket. At this point I resented giving those alien slaves presents but I did it not to arouse suspicion. Her daughter had just bought her a new car. I knew all about their way of getting people to buy things for them while offering nothing in return. For some reason, making up some non-existing itinerary, I had mentioned I wanted to go to Austin and now she expressed a desire to come along while I paid the bills.

I went along to her Baptist church where she put on a show of total dedication by falling on her knees and bow down like the Islam adherents do in the direction of Mecca. Sigh! By this time I entered the emotional phase of boredom with those characters. After I went to bed, she slammed a bunch of keys on the table in my room. This gesture was unusual for her to make and the emphasis I took as a signal. I read it as an invitation to take her car for a ride, which I did early in the morning while she was still asleep.

I anticipated serious trouble but for a couple of days, filling the tank without paying a couple of times, I remained free to drive through Texas and Oklahoma. I felt like Thelma without Louise. When I parked in a small town, a police car began to tail me. Then he turned on his siren to signal me to stop. Get out of your car, put your hands in the air, and lay down on the pavement! I hesitated at the last instruction. The culprits in movies had to do that but here I was imitating Hollywood!

Playing my new role of innocent victim rather than that of hardened criminal, I asked him softly what this was all about. This car has been reported stolen, he said gruffly, slamming me in the cuffs. Impossible, I said, and told him about my friend who suffered from Alzheimer's Disease and apparently did not remember that she had lend her car to me. The white lies came easier as I went along. It was similar to writing a fictional story.

I shared a cozy cell with two girls who were a lot of fun. To my horror, I had made the local newspaper though. If I had harbored any claims to fame, this wasn't the way I had envisioned it. Spirit did have a sense of humor.

Fortunately, they let me go after a couple of days as the woman did not press any charges. I imagined that she probably would not have liked to return other items I had given her; therefore she didn't make life too unbearable for me. My variety of experiences provided a peek in the system that revealed more and more the seedier side of what passed for justice.

New realizations
1) I noticed that the situations I had to handle occurred twice. It was the second time I 'borrowed' a car without the owner's permission, teaching them both a lesson in the process, engineered by my spiritual guide.
2) Truth hit the SSS-er. He would not jeopardize himself by reporting me to the police which he

would otherwise have done, as a perfect model citizen, in a heartbeat.

THIRTY

Living in Grace

As the seasons passed, I had to spend a lot of nights sleeping outside so jail became almost like a coffee break during a boring and long day at an office job. On another occasion in the State of Oklahoma I deliberately picked up two packs of cigarettes in front of a few people and walked out of the store. The manager who followed me told me to return and asked if I wanted to go to his interrogation room or be embarrassed in front of customers. He gave me a choice, believe it or not. I had gotten comfortable with the procedure and did no longer care whether people frowned on my actions or not. (One of the greatest common fears, apparently, is caring about the opinion of others!)

One experienced cop and a rookie came to take me to the local judge who seemed glad to see an offender he could give a sentence to. They took me directly to him. He offered me the choice of a $140 fine or ten days in jail. Lacking funds, I chose jail, of course.

I spent ten glorious days, dressed in white overalls, sitting in the holding tank as there was no bed available in the women's section. Since it was adjacent to the cops' recreation room they let me frequently sit there to smoke a cigarette, a habit I had not managed to shake off yet. I had returned one of the packages and kept the other one. When the rookie said 'Hey, you've got a pack of smokes just like the one you tried to steal', I found his comment endearing but very funny, perceiving the humor of spirit behind it.

In the morning I would get a choice of micro waved breakfasts, then lunches and TV dinners. One of the darlings brought me a fabulous book to read from his private library: The Haunted Mesa by Louis L'Amour. Altogether, I think with fondness of those cops who took care of me and played Scrabble with me to get me through my days.

On another occasion I could not get to a mall where I wanted to go shopping because I had no money for the bus and there was no pedestrian path leading to the stores. So a young cop stopped to pick me and give me a lift to the mall, not knowing he assisted a spontaneous shopper.

In Maryland I took two bottles of wine out of a convenience store and stuffed them in my back pack. A few minutes later one (not two, rather unusual) cop stopped to ask me if I had been in the store because he had received a call with a description of somebody who looked like me. Yes, I said, so he invited me politely to step into the back of his car so we could straighten out the situation. While talking to him I took the bottles out and hid them under a rubber mat on the floor.

He took a good look when he opened the door but didn't seem to see the bumps the bottles made. *It is possible to re-arrange molecules so the picture in front of one's eyes looks different than it actually IS.* Unfortunately, the ones with malicious intent have that ability as well, hence the phrase *hiding in plain sight!*

We went inside where I denied having taken anything and the manager apologized. In the car, the conversation had a lighter tone as he inquired from what European country I hailed while I did the reverse action of putting the bottles back into my pack. It was a very pleasant ride that I toasted to when I had my picnic near the Appalachian Trail.

After the cycle of trucking across country many times, getting to see the beauty of the North-American continent from a high seat, this new adventure prompted me to act independently from other people who would assist me with getting fed. Suddenly I had to adapt to an entirely novel way of survival techniques, my least favorite still that of stepping into stores where I had to pick up some food to get me through the days on the road. Nobody around to offer me a snack or meal other than the occasional jail stay where I had no choice but to eat whatever the authorities offered me. Freedom of choice got limited.

Since the boulders, stones and pebbles were thrown there by my invisible spiritual guide on the rocky road, there was no option in the matter other than dealing with whatever arose so I could measure my own progression in terms of the Law of Attraction, to see what or who matched my inner state of Being. Instant karma got delivered in exchange for taking mostly food by locking me up. At first, there was a period of getting used to it, to dissipate the fears that were connected with it. *My worst one was claustrophobia!*

--

THIRTY-ONE

Life in Reversal, then reversed again
After my main awakening, I got the impression that the world ran in reverse. To get used to that, I needed to iron the creases out of the fabric that weaves our society together. Concepts that were easy to communicate before became a major source of misunderstandings. The problem got exacerbated by the discrepancy of looking silently at a concept or mulling it over in the mind.

To make the whole picture even more complicated I found myself adapting to places like jail where a different reversal of society at large is at play. In western society, we are encouraged to grow up, to get an education, to be responsible for our own actions, and to take care of ourselves. In jail, one gets punished for making decisions and taking care of oneself because individuality is taboo. Naturally, it matched the hive mind of the simultaneous spiritual suppressors that run our societies. As soon as the door gets locked behind you, your life is in the hands of whoever is in charge of the cellblock.

I made the following mistakes when I got incarcerated in the Mickey Mouse city of Orlando, Florida, for accidentally mistaken a country-club under construction for a public restroom. I opened a door that was not locked. Within seconds I noticed a bar and a kitchen so I knew I was in the wrong place. Curiosity made me look around and I went into a larder where I located a tray of chocolate-dipped apples. I took one, turned around and looked into a blinking red light, triggering a burglar's alarm, before I heard voices and commotion coming from outside.

The building was surrounded by police with flashlights they directed through the windows to spot the burglars. Hesitating, lacking a frame of reference for the situation, I decided to walk to the front door to go outside. I held my back pack in my left hand and still had the chocolate dipped apple on a stick in the other. A crew of uniforms greeted me and the one female ordered me to drop my pack. I did not respond immediately so she moved as fast as a big cat stalking its prey to slap it out of my hands.

Gee whiz! Before she grabbed me by the arms I noticed in a fleeting moment a fire engine and three police cars. Where was the fire? I thought. An officer with a dog asked me about my partner in crime? They displayed prejudice in branding me a criminal without knowing anything about me, an attitude of moral superiority in their manhandling of my body and a naïve attitude towards the governmental hoodlums they were actually working for. My tax money had gone to pay for their salaries and here I was, being treated like a major threat to society.

Don't you know the difference between wrong and right? the female cop barked at me. I was too baffled to answer. Did she know she worked to protect and serve the criminals who rip off the population at large while harassing decent citizens who try to eke out a living? Next she explained to a rookie cop how to kick against the inside of my ankles to force my legs into a widespread stance. Is this an example of police brutality? I inquired. No, she said. Well, she could have fooled me.

    Nice to know I got handcuffed by a rookie cop who used me as a dummy before he put me on the backseat of the car. A man came by to tell an officer that he didn't know me so "I was probably some female hobo looking for food or whatever label they used to explain my presence." Whoa, should this be the owner who made this superb deduction? He claimed the door had been locked (lie) and I must be a street person looking for food (the apple)?

    Once in the station a sergeant lied through his teeth, telling me that if I would cooperate and write down what had happened they would let me go on my merry way. After I handed him my written paragraph I was guided back to the car that drove me to a place where trailers constituted one women's jail. For a second there I thought that maybe I would get the (belated) birthday party I had envisioned for my fortieth birthday. No explanation was forthcoming of why they brought me there.

    Recalling Seattle I knew the procedure consisted of an arraignment during which performance I would be officially charged with a crime. Here we were led in front of a TV screen while the judge read the appropriate line from an official looking document. Only in my case he made a mistake and charged me with murder to my horror. When I protested, he noticed that I was only guilty of breaking and entering, a felony.

Felony meant red overalls instead of the more benign looking blue ones. I had entered an intense version of a prison within a prison!

Next on the agenda was a "voluntary" I.Q. test we were forced to take. The person who oversaw the test did explain that if we would X-mas tree (a slang term for crossing off the multiple choice test by rote) we would end up in the hole, a prison term for being punished by spending two weeks minimum in the downtown, flea-infested cells. Bending over to the task at hand, I flash-backed to the receptionist job I held for the Muscular Dystrophy Association. When the telethon with Jerry Lewis rolled along on Labor Day, a one day job that paid the comedian more than his entire film career, I had gotten the order to answer the telephone on television to take pledges from people as a 'mandatory' volunteer. No pay for working overtime, slavery!!

Making little effort to answer the questions right, I still managed to get assigned to one of five training computers in the complex. Why don't you give my seat to one of the poor women from the ghetto? It'll be a great opportunity for one of them to learn a computer? I asked, thinking myself generous. I got slapped with a charge of non-compliance, punished with a stay at the downtown facility!

The next three weeks I sat on an upper bunk in a cell filled with black women. One gets additional days for minor offenses such as talking after the lights were out or protests against the control-freakish ways of the jail authorities. As the only Caucasian female in the cell, it gave me an appreciation of the experience of a black woman walking into a place filled with whites. Above my head was a flickering light that never went out. Apparently, I had looked so shell-shocked that one of them told me that my eyes had been as big as saucers, giving me the look of a crack addict.

A tough looking woman ordered me to bring her a few magazines to which I angrily lashed out with "get them yourself". Two days later when another white woman arrived, the new import complied with the same command only to be used as an errand girl by the bitch. By far, it turned out to be the worst place I had ever spent time in during my entire life, for more reasons than one:

1) With 12 women in a space that had bars on both ends, six stone tables with blocks that served as seats, one toilet, one shower, it followed there were constant cat fights.

2) We had nothing to do, no mental stimulation other than the Bible and brochures that were handed through the bars by Christian women. The compassion they should have handed out wasn't there while they looked disdainfully down on the inmates. Not one of them had ever been behind bars so how can anyone, who does not walk in the shoes of those they claim to assist, be effective? Handing out a brochure with a biased slant did not alleviate mental pain, loneliness and confusion.

3) The trays that featured chemically infused nourishments that had to pass for food got shoved

through a slot like we were wild animals in a zoo. Most of it was inedible.

4) The atmosphere permeated with anger, desperation and fear, dense vibrations that, as a collective, did not lift our spirits.

THIRTY-TWO

Three jails-a triple whammy

From a spiritual point of view it became an interesting sojourn. I befriended one woman who turned out to be very intelligent with three University degrees to her name, including one for criminal justice. She assisted me to find my way through the system and filled out forms in my name to request a sergeant for an interview and one Dutch woman to call the Consulate in Miami on my behalf. The latter refused to do so and looked upon me as an anomaly. I advised her to spend some time behind bars before she decided to 'help' people, perhaps her self-righteous arrogance would turn into humility.

The sergeant immediately demanded to know how I had found out about the request form before he answered my questions as to how I could be released. An honest man, though restricted by his function within the system, he proceeded to tell me that I could count on a minimum of three month behind bars, as Orange County was understaffed and behind schedule.

What? This news came in the second week and I didn't think I could endure being there for that long. He also gave me the tip, after I told him about the computer debacle, to *play their game* as they loved to rehabilitate people regardless of whether they needed it or not. Surprisingly, this was an insider's advice on strategy within the confines of a SSS-run facility! No bail had been set as the computer had assigned a car theft in

Dallas to my name. Extradition might be warranted if Dallas wanted me there.

As despondency set in, I attended a sermon given by an ex-prisoner. What a difference it makes when somebody has had a reality-check on the situation before they start spouting their own brand of wisdom. At one point, looking at me directly, she said aloud: I can't keep my eyes off of you. I knew this to be a signal to mean that I was not alone but protected in the endeavor.

The third Caucasian woman who entered the cell I recognized instantly as the programmed variety. Naturally, she parked herself in the lower bunk next to mine so I could hardly avoid her. The Bible was her weapon of choice. It is amazing how people can be seduced into thinking that a person is humane just because they're walking around with a Bible in their hands. Soon the woman next to her clamped onto her for guidance and she requested to pray together. So her first gopher was a big, crude woman who later proceeded to create difficulties for me, creating a skirmish by the instigator.

The latter had taken a hamburger patty from my plate with her fork murmuring something unintelligibly. Amazed, I looked at my educated friend who made a loud comment as to return the patty to my plate. I actually wanted to eat the piece of road kill as I was hungry but when the woman returned with it, my friend knocked her entire plate out of her hands. She doesn't need it anymore, she yelled.

Unabated fear shone in the eyes of the SSS-er, but I said nothing. At that point I found that type of person a nuisance, and a bore to have to deal with, a step up from fighting them. It turned out she was so afraid of me (or any person who was self-determined) that when we were both released at the same time and the warden cuffed our hands together, she broke out in tears and cried all the way down to the other jail. This did not prevent her, true to form, to bounce back and wave at me cheerfully as soon as we were back into the other women's jail.

My friend's action earned her another two weeks in that hell hole. At the slightest provocation the inmate would get two extra weeks to simmer down. This woman had already been there for over a year, and wasn't going anywhere for another six months. How could you spend so much time there without going crazy or doing something that would go against some stupid rule? I shook my head. What insane system locked people up and treated them like animals? Why didn't people wake up to the fact they were being lied to, robbed and used by criminals they (s)elected in office with a corrupt voting system?

When I entered that cell populated with black women I got a taste of what it must be like when the roles are reversed and a black person walks into a place filled with white skins. There is a slight feeling of misplacement, of being in the wrong place at the wrong time, of possibly being in danger. As I had grown up in a city hospitable to people of all colors and other ethnic cultures, discrimination had not taken root in my mind.

I did discriminate however, against ill-intentioned people. It would take a few more years before I could let go to embrace that enemy.

Back in the trailers, I lasted no more than a few days before they hauled me back to the hell-hole prison. Without the slightest provocation, a young, obese, black inmate who referred to herself as Biggie Fry, decided to unleash her hatred for white women onto me. She would steal my slippers and make comments about the things I said at every opportunity. I tried to emotionally detach myself and not take her insults personally, but I found her hard to deal with. One day, when I cleaned the floor and was about to dump the dirty water in the pail down the toilet, she ran over to me pretending to bump into me. In a reflex, I lifted both of my arms while holding the pail and a brush in my hands. Behind me I heard a scream.

The assault charge was a serious one. The warden behind me claimed I had attacked the woman so I went back downtown, protest or not. My chance to defend myself would come within five days before a committee of five women. Fortunate for me, when they put me in another cell I found my educated friend to be there. She knew all the rules the control-freaks were bound to. When they came and got me on the sixth day in the middle of the night, my defense was that they had called me in too late. Reluctantly, they let me go, sparing me an episode of solitary confinement surrounded by real crazies who threw their feces into other cells.

Just like in the other cell block, the only available bed turned out to be an upper bunk with a flickering light above it. My days of mental torture were starting again. The degree of difficulty had been upped also as now I had to share my bunk with another alien programmed woman in the bed below. Situations started to repeat themselves:

A huge black woman cut in front of me while I stood waiting for a lunch tray, turning around to elicit a reaction. I peered at the cops outside of the cell and wasn't going to take the bait, so I kept a straight face at the insult. On another occasion I almost kicked her unintentionally when she came too close near my bedstead. She did not know that it was unintentional so she offered me her place in the food line-up, to pay me a twisted form of respect.

The woman in the lower bunk bed was the type of Christian that referred to her idol as 'my Jesus'. When I gave her a book about the story of a young doctor from Miami who went to Calcutta, where Mother Teresa worked her miracles in the streets, she returned it to me after reading a couple of pages with the words that her Jesus would not have approved of it. I could not control my anger, ripped the book out of her hands, and called her a phony. My new acquaintance the bully ignored the SSS command to physically harm me which I found interesting.

In the morning, a ten gallon coffeepot containing liquid made out of hickory beans that passed for coffee was put in the adjacent room for us to fill our cups. There were about forty women in this cell block. One morning when I went over to get some of the hot liquid, two women picked up the pot to put it next to my neighbor. We started an argument about whose right it was to move the pot that got the entire block going. Within a few minutes they moved the pot back to their original spot.

Apparently, I missed a parade of naked women who came to offer my neighbor their pussies for some lesbian adventures. For somebody who imagined herself to be married to Jesus I regarded this as an odd diversion. Of course, she only used people and her Bible to control them!

I attended another sermon. This time the preaching woman was a Christian woman who had not done time behind bars like the other one. She did show me something new, however. A couple of the inmates sang in mockery and she refused to put up with it. She lashed out with the words: you will not mock my God. I peered at her closely to see a determined soul who allowed no interference on her path. *What she impressed upon me was her purity of purpose and her willingness to defend that!*

When I got moved again, I ended up in a third jail. This one was meant to be a show case and a money making venture that sold shares on the stock market. The State of Florida paid a certain amount of money to feed the inmates daily, provide health care and medicines, dental care, and other basic necessities. However, their rules were based on the "three strikes and you're out" concept. Anyone who broke their ludicrous rules on three separate occasions would return to the hole.

Within a couple of days I had two strikes against me and I sighed, not again. My first offense was an unmade bed when I stepped out of my room for a minute and the inspector passed by. I had to attend an hour's meeting conducted by the wife of the police chief. This dull woman, who had enjoyed a protected life without a lack of anything, decided to volunteer some of her time to instruct us on how to deal with life. Arriving one minute late at her first hour of dispensing personal wisdom, my name got entered for the second time in the black book of bad behavior.

She talked about how she went jogging in the local park. One day a man ran after her and grabbed her. Another one had come to her aid so nothing really happened. She never returned to the park to run again. I missed the point completely. She gave in to her fear after one mishap and tells a group of women whose lives were mostly lived in ghettos where they got raped on a regular basis, about how important it was to report those incidences to the police. The miscommunication became palpable when I noticed the sighs and lifted eyebrows on the faces of the inmates.

Her Christian upbringing with which I was familiar taught her the opposite of what should be done if one wanted to live a spiritual life. In fact, religions are the opposites of spiritual freedom. The road to spiritual power is to face up what you fear, to act from your heart, to come out shining. The main difference between the two approaches can be summed up in asking one question. *Religion asks 'who is God?' while spirituality asks 'who am I?'*

When I finally made it to court, the judge laughed at the written report in which they referred to me as "the apple bandit" and gave me time served. I was unaware that the felony had been noted on my record; I was "free" to go.

New realizations
1) Situations repeated themselves with less time in between. What are the odds of getting a bed with a flickering light in two different cells? Meditation got me through the torturous location.
2) There is nothing more demeaning than the jail system where you are barely allowed to go to the bathroom by yourself.

THIRTY-THREE

Back to the outdoor prison

After I got released I walked around for a while. I sat down on a park bench for about half an hour when a police car stopped near me. It turned out that somebody in a nearby retirement home had called them to report that I had been sitting on that bench too long.

They offered me a ride to a town on the beach, the name of which I read from a bulletin board because I did not even know where I was on the world map. I had already learned not to stick to the absolute truth in dealing with authorities who lied with such ease themselves. If you told them, for instance, that you did not have any money, you were automatically suspect. If you got stopped and interrogated with a fat wallet on you, the story had a more agreeable ending.

In popular lore, people referred to the courts as the 'injustice system' and the appointed public defender as the public pretender. My knowledge of the courts, lawyers and cops I gained over a period of four years after I got that felony on my record, opening up opportunities to witness many instances of injustice, of ludicrous accusations, of absurd charges, of incompetent and biased sentencing by judges who ignored the written laws.

According to my educated black friend, the jails were overloaded with African-Americans who got longer jail sentences for the same crimes committed by whites. Stories were abounding over cops who killed black offenders in the streets without ever having to answer for their deeds. Personally I did not fully ascribe to those theories because the only people who attacked me on three different occasions were African-Americans. I found them far more violent than white men who they habitually harassed. In the jails they ruled the whites and other minorities, duplicating the collective SSS behavior of the 'white systems' in society.

With the exception of some good, naïve cops who worked for low salaries, most of them were power hungry, lying, and corrupt men in uniform who harassed citizens who committed minor traffic offenses: shoplifters, drunks, and marijuana smokers. Dangerous criminals went free because cops were either too cowardly to go after their quarries or they took bribes. In modern society even citizens are now policing their neighbors and others over minor offenses. It is a paradise for power-hungry aliens, their gophers in selected bloodlines, secret societies, and the military who use high tech mind control devices in secret, somewhat like the wizard of Oz standing behind the curtain. Few people would even guess their presence, let alone their influence over most facets of our society!

Their human gophers are the ones who write our laws, design our jails, tell us what to do, how to live and which words to use to express ourselves in 'politically correct' language, control our University systems, media, and banks. Their gophers get rewards for work performed by others, such as University degrees, awards for the theatrical arts, are voted the most beautiful people, get media coverage and steer our planet towards a future where only people with a hive mentality are welcome.

    In contrast, the original, wonderful, irreverent and brilliant individuals who make sacrifices to create a freer world are put away in insane asylums, jails and prisons, modern concentration camps or get killed. Lies are told to cover up their murders by a biased media that is totally controlled by freaks or their puppets. The occasional idealistic journalist, who wants to honor his or her profession by telling the truth based on thorough investigation, as they are supposed to do, invariably ends up being decimated or punished in one form or another.

    So I told the two cops that I had just been released from Orlando jail and I was going home. It did not struck them as odd that a senior citizen had put in a complaint about me, sitting quietly on a park bench while minding my own business. I wondered what happened to the time when people minded their own business and were happy enough not to act out their irrational fears to call the law enforcers on every occasion.

    Enjoying the fresh air after having been deprived for months, I inhaled it as deeply as I could muster, filling my lungs. When I passed a mall I went inside to look around. In one of the stores a man followed me. I turned around to ask him why but he walked away. At the lingerie department I remarked that we must be sharing the same taste while I got positively annoyed. I went to the security department and wanted to put in a complaint. To my surprise, when I pointed him out, the guy turned out to be a security guard. His colleague told me that he was after somebody else but I did not buy that. I had to let it rest, however, as I was obviously not going to get any cooperation.

Taking a science fiction book with me, I walked out of the mall to a green, hilly area not too far from the parking lot. For a while I read undisturbed; the few pages of a book that promised to turn into an intriguing story; then the feeling that somebody was watching me hit me. I looked to the right and saw this huge alligator eyeing me. The only thought that crossed my mind in that instant was: "there is no fence in between us, this is not the zoo." My body froze, I could not have moved even if I had wanted to. With an air of boredom, I watched him turn to walk away in the other direction: I was probably not his type! A smooth green area in front of me turned out to be a pond covered with green algae I had not seen!

I could not return to the story in the book. The encounter with the alligator unleashed some fears within my body. Thoughts of what could have or might have been popped up belatedly. These thoughts welled up spontaneously to quell the fears my body harbored. Did I escape death or was I exaggerating? A moment in time that made a strong impression due to its novelty! How often did an alligator climb out of a pond to sit next to a human?

Compared to the two-legged erect reptilians these creatures did not hide behind a hologram. There was honesty about their simple survival need to eat meat unlike their two legged brethren who, besides using us as slaves with the aid of technologically advanced gadgets, they also used humans as food much like we eat cows or pigs.

New realizations
1) Game players, mostly people fearful of anything, were not trustworthy.
2) Impossible to share the idea of aliens with your average citizen whose veils were firmly in place, thinking everything functioned 'normally' as the eyes dictated.

THIRTY-FOUR

Las Vegas
Only a master stalker can be a master of controlled folly. Controlled folly doesn't mean to con people. It means that warriors apply the seven basic principles of the art of stalking to whatever they do, from the most trivial acts to life and death situations. "Applying these principles brings about three results. The first is that stalkers learn never to take themselves seriously; they learn to laugh at themselves. If they're not afraid of being a fool, they can fool anyone. The second is that stalkers learn to have endless patience. Stalkers are never in a hurry; they never fret. And the third is that stalkers learn to have an endless capacity to improvise." Carlos Castaneda

In the city of Las Vegas, made popular by gangsters such as Bugsy Siegel, where criminals habitually got away with murder and probably still do, I succeeded in getting arrested for grabbing a ridiculously overpriced Donna Karan shirt that sold for $255, 00. That price tag indicated a few dollars over the limit to be booked for petty theft in that city so I got slapped with another felony. I got booked by a cop who asked what my hair color was while I sat in front of her. Then she threw the pricey shirt on the floor while another cop irreverently stepped on it. I entered my phase of fighting the establishment.

On the way over to sin city, a SSS paradise, I had gotten a ride from a kindred spirit, somebody I could discuss some esoteric theories with. He was a man in his sixties who invited me over to stay with him and his daughter who was in her twenties. When he switched lanes he should have hit the car driving next to him but for some reason the other driver managed to evade him and the metals didn't clash. I don't have a mental image of an accident in my head, he told me, referring to the possibility of attracting that sort of experience if you gave it energy. I didn't either so we both looked detached at the upset driver who kept flipping him the bird: *fear always precedes anger*.

During the three days I stayed with them, I made an impression on the young woman who kept saying that she had never met anybody like me. What did she mean by that? My guess was that there aren't too many people whose guide steered them towards breaking the rules imposed by the system and then talked about it. Most gurus preach conformity to the system as if that is ***the*** requirement to make anyone see the Light! Learning about the system showed me how insanely it was put together, enforced by people who protect and service the insane without regard for decent citizens. If someone does a wrong, an accident occurs or a crime is committed, a new law is written based on the assumption that "everybody" else will attempt to do it too; it is written for our own good, no doubt!

In a country where the government officials lie about freedom of speech as a human right only to arrest anybody who criticizes their regime, a confused citizen is the result. Obeying the command of the sergeant in Orlando who asked me to write down what had happened when I accidentally mistook a country club for a public washroom, they used it as my 'confession to the crime'.

The father and daughter I stayed with for a couple of days never saw me again. Once again I disappeared behind bars. No doubt my fleeting presence had made an impact in their lives that would lead to new insights in the future. I filled out their address on a form so the police went to their apartment to inquire from whence they knew me. They claimed not to know me, of course. I never heard from them again!

Three hots and a cot was the slang term for checking into the jail hotel. Since I had a record with a felony on it, the female judge did not hesitate to sentence me to three months and probation. She actually wore a purple robe, the color of spirit, while her make-up and peroxide blond hairs impressed me as someone made up for a movie role: only in Las Vegas. But I merely wanted to use the bathroom, I protested to my ineffective public defender. A chocolate dipped apple and an overpriced shirt, stepped on by a burping cop, became the two items that branded me as a dangerous criminal that ensured me of an extended stay in the American justice system, dressed in red overalls.

As a novice in that system it is a chore to learn the ropes just as in any other profession. I noticed how repeat offenders came in and immediately got whatever they needed and wanted because they knew the wardens and how to work the system. Initially, I did not want to have anything to do with it but, later on, deprived of necessary hygienic items for which one needed to obtain permission, I started to pay attention on how to go about getting those items.

    There were two inmates to a room except for violent women who would be assigned to a single room or an elderly, homeless woman who checked into the jail every winter just to be off the streets. I spent a lot of time staying in the room if the roommate wasn't too crazy. There was a library in which I discovered the Dune books by Frank Herbert, an astounding science fiction tale that entertained and exposed me to many new ideas. While reading the series, I had a young Mexican woman as a roommate who liked to shoot the breeze with the other inmates so I had the room to myself most of the time.

    From her point of view I appeared as lazy and asocial but I explained to her, after she expressed the wish to go back to finish high school and obtain her American citizenship, that reading books were a necessary activity in achieving her high school diploma. After that lecture, she complained less.

    Naturally, I did engage in a skirmish. I would not learn anything if there wouldn't be obstacles to overcome or get my point across to others, regardless on which level of awareness they looked upon life at large. One newspaper got delivered for a crowd of about sixty women. Invariably, several of them would be fighting over the entertainment page which featured the daily horoscope. A white woman would lose the page or be ordered to give it up when a black one, belonging to a group of five, wanted it. Groups of blacks would terrorize single white inmates.

The skirmishes were about trivialities such as sitting down in an empty plastic chair that one of them considered as her property. I looked up surprised when one of them pointed that out to me. I refused to get up for her so now she accused me of "not paying her respect." This childish, arrogant behavior covered up a very low self-esteem but it was also deemed to be the way of the street. She would be 'losing face' if she did not object to me sitting down in her spot; so both of us had to put on a performance so neither one of us would get into trouble with other inmates or the wardens.

Cursing, she grabbed another empty chair next to mine and put it squarely in front of me to block the TV screen I watched. I said nothing but noticed out of the corner of my eye that four other black women were encircling me; the guards were in an adjacent room catering to an inmate. The coast was clear to teach me a lesson and, therefore, dangerous. She kept moving her chair a few inches closer to me until, finally, it touched my knees. At that instant, with all of my might, I kicked her chair away from me while shouting at the top of my lungs. The surprise attack and noise alerted the guard who immediately came running down and made the other four women move away from me. Nothing happened in fact, but we all 'saved face' and quiet returned to the cell block.

At suppertime I sat alone at a table when one of the four potential attackers wanted to grab a chair. I said something abrupt and she cowered, shaking with fear. This astounded me as I had not an inkling of the effect my defense action had on them that same morning. A simple kick and some noise changed the whole environment like the proverbial stone thrown in a pond to cause a rippling effect.

After a three month stay the judge added another couple of years of probation. I could not believe it. This meant checking in with a case worker and having to pay them a monthly sum for the inconvenience. Apparently, the case worker could also arrive at your doorstep unannounced to check and see whether you kept your promises or not. In other words, you suddenly became severely curtailed in living freely. Control, control, control—paying for a system that takes one's freedom away; one had to almost admire the ingenuity of a Dark agenda were it not so spiritually criminal!

I skipped town as soon as the cell door swung open!

New realizations

1) Most, if not all, people that worked for the government were obedient to lines on paper that basically took the breath out of anyone who inadvertently got in touch with them.
2) Any contribution any culprit had made to society, years of service, volunteering work, was totally overlooked on a rap sheet that only mentioned the actions against the system.

THIRTY-FIVE

Walking the coast of California

I hitchhiked west to Santa Luis Obispo in California, a Mexican town close to Hearst Castle, a tourist attraction. That's where I learned for the first time to visit the motels and hotels that served breakfast for their guests in the morning to get a free meal. Moreover, on Sunday afternoon volunteers served a hot meal at noon time for anyone who wanted to eat in a square downtown. That took care of my daily food supply. The universe will take care of one's needs while traveling the rocky road of spiritual progression.

As I arrived in spring time the weather was agreeable enough to let me sleep outdoors. I put a sleeping bag close to the area of the University where I, every now and then, ran into a homeless person. Most of the time I did not have much to say to them as my entire outlook on that situation was summed up in the word home free, not homeless. Instead of seeing myself as a victim, I paid attention to whatever was happening so I could learn from a situation.

After spending a couple of weeks there, I headed towards the coast where I met a brown owl. This animal exuded such powerful vibrations through its eyes that I got the distinct feeling it would attack me if I did not move. It is the only time I felt insecure about the intent of an animal. So I started walking again, down highway 1 against the traffic, in the direction of Carmel.

As the coastal highway featured two lanes and no pedestrian area, I had to step on the white sideline to move. Looking down on the spectacular coastline with its rock formations, I did not consider that a problem. Seeing some sea lions I moved into a grassy fenced off area where I could get a closer look at them. Lying down while reaching with my head over the side to look at them, they immediately looked up and exchanged glances with one another before diving under water.

I was impressed by that. How could they know I peeked over the edge while being only a dot to them? Behind me, a young guy kept changing positions and it occurred to me that his intention wasn't beneficial. The area was quite isolated and he could harm me if that's what he had in mind. Nobody would be around to hear my screams. In the learning process of trusting my Higher Self, certain precautionary measures were still in order so I ran back to the highway.

Any skill practiced often enough leads to mastery. Often I would be in an area attempting to enjoy some peace and solitude when suddenly somebody would pop up to present me with a problem I needed to handle. One day I walked into a forest to get away from the hustle bustle so I could spend some time alone reading a book, affording me the luxury to retreat in my own universe. A car kept following the road going in the same direction I walked and, finally, I took a turn to disappear. Fifteen minutes later I heard the steps of the driver as I spotted the parked car in the distance. I got furious and yelled I didn't want any company: unfortunately that did not deter the guy from pursuing his selfish desire to bother me. No choice but to get up and walk away without being able to get any reading done.

Sitting on a sand dune, a distance from a parking lot near a beach, I marveled at another fantasy book. Some of the writers of fantasy trilogies put so much truth in their stories it beat any so called non-fiction book that claimed to do so. I could relate to their stories which gave me comfort on my solitary path. Just the knowledge there were others like me who perceived similar and different situations reinforced the sense of Oneness in the spiritual realm.

Thinking myself to be alone and safe, I became aware of angry footsteps near the parking lot. A guy walked in my direction but he was so far that I didn't pay him any attention until he got so close that I looked around to see where he was headed. When he yelled for me to stay put, I did the opposite. Alarmed, I jumped up and wondered what was in store. Take your pants off, he ordered. What? I said, in total disbelief. I mean it, he replied, either you give me your money or we will have sex. Having just comprehended how the two most intrusive control mechanisms in society were sex and money, I knew a (Higher Self conducted) test was at hand.

I refused to budge and started screaming to match his reality; in other words, he counted on getting me scared so I played along. Nobody can hear you, he stated. I watched him pick up one of the two bags I had put on my blanket. I had just finished packing the contents of the bag he picked up into a new one that stood next to me. He grabbed the one filled with some old clothes and a couple of bags of chips and stormed off while opening the bag, dumping its contents and announcing loudly that "I had no money." Phew!

    In the beginning of my journey on the road, I had a strong need to spend time alone and I didn't like to be constantly surrounded by people. The only way to erase that need is to look inside, locate why the need existed and get comfortable within. This was one of the issues I had to deal with so it kept happening. As soon as I sat down at a table in a diner, café, bowling alley or restaurant, some large group of people would join me. Exasperated at first, I grasped the significance of having to deal with this issue to get focused enough to keep on reading without allowing outsiders to interfere with my concentration.

    As time went on, I spent more and more nights outdoors. Not knowing how to live like a homeless person, I would stumble on something that looked like a reasonable area to take a nap and I would lie down. I have slept on dirty mattresses in populated areas not feeling any sense of danger, plausibly because I would be too tired to question it. Later on, as I became more grounded and independent, I learned how to be more discriminatory about my choice of rest area to the point where I 'felt it would be my spot'. It happened quite often that I would go to sleep somewhere and be run out of town, especially in Pleasantville types of places. Resting in somebody's pickup truck while I crossed a city resulted in a ride out of town so I never did that again!

I enjoyed walking the coastline for the exercise, its beauty and the challenge of watering and feeding myself as there were only a few stores and one camping ground where I took a cold shower and helped myself to a few cans of soda pop. Somehow I got through it being underfed until I hit the beach of Monterey where I met a young guy whose mouth contained a couple of teeth that made me think of the sea lions. Perhaps he had been one in another life?

He explained to me that he waited for a check so he could get off the beach where he had been sleeping for several weeks. Waiting for something to happen as opposed to taking action is no indication of an energetic mover; it is a sign of apathy. This man could not proceed without the (false) security of having money in his pocket.

I stayed with him behind a couple of wooden planks he had put up as a protective shield against the wind. In the morning an elderly SSS guy who lived in one of the nearby condominiums, groped through a trashcan that stood near our area. He came over to talk to my new acquaintance who deferred to him by answering his questions about his check. He leered at me and I began to get angry at this man because with so many trashcans why would he pick out the one where we were trying to have some privacy. We were not going to his condo to do the same thing? I willed him away.

For me, it was impossible to take the stance of so many of the homeless who suffered from low self-esteem. Later on, I would experience the charities that catered to them, without exception run by SSS adherents who did so with a smile, offering a sandwich while forcing their religion onto them. It was an effective way to make them feel like second-class citizens. The dose of sneering by the middleclass people who looked down on them was the worst part of the whole sorry existence and guaranteed to instill a sense of exasperation.

New realizations

1)   I did not want to get involved in situations my body considered unpleasant or confrontational. To be constantly surrounded by people or being sought out by them, even in remote areas, I considered an affront I had a hard time dealing with.
2)   I knew there was invisible protection as my vulnerability never got compromised and even people who wanted to harm me were deterred. Usually, I felt my guide's presence.

3)   Food always came when my body really needed it, regardless of my whereabouts. The most remarkable moment came when I got lost in a desert to find a bush adorned with candy canes; a gallon-sized bottle of water standing next to it.
4)   People who needed my assistance to understand something or evolve to the next phase in their lives would invariably cross my path at strategic points.

THIRTY-SIX

More Adventures on the road

Somewhere between Monterey and Carmel a young guy offered me an overnight stay at his beach front cabin. He dropped me off and left. A female neighbor wondered about this after I told her how we had just met. As a joke I told her that I was a walk-in, a phrase I had picked up out of the last book I had been reading. It turned out that she was one. In such instances of synchronicity, a veil is lifted to reveal that the *process of the spirit was perfect*!

A walk-in is a spirit who takes the place of the one who no longer wants the earth experience in that particular body. The woman explained to me that her body was sick with diabetes and how she had to spend a lot of time in the local hospital. Since she had the ability to perceive spirits who had left their bodies after death, she functioned as a messenger. Lots of people do not know they are dead like Bruce Willis in the movie The Sixth Sense. She told me about the spirit of a man who had doled around in the aisles of the hospital for over twenty years.

My next stop was north of San Francisco in Marin County. There I spent a few days in a park where I encountered a woman with a German accent who walked her dog every morning. The second time she passed she asked me where I was staying. In the park, I answered honestly, to her consternation. When truth enters a scene, vibrational ripples can be felt. The next morning she invited me over for breakfast and I followed her to her house, where her husband awaited.

Again, the malicious intent was palpable as I got ushered into her kitchen where I got served one piece of wheat toast with jam. After answering their questions about my reasons for staying in the park, she told me to return the next afternoon to take a hot bath if I wanted. Then she asked me again if I was really sleeping in the park. Yes, I said. Then she related how she had told her friends in church how she met this extraordinary woman who, like Jesus, slept in nature; her friends, naturally, made fun of me.

I knew her SSS husband kept her in spiritual chains but she was ready to break free; so it didn't come as a surprise that she told me in private about her intention to get a divorce. With a whole house at her disposal her attitude towards money was very poor. This she demonstrated in putting a price on everything. She told me that she had not enjoyed a new piece of clothing for years as her husband regarded that as a frivolous interest. (Law of Attraction at work as that happened to me when I had to wear clothes my mother sewed!) I perceived her as a prisoner in her own home who was too afraid to live or do anything that would give her joy. This became very obvious when she almost gagged when she saw me doing a crossword puzzle, a form of meditation for me. Entertaining oneself she considered a waste of time and selfish endeavor!

I went shopping for a couple of new jogging suits and returned the same day. She had invited me to join them for supper. Her husband looked at me, said sarcastically that I had more money than they did which I answered with a smile. The weather forecast had announced that a bad storm was brewing and she asked me again whether I planned on staying in the park. Surely I had the money to get a hotel room if I could afford to give her a new jogging suit. No, I shook my head. That left her with the choice to offer me a bed or sending me away.

You cannot buy me, she told me stubbornly, after I offered her the jogging suit. Yes I know, I answered, thinking how her husband had still a dark hold over her. I'll be leaving the area soon to go up north, I reassured her, so do you want it or not? Glancing longingly at the suit, she finally took it out of my hands, but she did not offer me a stay in her house. Despite her intent to leave him, she clearly had adopted several of the traits that are so effective to divide and conquer us: when I did a crossword puzzle while she ran a bath, she went ballistic, ripping it out of my hands, telling me 'the bath was ready'. Her irrational behavior showed me how agitated she really was beneath the veneer of conformity! I was not allowed to enjoy myself.

One hour later the storm hit and I found myself outside. Seeking shelter in a nearby portable, free standing toilet resulted in a collapse after a gust hit it and I screamed, thinking I would be covered with shit. Fortunately, it had just been cleaned and the water in the container did not reach me. I scrabbled up and got up.

Not being able to see anything through the curtain of raindrops pelting down the streets, I groped around and finally decided to try out empty cars in garages to see if one of them would be unlocked so I could stay inside until the storm subsided. I found one and slept on the back seat until dawn. Lo and behold, in the morning when I looked outside I recognized the house of the German woman. Destiny had brought me to a sedan that was parked right across from her house. Such irony!

New realization
1)   Giving without expecting anything in return was the lesson here. How can anyone with empathy allow someone to go out in the storm while you had several unused bedrooms available? No matter, I got it so didn't feel taken. I had offered the present in return for the toast and coffee, more than enough to keep a balance in.
2)   Her lack of joy was tangible; no amount of money in the world could fill that emptiness inside.

THIRTY-SEVEN

Forced return to Las Vegas

After moving to the town of Napa, I got arrested again for the petty theft of food and I landed in the local jail. This small jail only housed less than fifty women in sections of six and I was getting used to them by now. However, a new scenario loomed: extradition to Las Vegas.

The overpriced shirt for which I had done three months of jail time had not been sufficient to pay my dues and the humorless social workers in Las Vegas could not stand anyone who did not show up on their doorstep to start their rehabilitation program for re-integration in an insane society or some such nonsense. So they did not mind 'doing the right thing' and use tax-payers money for an airplane ticket to haul me back to their city to restart my probation program.

A young lawyer fresh out of school did his best to find the loophole in the law to get me out of this predicament and he found one. An idealistic guy who fully believed in the righteousness of the laws, he got a shock when he heard the nervous judge decide, going against the law, that I had to be extradited.

For a couple of weeks I enjoyed their hospitality before a paddy wagon came to drive me to Reno where I ended up for another week in an isolation cell after I ignored the order of a guard to step down from a chair I stood on. I enjoyed the single room which provided me with quiet time to do some reading, a time to recharge my batteries. Jail was no longer the horror I once regarded it to be.

I marveled at the plane ride. Anyone who saw me in the cuffs would have assumed me to be a dangerous prisoner. In Las Vegas I got dropped in the now familiar waiting tank where I had to go through the whole procedure of being fingerprinted again. You wonder why they don't file them somewhere in their system:

(The system likes to collect that information and it is a redundant system, with fail-safe, redundancies built in, to collect as much information to cross-reference and track their cattle, as possible. Now the system has the 'finger print' of a user's cell phone, to dial up, whenever they need to protect us from ourselves.)

Spending time in the Las Vegas holding tank must be one of the most frustrating and funniest experiences on the planet. Most of the women who came in there were brought in with the most ridiculous criminal accusations I have ever heard. Obstructing the path of a pigeon or defacing a hamburger were two of them. Can you imagine getting arrested for throwing a slice of tomato on the floor because you didn't like it on your hamburger patty or stepping in front of a pigeon? Then there were the poor girls who tried to make some extra money hanging out in the casinos trying to hook onto some high roller. Guess the casino bosses did not like competition. Most women sell their sex or marry wealthy guys. This is what Las Vegas is all about: **money and sex, the two major control mechanisms.**

The worst offense in Las Vegas is appropriating money that does not belong to you; this included picking up a chip or a token out of the tray below a slot machine. The casinos actually hired undercover detectives to keep people who made a hobby of picking up loose coins out of their play halls. The Eye in the Sky referred to cameras strategically installed at every angle covering play areas where employees stared all day long at screens to determine whether somebody cheated or did anything against their casino rules. For some reason, they habitually missed the crimes related to people getting murdered in hallways or parking garages.

So here I was again, arraigned by the same female judge who noted my disobedience. The same public defender was assigned to defend my case who announced that I would not get a court date until I stayed as a guest in their cell for at least three months. Not surprisingly, several faces were familiar from the last time I had been there and I even shared a cell with some women who had been my roommates on a previous visit.

One of them was a young woman whose upbringing by a jewelry thief had resulted in a major confusion regarding ownership. Whatever we had in the room and belonged to me or had been given to me like several pairs of socks, would disappear systematically. It was futile to talk to her about it as a vacant look of non-comprehension would appear in her face. Only after I told her about fifty times to stop taking my candy, did a split second of light shine in her eyes. I regarded that as a breakthrough in her case.

    A female bank robber also shared my space. Her mother had taught her the art of living the double life of a respectable woman who robbed banks on the side. I considered it a bit more original than going to bars at night to sell your body so we could get along just fine. She told me that the jail was the worst part of a sentence as the stay in prison was a cinch, with TV, any drugs you wanted, and three meals, etc. She could not convince me of that and let it rest.
    I drew pictures of the girls who paid me in candy bars and other necessities such as deodorants and shampoo. It provided me with an opportunity to beautify them so they would get a boost in the way they looked at themselves.
    Then there was the case of a middle-aged woman who had been kidnapped by a former schoolmate. She had refused his advances and he would not take no for an answer. So he bound and gagged her, threw her in the trunk of his car and drove cross country robbing convenience stores and banks. That woman had to proof in every town where he had made a hit that she was his victim and not his accomplice. At night he had taken her out of the trunk and allowed her to share his motel rooms, or so the story went.
    I got an interview with a counselor who would do his best to get me signed up for another truck driving school to get me 'rehabilitated'. Could I tell him that I served my Creator by spending time with spiritually

neglected women? He wanted me to undergo a psychiatric observation for a ninety day period in prison after I asked him if department stores owners ever got arrested for overpricing their merchandise? He conveniently forgot to recommend me for truck driver's school since, according to him, I demonstrated a lack of remorse: non-conformism is lethal in the (in) justice system!

Then the letter writing started. My lawyer recommended writing to the judge why I had not shown up for probation so I followed his advice to write a couple of requests soliciting her understanding about my position in society as a down-and-outer. Here the saying "when you do the crime you have to do the time" means you are being forced to take responsibility for your own actions. But, once in a jail, it is contrary to their rules to make a decision based on one's own cognizance! Does anyone notice a major cause for confusion here somewhat like the rules other places like Scientology enforce? **Spirit cannot be forced!!!**

It introverts and is a trap for the spirit so the rehabilitation process is a complete failure! I had to beg for forgiveness for taking that overpriced shirt which I could not do. However, I could mouth some apologies to match their warped reality. Coming across as a victim who had been misguided by a set of ignorant parents is an acceptable strategy. Thus I complied, knowing from my experiences in Orlando and other jails, that to rebel was senseless and ineffective.

Another three months passed and again, the judge gave me two years' probation before she released me. And once again, I did not show up and left Las Vegas.

New realizations
1)   My claustrophobia slowly disappeared during the time I spent behind bars. I began to enjoy it, since I could assist some women in dire circumstances who were grateful for the attention. It felt like living in grace!
2)   The justice system reflected the same modus operandus of the government at large, the military, corporations, and churches. They were microcosmic prisons on a prison planet.

THIRTY-EIGHT

More Encounters

I walked down the streets of Sacramento after a driver of a van had given me the option between grass and ass which I had rejected. Crossing a bridge in the early evening I noticed a sign that said that the Pentecostal Church held a service at seven o'clock. Without an idea of where to spend the night, I decided to attend the sermon.

It turned out to be an African-American church in which I got welcomed by the pastor as the only white new face. He put me on the spot by asking me to introduce myself to the congregation. Making something up instantly, I took a seat once again. *These situations did wonders for me to learn how to stay in the Here and Now!*

A couple of minutes into the service a young woman with a toddler ran down the aisle in my direction. She told me about taking her child to the hospital the next morning to have his tonsils taken out. I looked at the boy and shook his hand.

After the service she invited me over to her place where I stayed and accompanied her to the hospital the next morning. Hands on healing, channeling permission from above I touched the boy while sending him a thought of love. Then I heard the nurse say that the boy had enjoyed an unusually speedy recovery after the operation. His grandfather came down to visit and thanked me for my support. My function ended, I bid them farewell.

Thoughts must have crossed my mind regarding missing weddings in my life, because on two separate occasions I inadvertently crashed wedding receptions.

The first one was held in a country club I strolled into on a beachfront in California. The beautiful setting enticed me to take a place in one of the chairs on the patio overlooking a lake. I disregarded the joyful activities around me and did not partake in any conversations, nor did I take any beverages or food that was served. Rather naively, I thought I would not be noticed by the invited crowd but I proved myself wrong as the bride came over to inquire if her groom had invited me. Yes, I said, while offering her a beautiful ruby ring I had borrowed from a store that specialized in fakes of authentic priceless creations. She thought it to be real and did not hesitate to immediately put it on her finger, walking away with it.

The next one in line was her mother who I also presented with a ring she accepted. Still I was not offered any refreshments or food but now I got the grandmother who asked who I might be. Just a friend, I answered while saying that her son, the bride's father, had been rather uncouth towards me regarding my presence. It is utterly amazing how upset many people can become regarding someone's presence. If they didn't want me to be there why did they take my gifts?

It didn't last long before the bride, new ring on her finger, told me that her father would escort me out of the country club. I told her that since I didn't like his attitude towards me I would not allow him to do that. Have you forgotten what a real lady is like? I asked him, referring to a female with certain manners, quite unlike the females in his own family. So I donated two fake rings without getting even a cup of punch.

The second time I waltzed into the wedding of an African-American family in a public building in Seattle where I had the only white face, just like when I entered the Pentecostal church in Sacramento. This time I asked the server for a glass of champagne without further ado. The lie that kept me going for a while in this reception was that I worked as a janitor in the building so they accepted that as a plausible explanation for attending their wedding. Basically, I considered both weddings as lame affairs that bonded two people with a piece of paper. I was actually glad to have escaped that scenario in my own life.

Still busy studying and fighting the alien-allied SSS humans, I ran into another one who invited me over to his place to consume a couple of beers. Inside the house, I met a mulatto woman who informed me that she hated beer drinkers because she had grown up with an alcoholic father and her memories were not very pleasant. I listened and drank the beer waiting for my host to make a pass on me. There has never been a stranger who offered me liquor without wanting to be compensated with a roll in the hay.

In this case, things turned out differently as I did not get drunk. Waiting for a chance to talk to the woman, she noticed that we had exactly the same body type, same height and same measurements which prompted me to put a whole new outfit on her bed after she left for work the following morning in exchange for letting me bunk in her room. During the time spent with her she mentioned that her SSS roommate was an odd fellow who was not the person he seemed to be which pleased me a lot. Impressed, she noted how fast I had gauged him. It took me several weeks, she said. Are you kidding? Most people spent lifetimes with them without noticing anything different about *them*!

On another occasion, dressed beautifully in expensive clothes, I went home with another one of those characters. He lived alone in a house in Eureka, California and he offered to take me out for a drink. A similar scenario had been planned with the saying Candy is dandy but liquor is quicker. For some reason, I made the mistake thinking that we would be going to a fancy restaurant where I could show off my clothes. Instead, he took me to a couple of seedy bars, one of which turned out to be one with karaoke facilities.

I dared him to sing the song Sweet Dreams written by the group Eurhythmics with me on stage, knowing they never ventured to do something new. Under heavy protest I dragged him along, even though the place was nearly empty. We read our lines and sung our song, then headed home where I took charge to order him to sleep in his master's bedroom while I bunked on the couch in the living room. *(Once again, they do respond to direct orders if delivered without hesitation.)*

'If the nature of the beast is predatory, convinced that sex is its mainstay for survival, then the prey better pay attention', I thought. Telepathically, I heard the words 'get out now' when I sleepily awoke to use the bathroom. NOW, a voice thundered inside of my head; it was past three in the wee hours of the morning. I got dressed and got out in the chilly night, knowing I may have escaped rape or a worse fate.

New realizations
1)   If I wanted to keep a SSS gopher or alien at bay, all I had to do was to give them a direct order.
2)   My guide showed me how to erase a prejudice by staging a situation, in this case drinking too much alcohol with a SSS-er, but somehow, I remained sober. The simultaneous woman got an AHA moment out of it, putting her spirit more in control over her personality.
3)   A direct order to me telepathically given by my guide I had to obey, otherwise troubles awaited.

THIRTY-NINE

An island visit

Simple necessities like relieving oneself became yardsticks to measure my own progress in maturing as a spirit. Before I took the ferry that would take me across Puget Sound to one of the islands off the coast, I spent a few minutes in a public bathroom not knowing there were many women in line to use the facilities that consisted of two bathrooms. I took the opportunity to change clothes as I often did, and got cursed out by the crowd as soon as I re-emerged from the stall. A bit taken aback but no longer completely intimidated, I went on my merry way to the ferry. In hindsight, I merely did what any homeless woman does in the stalls but, to me, it was dipping into an unknown type of existence, noticing that every stratum of society had a set of rules for accepted behavior.

Once on the island I ran into a guy, another SSS character who invited me over to his home where he lived with his brother. His brother functioned as his gopher and protector, taking care of all the problems he instigated with his neighbors, acquaintances and authorities. He showed me a book that had been signed by a number of people he admired to impress me with his popularity. For the first time ever I stuck my neck out by taking the book, just to see what would happen!

It created a huge problem when I appropriated the book only to throw it alongside the slope of a dune in the bushes. Telepathically, I had been advised to do so

Ayla's Quest

while I balked because I could foresee the oncoming emotional freight train headed in my direction. But I complied. I did not have it in my possession so he could only accuse me of taking it without any proof that I had actually done it short of a confession. I was not willing to provide him with one.

Nevertheless, he kept on talking about that book no matter how many times I told him to shut up about it and look in a different direction for a solution to his problem. His brother looked at me closely, interrogated me separately and swayed by my answers finally offered to buy him a new book. Of course, the signatures were missing and although I marveled at the fact that those characters always found somebody or a way to leech onto someone to keep them in the material goods, I felt somewhat guilty about the fact that the brother had to give up some of his money; still had to overcome that good, old guilt.

I left but didn't go very far when I noticed a car that followed me. I turned around to confront the couple that eyed me as if I belonged to a clandestine operation. Shooting them one of my glares they ducked and the driver started the motor to get away in case I ....became dangerous? Not long thereafter, reaching the ferry, I found my former host waiting for me to accompany me to the city. Again, he began to grill me on the disappearance of his beloved book. I wouldn't budge.

He asked me whether I wanted to accompany him to the apartment of a friend who lived alone as a paraplegic, bound to a wheel chair. I knew the 'assignment' not to be over and reluctantly consented to do so, expecting to be treated to a staged play. This is what happened:

He got on the bus without paying because he took control of the situation, advising the bus driver of some excuse that the latter accepted. They like to live for free or have others pay for them! I actually marveled at this because it had never occurred to me to attempt to get a free ride in my entire life. I just followed and observed what was happening.

Living at a second floor, one bedroom apartment downtown Seattle we found a paraplegic, long-haired, attractive man in his early twenties. My companion put on a show of embracing him while making him promise to be a good host which amounted to him handing over all of his cash money to buy beer, whiskey and food. The man left the apartment to spend his new-found treasure to start the party.

Not knowing anyone with that disease I looked at him and wondered how he could swallow alcohol and medical pills simultaneously without getting seriously ill. Not knowing that my companion was forcing him into that position, spending money he could not afford to spend on alcohol, I sat back wondering what scenes would follow next. As the SSS-ers are very predictable, I assumed that the consumption of alcohol in which I cautiously participated would lead them to look upon me as a possible available sexual partner. Even in my most generous moments I could not envision merging with just anyone who came along to practice "loving one another."

When I declined their invitation, my companion lurched for my lighter that had an embroidered cover with a Navajo design he had given me for some reason. He "stole" it back when repeating the refrain of the lost book so I did not object. The sight of a young handicapped man who was swigging away at the whiskey, getting drunk while getting additional liquid amounts force fed by my companion, was disturbing. But I wasn't sure what to do here. Apparently, they both consented so I could not interfere. Asking the question about whether he would get a physical problem was met with silence.

Disappointed at my refusal to engage in sex and the depletion of the host's money, the island man decided to take his friend out for a ride on the bus. I accompanied him and at a given point, he disappeared to leave the handicapped guy in my capable hands. Needless to say, it was a big problem for me to get him back on the bus, drunk, while trying to convince others that this was not the case and please, could anyone give me a hand with getting him back home? Our mutual contact had disappeared for good and did not return.

I let him sleep and called his father the following morning while I used my own money to buy him a steak and one bottle of beer which surprised him a lot. I told him that drinking one beer with a steak is a different approach than getting drunk and out of control. It turned out that the family knew about the destructive behavior of the island man towards their son but could not control their son's life nor protect him against such predators. For me, it reinforced my already expanding knowledge of the simultaneous spirit suppressing, parasitic behavior I observed.

FORTY

Encounters with animals

During the nineties when I did my studies in the field so to speak, there were many encounters with animals. Most of them acted towards me as just another creature passing by, but every so often there would be a moment of hesitation from my part as in the aforementioned case of the brown owl. Even the alligator did not upset me as it simply moved on in the opposite direction while I read my book.

Twice I got bitten by dogs because of their training by their owners. Once because I desperately needed to use a bathroom while waiting in a car, the dog defending the house did not know me so he lashed out; on another occasion I asked the owner whether his three Chihuahuas were friendly to which he nodded. When I bent down, looking at the rat like creatures, beady eyes staring back at me, they bit me. As expected, the owner merely smiled, offering no apology before he walked away.

A revealing moment about snakes presented itself when I sat on a blanket in the desert. Having no experience with those critters other than a snippet recall of a life lived as a female snake handler in China who sold them on markets, I watched two of them slither by, but when the third one arrived, I heard the inner voice telling me to get up. I did not hesitate and watched it raise its body in anticipation of my removal before it came slithering over my blanket. I realized that snakes had different personalities and possibly a similar pattern within its ranks as its human counterparts: a controller, a gopher and an individualist.

A particular vivid memory is the unexpected banana slug I found in my hair when I dozed off. Just the feeling of the slimy creature when I wanted to push my hair out of my face stayed with me for years to come. Such impressions are very difficult to erase from your inner radar, but they do, when I no longer pay attention to them and suddenly find one day that there is nothing left but a gentle memory. The texture of the slug is gone!

I met many squirrels along the way. I had the mistaken notion that they were cute critters until they started to complain about my presence in their territory with loud chirps that could last for hours.

There was a similar problem with raccoons that barked like dogs and fought hard when they got mad at each other. I lived with a couple for several weeks in a forest under a wayward willow, a fantastic tree that provided shelter from inclement weather. Often those two came rolling down a branch right behind my head when they were playing or interacting in some way.

Animals also became symbols for my progress. In shamanism, a specific animal comes forward to the seeker to become his ally, referred to as his power animal. Every time I finished a cycle or learned a lesson successfully the power animal would change, combined with the numbered phase I was on; for instance, recently I finished four months of living in a tent while it rained daily on the west coast of Ireland.

Had I been griping about rainy weather before, not one complaint crossed my lips while being inundated by rain for four months straight. The butterfly stands for lightheartedness and transformation, indicating my power to transform myself and anyone who asks for my assistance. Eleven butterflies surrounded me when I got ready to pack up my tent!

New realizations
1)   Animals understood the natural Law of Allowance perfectly: they would allow others to be themselves without bothering them.
2)   Amazing synchronicities occur at specific moments in one's life when certain animals appear, according to shamanism.

FORTY-ONE

Breaking eating habits

    Anything we do and did is related to thoughts and methods role models provide us with during our early years while our subconscious plays an additional role. *No form exists apart from consciousness.*

    Growing up with parents who liked a certain type of food becomes a main staple into our diet until far into adulthood. When we feel depressed or sad, there is a tendency to start eating something our bodies crave and we refer to it as comfort food to make us feel better. For me, without question, a bag of French Fries with mayonnaise did the trick to put me back into a more cheerful mood. It also served to fill the emptiness inside I felt when love was missing from my life.

    A necessity in changing my eating habits came when I moved to the USA: the French fries were now delivered with ketchup while the potatoes were of a different quality. Although there wasn't a big difference, the American method of preparation and cooking was different. Then there were considerations relative to such items as corn, a popular vegetable in the United States but looked upon as slop for pigs in The Netherlands. So I wouldn't eat corn until I finally tried it after several years. *One simple thought prevented me from eating it!*

    We all can think of examples when we are eating something that may be delicious, only to immediately take on a disagreeable flavor when somebody reveals what it actually is that we are eating. Snails and chocolate covered ants may be delicacies in some countries, in others they are regarded as trash.

While in my twenties I had a craving for salty licorice, a popular candy in my country, raw pickled herring with onions which is a cultural mainstay and cheese, our pride and glory. Over time, it diminishes somewhat as the body gets used to other types of food but it takes a long time to really reduce it to a gentle memory without the accompanying cravings.

In the mid-seventies I moved to Hawaii where the climate and local food created another type of palate. Getting curious about the impact of food on my body, I studied it while I worked as a licensed massage-therapist. As with so many subjects, most authors write about what they believe is right and what works for them; then they set out to tell others how to go about following their example. I read so many contradictory opinions and findings that I decided to simply try the different diets to determine what would work for my body. A vegetarian diet lowered my level of energy while I almost got sick on a fruit diet. The best one for me at the time was based on my blood type which consisted of a protein diet with a helping of salad and fruit and a few hours of physical activity daily.

However, other factors came into play as I grew older and traveled to places with different climates and I learned how to listen to my body: if it really wanted or needed something I would simply get a taste in my mouth. This was a fool proof method of communication as my energy level would remain constant and my body was happy.

After my awakening when I deliberately set out to free my body from any form of want and/or need, the whole food picture changed. I recall standing in front of a store with my favorite candy and I did not have money to buy it. It was meant to assist me in overcoming a habit. Emotionally, it didn't feel too good and I ended up cursing under my breath as my saliva ran amok but I didn't touch it, an exercise in building up inner strength to resist temptation.

During the years when I had no money to spend, I had to rely on whatever came my way, as expressed in the cliché "beggars cannot be choosers"; however, I never begged. When I am truly hungry and in need of nourishment it doesn't matter if it happens to be food that I normally would not eat because it doesn't taste too good.

Ideas about eating health foods, freely run chickens, unsprayed vegetables and fresh items I eliminated entirely. I ate what I happened to find or get, regardless of any considerations pertaining to health issues. In the period after the jails, cops and helping myself in stores, I got gradually introduced to eating out of trashcans, a move farthest away from the way I was brought up because 'eating without washing your hands' or dropping something on the floor, then eating it, would be considered unhygienic. *If mom could see me now, opening dumpsters searching for edibles!*

Initially, I could not even bring myself to open the trashcan when I got stuck in an area where there were no edibles around for miles. When I finally did, a wrapped chef salad stared back at me, so I consumed my first meal out of a collection of thrown out food. Again, it was directly related to the idea that it was not healthy to eat out of the trash, an almost impossible notion to overcome when you are convinced that you are going to get ill if you do. In my case, this is a DNA command, a thought determined by someone else that influenced my behavior and took some of my freedom away.

It took a while before I could get used to actually looking through trash in moments of necessity but I soon found that dumpsters from restaurants contained lots of food that got discarded after the business closed at night. When I got caught in the act by employees of restaurants I would offer some glib excuse of 'looking for meat to feed my dog'; initially, embarrassment was still a part of my inner landscape. Slowly but surely, this dissipated and then disappeared after practice. When I completely let go of the fairy tale that one would get sick when eating the way I did, without refrigeration and disregarding all rules and guidelines of the governmental agencies, I enjoyed optimum health, of course.

Finding places to sleep when night fell remained for a long time a worry I could not get over, even though I usually ended up in some safe spot. The worries about my eventual lodgings that same night occurred often during the day so, basically, I was living in the near future. It was very hard to get control over them especially since I kept moving around in areas where I had never been. Telepathy, that initially started with spoken words, and then with nudging and impulses and eventually tapping into an inner knowing was used to direct me towards places. However, my mind kept wondering at least several times a day about it.

It did happen that I had to stay up all night or that I wouldn't get much sleep but those occurrences were the exception rather than the rule. Sometimes I misunderstood or made a mistake: once I went into a fancy hotel to the top floor where I found a dark area behind a curtain only to find that two employees turned the light on as soon as I lay down. Immediately, they escorted me out of the hotel into a dark and very cold night. There was nothing for me to do but to walk most of the time to get through. These were endurance exercises that I learned how to handle without complaints but I did not like them; if given the choice, I would have opted for more luxurious surroundings.

During a rainy night on the coast of California in a well-to-do resort town, I put my sleeping bag in a shack and woke up at the screams of a maid who thought she had found a stiff. A cop I had spotted earlier while walking around town looking for a place to stay out of the rain came down to run me out of town: my sort was not wanted, he said. He told me that he had assumed I stayed in one of the local hotels when he had seen me the night before. This encounter changed my entire attitude. Had I gotten upset before, angered at the arrogance of treating me like a low life, slowly I learned to accept the inevitability of the course: I really did not have a choice in the matter. My requests to get settled and be spared the further ordeal of constantly moving around, remained unanswered.

Years earlier I had expressed the wish to know as much as possible while on this planet and I had assumed that I would glean this knowledge from books, teachers, videos and movies. Assumptions, projections into the future while not knowing if they would or would not materialize, it became one of the mental configurations I had to let go of. Assumptions slipped in sideways in many instances, it took a while before I could control them.

One of my intensive cycles consisted of simply walking to observe people's behavior silently. There were people who jumped in front of me and made me move aside to get by them until I realized that they were inconveniencing me and not the other way around. So I had to learn not to put up with that and let them have it, aware of their intent to control me (possibly unconsciously) but not allowing them to get away with it. As soon as I got that under control I became a bit overly assertive by starting to push them away from me, bumping into them to make them move. When a man ran into me to knock me down I got the signal to stop: enough was enough, point made.

There always seemed to be one obstacle even when I walked down an area alone. If I wanted to cross a street, a car or bicycle appeared out of nowhere to block my path. If someone approached from the opposite direction, they invariably walked towards me no matter whether I made attempts to avoid them or not. For quite a while this minor irritation would upset me so it kept going until I no longer reacted to it. All these seemingly trivial matters served to empty my mind, creating space for my spirit, cleansing out my inner cobwebs to be replaced with inner freedom.

As anyone can attest to, clearing your mind and body from worries, unwanted thoughts and commands is a humongous undertaking because it sometimes seems impossible to depart from that battlefield. When a loved one, for instance, stays out too late, one frets about his or her whereabouts; when you take an exam you wonder if you passed it; if there is a bit of pain in some area of your body you worry about your health. On and on it goes, swirling like a tune that keeps playing like a broken record. Commands, intentionally repeated over and over again, affect one's behavior unknown to the conscious person. The body stores all kinds of emotions, phrases, impressions of situations that come to the fore at awkward moments or when alcohol is consumed. To be free of all of their input is a worthwhile quest that leads to peace of mind and an integrated personality whose intent is laser sharp.

New realizations
1) Battles were fought in seemingly innocuous actions such as passing someone in the street.
2) The stiller the mind, the less obstructions presented themselves, the more peaceful life becomes.

FORTY-TWO

Breaking the money habit in Las Vegas
　　The tip of the pyramid-shaped hotel The Luxor on the Las Vegas strip, my former hangout, draws in an electrical current. The Luxor is an energy harvesting Star gate vortex not far from Area 51 and S-4.
　　The last years of my intensive journey were spent on the Strip of Las Vegas as a home free person, someone who had stepped out of the box with enough inner strength to deal with the temptations of this neon city that was very Dark in its intent, sucking in anyone who harbored weaknesses. Therefore, it made a great Teacher.
　　The lack of identification papers made my presence officially illegal. The casinos insisted upon visitors who could flash credit cards and official papers; it would not be possible to get the money from a jackpot without identification. Somehow I managed to be there without those papers for years, avoiding all confrontations other than some minor run-ins over trivial matters.
　　My chosen 'home' was the Luxor hotel, a place I learned inside and out so I could use their amenities. I played the slot machines and poker machines with money I found on machines left behind by negligent tourists who did not pay attention to what they were doing. I tipped the employees with that money so they would give me pointers on what machines to play, the ones that were likely to pay off faster (not that it

mattered.) I used the swimming pool and the Jacuzzi to keep clean and occasionally found tickets for the spa. Room service left a wealth of sandwiches and leftovers while I also got tickets for the excellent buffets that were offered in one of the restaurants. Fruit baskets, tickets for shows, all free, simply by looking around. Never did I encounter one problem in this hotel and I feel fortunate to have 'lived' in that place.

My relationship with money has been a roller coaster ride. In my family the subject was considered gauche, one did not talk about it. Neither parent gave me a future reference on how to handle it, invest it or hang onto it. Consequently, I never developed an interest in it. I do recall mother complaining about being poor but that seemed unreal as they paid cash for anything they wanted to buy: motorcycles, boats, and other expensive toys.

The more imaginative approach of a frequent visitor, a hunchbacked man who did magical tricks that created coins I found underneath pillows, in pockets and grabbed from behind ears out of thin air, appealed more to me. I made him promise me to tell me the secret of his tricks on my twelfth birthday, considering it the smartest move possible for a sunny future. When he gave me my first bike as a present which I could use to deliver newspapers without telling me his secrets, the letdown was complete.

A series of jobs followed to get through school providing me with extra pocket money before I got forced into my first position as an overseas operator. Disliking telephones and having to give most of my money to my parents to contribute to the household, I responded to the inner command of "I have to get out of here." Leaving the country was not an option so my next move consisted of joining the Air Force where I did a stint as an Air traffic controller.

Until I set out on my guided journey at the age of 41, I worked various jobs and spent three years as a student in two Universities. There were high paid and low paid jobs but, for some reason, I could never get a credit card despite the fact that there were bankers in my family. There were some poor boyfriends and some very wealthy ones while my highest paid position gave me a taste for the high life. But no matter how much money came in, it went out just as fast and I usually felt like my left hand was taking it while my right hand would relay it to someone else in payment for something.

Many attempts to save some of it failed miserably. I always seemed to have enough to meet my needs but nothing more. When I bought extravagant, specially designed furniture for a townhouse I rented in my twenties, it got stolen when I left on a trip to Europe. That prompted my decision not to bother with buying furniture until I would get settled. Little did I know that the concept of 'getting settled' did not appear in my future? Astrologically, the square between Uranus and my Sun in the fourth house of the Home, combined with my Moon there, indicated a variety of different living areas as well as conditions. I kept moving around after I fulfilled a specific purpose in a certain area and I noticed that, in my mind's eye, I'd see a golden circle, indicating the end of a cycle.

Lots of money has been stolen from me by friends, acquaintances and strangers. I lost many wallets and purses before I learned to start paying attention and be less trusting of others in financial matters. Yet it had little meaning for me other than wanting to buy certain things, mostly books that would teach me something or inform me of alternative ways of living. When lots of money came in I spent it on courses and therapy. Within a fairly short period of time I managed to shift my life into an entirely different direction.

I had to work the hardest in jobs that paid the least amount of money, a fact that I reconciled with the idea that it was slavery. Invariably, I worked for people who were less skilled and intelligent in comparison and who got paid a lot more while my skills, like speaking and writing four languages fluently, would be used just because it came in handy. I regarded this as a form of legal theft.

In my thirties, I did not even apply for jobs any longer. It seemed that I would run into someone or a situation and, somehow get a job. Case in point was my visit to a piano bar in Honolulu on a Sunday afternoon in 1981, when I grabbed the arm of a man who was about to fight a much larger, drunk navy colonel. This move landed me a position as an assistant in his office of filling out tax return forms. It turned out, miraculously, that this man occupied the exact same apartment I had vacated a couple of years earlier before

I decided to return to California. What are the odds of that happening?

For two seasons I functioned as his 'scream tree'; he took all of his frustrations out on me because I was the only employee who could take it with a smile. I learned something about the way people spent their monies and I found that mildly interesting. The owner who used the loopholes he had learned at the IRS in favor of his clients, made some spectacular bad investments for himself. What I did admire about him was his integrity as he paid off every penny he owed to his debtors. The best thing I did for him was make him aware of the fact that he gave it away to support an ex-wife and two children who lived in a fancy house while he subsisted in a modest apartment. He bought his own condominium and went on vacation to Australia right before I left.

So the novelty of having to live without any money for several years was both frightening and an eye opener. As described before, once I got the hang of exploring alternative ways of doing things like free shopping and inviting myself to parties and breakfasts for hotel guests, stints in jails and the occasional gift from people along the way, my fears of survival without paper and plastic gradually subsided, and then disappeared altogether.

By the time I arrived in Las Vegas for an extended stay, I had been grounded and deprogrammed sufficiently to be able to withstand the onslaught of noise, neon lights, and gambling. For the casual tourist who comes to spend a few days sampling good food, watching shows and playing the slot machines, it can be a lot of fun. However, this city has an underlying seedy side that becomes apparent to the person who decides to spend an extended sojourn observing it.

How unlikely it may sound, for a spiritually inclined person on a higher level of awareness who is determined to learn how to blend his Dark energies with those of the Light, it is a paradise. It is exasperating, enervating, funny and joyless. The Strip where most of the big hotels are located with its variety of lures for the curious tourist is a magnet for bodily satisfactions. Anything is available that caters to physical needs and desires, for a price. Hence, it follows that someone's penchant for a certain taste in sex, foods, clothes or other forms of entertainment will be easily satisfied. For someone who abstains from such temptations and who has no money to spend, it can easily turn into a hell hole.

I experienced the worst moments when I did have money. I recall finding $500 which I proceeded to gamble away within one night. Not one machine gave me a winning hand; I drank too much wine, lost my coat and purse, gave a barmaid a hundred dollar tip (actually she had served quite a few free glasses of wine over months so I created a balance here) and ended up in the desert poorer than the day before. It served to make me wonder why I would bother wanting money as it did not seem to do me any good.

Then I actually got the unusual experience of not being able to lose for one New Year's Eve in Laughlin, a gambling town on the border of Nevada and Arizona. That night I found $300 and I happily started playing poker. After a while I had tripled my money by hitting four aces and my winnings kept increasing. Not far into the next hour a SSS woman approached me who told me to be grateful to God so I gave her the direct order of taking a long walk on a short pier. I had spent about two years sporadically hitting anything and this was the first time I actually had a golden touch; nobody was going to stain that moment of victory and *nobody was going to take my power away*.

    The experience turned into a two edged sword, as usual. After hitting several Royal Flushes I began to attract the attention of the regular players who were getting mad at me since I diminished their chances of hitting anything relatively big. Switching to other games, I kept hitting the bonuses and other features until I gained thousands of dollars that I shared with others: I tipped C-notes and made a lot of people temporarily happier. After all, it was New Year's Eve and I enjoyed the party thoroughly until the wee hours in the morning. Then I had to go into Arizona to find a hotel that would give me a room as I could not get one in Nevada without my papers. Four days later, back to 'normal' I had to spend the night outside in a storm!

    As the global monetary system has been put into place to control people's actions, glorifying the lifestyles of the rich and famous, it follows that this city of neon light was created to underscore the illusion of happiness through the appropriation of money. High rollers get rewarded; winners get bonuses and freebees while losers are discarded as fast as possible. On the surface, it is all smiles and lights, fun for "everyone." There is no encouragement for integrity, humility, honesty, perception, and mental courage, the finer traits of people that would create a healthier society. It is a topsy turvy reality!

    Tourists consider themselves forewarned about the temptations the Strip has to offer so they do not feel free to really enjoy themselves. Most of the middleclass that works for a living feels guilty about spending money on gambling. They do not like to lose their money in noisy machines as their brain then starts to calculate what other things they could have bought for the money they lost. They walk around arrogantly thinking they know what the scoop is and that they are in on privileged information. Of course, they usually are not cognizant that their way of thinking is already a form of having been brainwashed.

    What is money but an idea? Why can't you live without it in any of the western societies? Most people limit their actions to the amount of money they think they can afford to spend on an endeavor. Few have the mental courage to hit the road and live happy go lucky without being concerned about it at all. There is nothing wrong or right about money itself as its true value depends on the attitude of the holder, but it is *the symbol for power outside of oneself.*

    People who pursue that type of power and the accumulation of money are chasing a rainbow forever. The rich ones I've known are constantly preoccupied with holding on to or increasing their possessions without ever spending a moment in the present to see what is in front of their noses. Emotionally, they are completely controlled by whatever game they are playing: the fluctuations of the stock market, interests on their accounts, investments, their holdings, businesses, funds, etc. When I listen to members of my own family equate its value with success I get bored as I know that they are deaf, dumb and blind to what is truly important!

For me to be surrounded in Las Vegas for four years by literally piles of money without having access to it, my observations on how it has a stranglehold on people, was priceless. Whenever I mentioned that I didn't have any, the attitude of those I dealt with, immediately changed as I have mentioned before in some examples. The air positively turned chillier, as if a ghost entered the room. The lack of money is generally looked upon as a fault of character: one has to take the responsibility of taking care of one's own needs rather than expecting someone else to provide it for them. In fact, I did take care of my own needs but I did it without money! I learned how to live creatively, without considerations about what is acceptable and what is not.

There are wealthy people whose attitude is similar to that of the poor as they compare prices to save a dime. It is a matter of principle, they say, while breaking out in a sweat over losing a buck. Where is the joy in spending it? What is it good for if it creates such anxiety and fear?

FORTY-THREE

Back to jail

    I knew it would just be a matter of time before I would get hauled away again to jail to confront my disobedience to the court for not showing up for my intended probation/rehabilitation. This fear made me attempt to leave the city but it backfired when I could not get a ride out. I didn't want to be there but had to grin and bear it until I finished my assignment. The cop who accosted me in the desert one morning and checked my name on his computer to find that I had violated my probation terms by not showing up, arrived about a few months later.

    So off I went again to spend the winter with a roof over my head. With a stay of three months minimum to look at before anyone would bother to give me a court date, an automatic penalty for disobedience, I sighed and opened up to the most difficult and last experiences I would ever had confined behind bars.

    It started out with a new procedure from the last. Again, I had to be fingerprinted and booked. Maybe the system is just invented to create problems for non-conformists, while employing the "individualist challenged" ones? To think that they got paid from money collected from spirits kindred to my own was an irony indeed. Unfortunately, too many people think that society is "the real thing" so it would be near impossible to explain that it isn't! As long as the mind is programmed to believe that government employees are superior to us while our spirits are asleep at the switch, who would our worst enemy be?

An elderly, nicely dressed woman, looking uncomfortable, sat across from me in the holding tank. I wondered what crime she could have possibly committed and questioned her. The interest unleashed an emotional response connected to some argument she had had with a guy in the church, when she slapped him after a disagreement and he had called the police on her. I thought it funny as now the interest had been piqued from other women and she started to feel more comfortable; my presence could create a bit lighter atmosphere occasionally.

But the degree of difficulty during this incarceration had been upped and I found myself soon in another tank without any comfort, engaged in a battle of wills with a control freak. After I had gotten the familiar red overalls of thin cotton fabric, shivering, I was told to sit on the floor by a black woman who had taken it upon her to play the boss in this air-conditioned tank. Two other white women who entered alongside me obeyed her but I sat down on one of the benches, asking her why she was giving orders? Watching two other black women at her bidding, ready to teach me a lesson, reminding me of other times that I experienced that predicament, I continued questioning her. It mattered none as their hatred was now unleashed at me, calling me names and throwing insults at me. Grow up and get a life, I countered, refusing to budge. Then the door opened to several other women who immediately joined me on the benches and the subject became moot.

Soon I got a roommate whose main interest in life was the group The Sex Pistols. I could do no wrong after I let her know that I knew about the tragic demise of its leader, Johnny Rotten Vicious, who had committed suicide after his girlfriend died. This contact was instrumental in telling me about the money left on machines by tourists, something I learned how to look for once I got released.

Several years after my last incarceration I got the same public pretender, a guy whose money was earned by pushing pencils and filling out forms while giving me the standard talk about being good, writing apologies to the judge and being just about as ineffective as they come. This time I listened to him in silence, non-resistant.

I refused to write more apologies knowing it had no influence whatsoever on the outcome and I did not care what they had decided in their prejudiced minds; that it had little to do with my actual case was obvious. How many times did I need to get punished for taking an overpriced shirt I wanted to give as a present? I had already spent six months in jail and now I would do an additional three months before I would get, no doubt, more probation and/or a prison sentence?

My attitude was different, a terrific yardstick for my increased self-confidence during years of absence. My point of view had changed drastically. No longer did I enter the 'Holiday Inn' jail with hesitation, not knowing what to expect. I decided to hold my ground while being a player on the peripheral; one foot in and one foot out. Firmly giving the reins to my Higher Self, not caring what would happen to me, I took a leap of faith!

Unlike my other visits I got the order to be available for work, six hours of folding laundry which I refused. Just like the Orlando jail I was slapped with a charge of non-compliance but instead of sharing a cell with twenty other women, I got thrown in with one complete nutcase who kept screaming about sex through a pipe that led to the cell of a male inmate. There was no way I could get her to shut up or pipe down on her volume so I had to spend the weekend retreating into my inner sanctum to endure this onslaught of noise. Some communication in between the telephone sex made her show me a letter from her adopted mother whose venom against humanity jumped off the page so I knew I had a problem.

When I could no longer bear it I rang the buzzer to summon the police who did not come to my aid. My program as conducted from above pointed to self-reliance so I had to figure out how to solve my own problems. She turned around to whine that she hated the police, clearly shaken up at my audacious act; her reaction made me aware of the terror behind the loud façade. When a warden finally arrived about a half hour later after she had quieted down, there was no longer a need for interference. The next day, after she had yelled all over the cellblock that I had ratted on her, life became just a tad more difficult before I decided that I'd better take the job.

Off to the laundry mines where another challenge awaited. As is so often the case where the have-nots congregate, the controller is a SSS freak whose authority is confined to a small segment of society; they, in turn, are controlled themselves. Oh joy, I thought, when I saw the mulatto female who was slated to become my next tormentor. Her eyes and that of her gophers never left me to notice and remark upon every move I made so she could admonish me about it. From my shoes (she actually questioned why I wore shoes that had a line on the side) to the time I took to fold the laundry, going as slow as I could, it got recorded. Everything I said was reported to the woman so I made a point out of making remarks about what I thought about the whole set-up. Naturally, I got thrown in the hole again.

    This time I got hooked up with another screamer but her communications included more subjects than just sex before they decided to use my services for folding again. Unlikely as it may sound, I did enjoy myself noticing the subtleties of my surroundings, the patterns, the modus operandus and the awareness levels of the inmates. At this point in my own development I could handle already a lot of distraction.

    Some of them agreed with me when I talked about how we could all get out of that place if we physically united to overcome a few guards. Most of them were so introverted as to only consider themselves and their own situation combined with fears, a symptom of the divide and conquer technique our controllers have been using over a long period of time, and victim consciousness. Oh, but I have only a few weeks to go before I am free again and I can't risk that, would be one of the most frequent excuses not to participate. Impossible to get people organized nowadays to stand up to authorities they paid to service them and who actually expected them to kowtow to them.

Occasionally, I would run into someone whose spirit I could assist with a well-placed remark. I recall a first time offender who had to fold with me while telling me about her situation. When I offered a slant on her point of view she lit up with a new AHA moment and glowed in this unnatural environment, ready to share her new insights with the rest of the world. Spirit will not be denied!

When I attended a sermon from the Bible on Sunday morning, another control freak who had promised to discuss a specific topic, decided to do something different and started reading from another book. I objected on purpose. They are rule bound (see list) and the only time the opposition (in this case yours truly) can win is to point out that they are not keeping in tune with their own rules. I got up and refused to listen to her ranting until she changed back to the Bible to give the announced sermon.

This is the whole premise the laws are written for: to obtain obedience by agreement from society at large. If you are a citizen of a particular country you shall have to abide by their laws. At present, laws are amended without knowledge of the population and the opposition is harassed or eliminated. This type of news does not make it to the airwaves on which the media spout their nonsense so a hidden agenda of enslaving the population is simple to do.

My experiments in going against the grain were rightfully penalized by the system as I decided intentionally not to obey the laws. In doing so, I got an eye opener to the suppression of spirit, the notorious lack of freedom and almost total control of individuals who sported a hive mentality and had no business in suppressing others in living their lives the way they saw fit. It is too late to change it but understanding helped me accept a sordid reality I refuse to be a part of. Later on, I stepped out entirely to become an observer.

On my way to court I got cuffed to a huge girl who yanked me along to make me walk faster. I objected to her treatment which she tried to turn into a veritable war during the rest of my stay. I refused to fight, not avoiding her but applying principles of non-violent warfare. Watching her intently, I sidestepped any trick to get me in a compromising situation so as to be hauled off to the hole again. Practice makes the master in any situation.

When I heard the same female judge mumble something threatening about my return to her court room, I could care less. At this point I felt it no longer worth my breath or attention to defend myself in a corrupt system. I did pay attention to the TV-cameras in the court focused on an inmate who sat next to me. If they would get my image on the evening news I was prepared to sue them.

Apparently, the guy had sold his baby daughter to a childless couple who had paid him with cash and a car. Later he wanted more money and demanded his daughter back when he couldn't get it. Somehow he managed to kill her after which he put her body in a dumpster where he set fire to it; the burned remains were found by a couple of guys who reported it to the authorities.

This particular judge was prejudiced in such cases. She would dole out the maximum prison sentence regardless of the facts and evidence to the contrary, taking it upon herself to avenge the victim. The prosecutor wanted to make a deal with a nine-year sentence which he refused, confident that he could beat his case. I shook my head knowing he made a big mistake and later followed the case, out of curiosity: the judge gave him a life sentence, after which he attempted to commit suicide by jumping off a second-story railing which resulted in a broken leg. Now his defense centered on the pain he suffered, making him appear as a victim. It was in vain.

For some obscure reason she gave me 'time served' while telling me to put my talents to work. My own explanation centered on the fact that I no longer fought the system as I could not fathom engaging in another battle with the system. If someone lacks the perception to understand what I am saying or writing, there is nothing that will lead to that understanding: it is simply not their time to 'get it.'

As soon as I left jail I went to a stretch of land in the desert close to the north end of the Strip, close to the Luxor hotel. At night, a noisy helicopter that habitually flew over the area shone its strobe lights on my sleeping bag while giving me directions to get up. I ignored it, cursing under my breath. There comes a time after being harassed for years by authorities that a fantasy of mowing them down provides a particular satisfaction. The helicopter landed and I got surrounded by men dressed in black. No chance to avoid this display of (external) power so I got up, hands in the air.

    The leader of the pack said through his wires that 'this is not him, it is a female.' Explaining to me that they were 'looking for a bad guy' he asked why I slept in the desert. Not looking like a homeless person people were perpetually amazed when I told them that I slept outdoors, enjoying the Earth's energies. I had to give him a plausible explanation otherwise I would have been arrested again by this paranoid crowd, the truth always worked. I said that I had just been freed from the city jail after which I found out that my (non-existent) boyfriend had gambled the rent money away, losing the apartment. He nodded in understanding and wished me good luck!

New realization
1) At this point, I got awarded with a dismissal of the charges so no longer did I have to return to jail. Non-resistance was more effective than combat.

FORTY-FOUR

Allies on the Strip

When I first returned to the city I found a couple of blankets and found a spot in the desert behind the MGM hotel. About half an hour later a bespectacled skinny guy, obviously drunk, staggered close to where I had made my bed. Without any further ado, he plopped down and clutched his thin shirt while shivering. After some inner probing, I decided to make him more comfortable by offering him one of my two blankets. It became the start of an odd friendship.

Knowing that I would get the aid of somebody to show me around the new territory of Las Vegas, if you will, I did not regard this alcoholic man as a candidate for that position. He seemed nice enough but his demeanor was flighty as if he was persistently late for an important appointment. A few days later I met him again and it turned out that he was indeed my 'ally' to make me aware of how to go about taking care of myself while living in the vicinity of the Strip. There were lots of free things that were offered if you knew where to look. He pointed me in that direction.

This middle-aged guy looked like a mess. Speaking with the New Jersey accent of a mobster, he told me that he had worked for years as a dealer in the Trump casino in Atlantic City. His ex-wife had wanted to move to Vegas where she met another man, leaving him. He started drinking heavily and ended up not being able to hold a job and losing his home and possessions in a divorce. I could no longer feel sorry for anyone as I had seen too much misery in my life and knew from experience that one could not force another human into letting go of something they were not ready to do. He felt so bad in the morning that I could almost understand his need for beer just to keep going and numb the pain.

Walking the Strip is an intensive exercise. About seven miles long just going past the hotels and casinos could be the daily exercise program of a fitness fanatic. If you walk through the hotels and areas in between, checking out to see what is available, you could easily add another five miles. By the time you go back and forth your feet hurt and you feel depleted of energy, without having done anything besides looking around. Oddly, it reminded me of being on the trucks, in perpetual motion!

Often I wondered about my presence there as I could not read books or write my thoughts down as I did not have a place to put anything. It seemed rather futile. But the place offered me opportunities to strengthen any inner weak spots in an unrelenting manner.

My first concern was food but, as I had dropped my aversion of eating anything that came not wrapped in plastic or had been freshly prepared due to necessity, it turned out to be the least of my upcoming problems. The colossal waste of food on the Strip could keep a small nation of hungry people alive for days. However, all the food that was ditched from the daily extravagant buffets in dumpsters was inaccessible because of padlocks. I learned later that food banks that begged for donations were denied those left-overs due to hotel policies, whatever that meant. Even when they offered to pick it up in vans they were refused.

Needless to say that this policy had everything to do with control: people without money were not welcome and were not going to be fed. They had the right to decide this regardless whether anyone agreed with it or not. From listening to cases in court I had surmised that a harsher penalty was given to someone who inadvertently picked up coins or stole money rather than a murderer; after all, somebody will inherit the dough after the hapless victim has passed and therefore, there will be a new customer who could spend the money. Business is pleasure in Vegas.

When I took an elevator up to one of the floors in a randomly chosen hotel-casino, I immediately ran into a cart used for room service that featured half a delectable roast beef sandwich. I picked it up and got the idea to start looking for food in case of emergency along the aisles of the hotel rooms. So for several weeks while doing my orientation of getting an overall impression of how things functioned along the Strip I would check room service in the morning or evening hours to provide nourishment for my body. I never failed to find something not only edible but good tasting. It was a paradise for those homeless who were savvy enough to blend in with the tourists.

Forty-five

An alien ally

In 1999, when I entered my last year on the Strip, I met an acquaintance of the ex-dealer who had introduced me to the code of homeless Strip living. A guy in his early sixties who looked ten years younger referred to himself as the best dressed bum on the Strip. He was a reptilian.

For me it was the first time I could deal with one while remaining emotionally neutral so I got a lot of information from him. This guy lived an entire lie. When he invited me over to his pad it turned out that he had a couple of sheets wrapped in newspapers hidden behind a dumpster. He fetched them and put them in between a couple of restaurants just off the Strip in plain sight of passing pedestrians. The audacity of it floored me but, being game, I consented to sleeping there for a couple of nights just for the experience. Nothing happened, no police, no problems, just two people sleeping a couple of white sheets. Simply baffling!

Again, he was a contact I had to deal with as indicated by my guidance number of 23: his birthday was on the third and mine was on the second of October. The fact that my birthday preceded his indicated a tiny victory for me after almost five decades of dealing with them. However, it also stood for 2 (double-dual universe) and 3 (dimensional bowl.) He lived entirely for free as most parasites do, depending on their gimmicks, backgrounds, modus operandi and status in the communities. The females usually become pregnant to lure some hapless guy into marrying them, divorcing them, then using the offspring to secure a free meal ticket for the rest of their lives. The males have various ways of securing themselves of income through intimidation and manipulation. Never did I encounter two reptilians marrying each other; they always leeched off of one of us.

    He interviewed me for the position of becoming his partner, asking if I harbored fears of getting caught if I went around looking for coins in trays and playing machines that still had credits on them. I shook my head truthfully, having endured jail sentences and the exposure to authorities for several years. Taking a deep breath, I found it ironic that a reptilian, once my sworn-to enemy, was going to show me the ropes about how to go about making a living on the Strip, my second teacher.

    Curiously, the strip searches done in jails actually assisted me in overcoming my emotional reactions to being touched involuntarily. Upset as I became at first, feeling violated or demeaned, now somebody could touch me, even squeeze a breast while I would not react to it in any way, taking their fun away. There is nothing more boring for a predator than somebody who offers no resistance or reaction to their provocative actions to humiliate the victim.

    For starters, he showed me a store where he changed his clothes every two or three days. He would go in, pick out clothes to wear and exchange them with the ones he had on in the dressing room. At first, I thought it hilarious and couldn't believe he did that so often but I saw him do it so I followed his example. No employee ever stopped him from doing this; it eliminated washing clothes, a closet to store the clothes or any other maintenance like darning or mending. What a lifestyle!

His identification sported an address in a fancy neighborhood where he did not live. However, just the fact that this address was uptown it prevented him from getting into serious trouble as any authority would think twice before he decided to create difficulties. His eloquence and intimidating tactics- the "or else" threats- would steer him clear.

I only met two reptilians behind bars as they usually are assigned to other areas. The last one in Las Vegas was a pick pocket who shared my cell two days before I got out for the last time. I managed to convince her by mimicking her behavior that I was her superior and she let me be. *One of their tests is to point out 'a spot of dirt' they notice to see if the person/victim reacts/responds with emotion or guilt feelings.* No difference here: I used the toilet, flushed, after which she noted the spot. I merely returned, looked and said nothing. That was her clue that 'I was one of them'. (Recall that the SSS truck driver who hit another truck did the same thing: he never spoke a word, moving on, refusing to acknowledge a mistake!!!)

She told me how 'they' – us humans – liked hearing the word *remorse*, a word she liberally used in letters she wrote to men who sent her money. It is the only person I ever met who accumulated wealth behind bars from men through the sheer power of the word. It horrified me to learn that she had a writing style similar to my own, alerting me to the fact that it was extremely difficult for a less perceptive person to discern *the intent* of two diametrically opposed people who sounded almost identical.

I ordered her out of my cell and into another one a few hours before I was scheduled to leave; this move earned me the admiration of other inmates who knew how manipulative and difficult to handle she was. I considered this another long awaited personal victory leading me out of the entanglements of the matrix.

With my newly acquired knowledge, I started out on the right foot by 'finding' a large amount of money, abandoned by a player, on one of the machines so he thought I would be a future goldmine for him: a sap who would take care of his needs while we were partners, providing him freely with sex and money. I knew that I piqued his interest to make the association easier to get into, setting me up as bait. For me, life became a bit easier as I could now spend time in hotel rooms that he rented from our collected monies.

His routine included going to Laughlin twice a week on a free bus that included buffets. So I had to adapt to that schedule. Suddenly I looked like a member of a married couple with the one bum on the Strip who slept there outdoors. One day he got stopped by the police and he told me that he almost peed in his pants because of his fear. He was truthful. It reminded me of the appearance and inner factors; we both looked cheerful but I was the one who had the inner serenity while he was petrified of making mistakes, jails or anything that could expose him to his true image: that of a reptilian.

One day I wanted to use the 15 cents credit on a nickel machine next to the one I was playing but he came over to elbow me away, acting as if he had never seen me before, amazing. We both ended up not getting the nickels as the person who played the machine turned around to return but the event shook me up. For a few seconds his cruel and aggressive nature shone through in a manner that left little doubt about his inability to give or receive love.

Sometimes I did not mention money I had gotten, just to see whether he would find out about it or not. I took care of myself and he could do the same as far as I was concerned. We did pool together when we wanted to share a hotel room or eat dinner. This was remarkable too as I had never had a relationship with one who did not expect me to pay for everything. They will never tell you to pay bills for them; they make oblique remarks that make you offer your monies to help out, giving you the impression that you offered it out of your own free will (see list).

His eyes were glassy, dark, no light in them. Of course, I kept seeing the reptilian image inside the human body so I did not dwell on that. As his hair was long it fell over his face until we visited a beauty salon together where one of the two women almost gave him a be-bop cut. When I looked at him I couldn't believe how ugly he looked but I didn't say it. It would be contra-survival to insult someone who is violent by nature and lived for his looks…it is asking for trouble and I wasn't that dumb.

I did, however, inquire why he had allowed the hairdresser to cut all of his hair off. He started to curse which surprised me too as he had not uttered a word about the whole affair since the deed was done. The hate for the female hairdresser came out but since there was nothing he could do about it at that point, he let it rest. I laughed, to which he did not react. In fact, when I got tested on my ability to remain motionless like a Ninja, it occurred to me that all that inner work had provided me with the ability to duplicate their behavior *knowingly*. No wonder they saw me now as one who aspired to be like them. Irony!

Whenever he saw something he knew I loved, he would take it away from me, just like my mother used to do. Nothing escaped his roving eye, nothing to the slightest detail: knowing what page of the newspaper I liked, he would make it a point to get it before I could get to it. Besides exerting his control, it also occurred to me that he could not tolerate my love for something or someone. No wonder true lovers were always torn apart in our dark society. And this has seeped over into the behavior pattern of people in society at large, through the media, thereby forfeiting their own individuality.

His propensity for sex he expressed through watching the female bodies in the swimming pools, on stage and in the casinos while telling me how he was a 'one woman man.' I could care less, wanted to get rid of him so he could sleep with other women. He claimed to have two children, two sons who worked in the post office and as a computer engineer. I knew this to be a lie; he didn't have any pictures and every time the boys would come to see their father, I happened to be elsewhere, either going to the bathroom, playing a machine or walking around. He ignored any question, refusing to answer.

Sometimes I did not see him for days and then would run into him on the bus to Laughlin or in one of the casinos. There would never be a question, reproach, interest or other emotion indicating that he was glad to see me, wondered where I had been, nothing. We just existed, side by side. In hindsight it occurred to me that he had done me a favor, *one could use the reptilians as teachers to a certain extent to get desires under control.*

Before I left, he mentioned that he had never taken advantage of me. He was right, he had not. He was the first and last reptilian I spent any extended period of time with who had not controlled me but had functioned as a partner. *No doubt, I had been thoroughly tested by my Higher Self to see whether I had truly left the aliens behind.* I passed, noting that the only thing missing in the partnership was the necessary ingredient to make a spiritual soufflé rise: magical affinity!

In comparison, the kindred dealer was more difficult to deal with as he could only function with a certain amount of alcohol in his system. Whenever he reached the level where his inner pain got sufficiently numbed, his sense of humor would shine through. Since his emotions were repressed I found it even harder to spend time with him. Jealousy at my association with the best dressed bum, never having made a romantic pass at me, he acted possessive toward me for no reason at all. Of course, there was no opportunity nor inclination to tell him what was actually going on – my final interludes with a breed I had watched, studied, fought and interacted with most of my life – because he would have called me crazy. Instinctively, he (as a simultaneous incarnation) did not like him!

FORTY-SIX

Life on the Strip

The noise of the slot machines was ear deafening and one of the hardest things to deal with in the beginning. But, again, one gets used to (almost) everything and although I never reached the stage of totally blocking it out or getting totally comfortable with it, I could block it out of my mind. Similarly with the artificial lights that shone twenty-four hours a day, seven days a week: there was no getting away from the neon and glitter on the Strip!

Every day when I got immersed in crowds, the inner command of "I have to get out of here" would flash before my mind's eye. I couldn't leave on my own cognizance; it was 'grin and bear' it time. I had successfully passed my tests of walking and handling situations with people subconsciously controlling the sidewalks, so I could easily maneuver through the pedestrians walking through and outside of the casinos. The occasional run in with some dominating control freakish female I handled by pointing out in exact words to describe their actions. A strange thing happens when you hit upon a truism with the exact words that are somewhere buried in the opponent's body: it takes the wind out of their attack.

I watched and listened to many mediocre performances and bands in the nightclubs, its appeal based on the hit du jour on the bestseller lists. Most bands just sang the songs that were popular, most of them emitting a sense of boredom that was unmistakable. Occasionally there was a truly good one but they never lasted long. Then there were the Elvis Presley impersonators. They are a staple on the Strip and almost every self-respecting casino has one in storage.

The first hotel I got ever kicked out of was the largest hotel in the world: the MGM, for no reason other than picking up a coin out of a tray. The gangster-type that came after me may have seen me there before but he didn't give me a chance to defend myself, loudly speaking and pointing to the door. This I considered a nuisance as the only sky train that ran at that time was connected to that particular hotel. I also found a wealth of food in unconsumed room service, mostly from drunks who got hungry late at night and then fell asleep before they got a chance to eat it. So I didn't take the guy seriously and continued going through the casino.

Several times they got me, once when I picked up a daily newspaper, another coin in a tray, really trivial stuff, falling asleep near the pool and once when I jumped up when a security guard I had talked to before passed by, immediately alerting him to my presence. Thus I learned not to make any sudden movements when those uniformed robots were in the vicinity. Every time they took me into their interrogation room in the back of the high roller section to discuss my crimes, threatening me with jail. Subsequently, they would let me out through the door that lead into the parking lot. Funnily, they never stopped me from entering their high rollers lounge where I would stack up on hors d'oeuvres and fine wines.

Fabulous foods, Jacuzzis, swimming pools, nice clothes, shows, and other people's money to play the machines with: I enjoyed abundance on a daily basis. I made friends with people who worked in strategic spots who had no idea who I was or where I slept. I even had an occasional escort to reinforce the image of a self-confident, good customer who tipped well.

I learned how to relate to and explore my feelings concerning money. I played and reacted to winning or losing. To be in a casino is like stepping into an entirely different dimension, a different world. Intentions to be frugal and limit your losses disappear after the shrieks of winners would be broadcasted. Alcohol would trigger the uninhibited confidence of "letting it all hang out," ruining many people whose perception got instantly warped: a hundred dollar bill looks the same as a one. As I never got to keep my winnings it should not have made any difference but anger, enthusiasm, boredom, amazement and a few more of those nuanced feelings would battle alongside the games I played.

I recall a woman who lashed out angrily at a slot machine, calling it a bitch and telling it to 'give it up.' To my amazement, the machine responded to the abuse and started to pay off. It didn't work for me. Numbers never worked for me either but my presence seemed to be lucky for others. When I sat down in a Keno area, suddenly people would start winning all around me while my own numbers remained near misses. Disappointment would set in and, occasionally,

Ayla's Quest

amusement. Point is that I would react to those situations, allowing them to influence me. When you are surrounded by a group of people who are enthusiastic your own spirit gets a boost but when the group is sad they will get you down, no matter how happy you may be. One can imagine what kind of effect it has when you are daily surrounded by crowds of people who are fearful, going through the motions of life and who respond to neon and glitter as a form of entertainment to escape from their trials and tribulations.

There was fun in playing computer games that offered bonuses and when a new bingo/slot machine combination hit the market, I found a source of income that was steady and reliable. This attractive nickel or quarter machine had many features that any beginner overlooked only to create an audience of savvy customers, including myself, that would patiently wait for someone to walk away when the machine was ready to pay off after it had taken a fair amount of money from the customer. The only uncontrollable trick was that one had to make a choice between five pictures at the end, two of which paid low, one a medium amount, and two that paid high amounts of money.

That's where the gamble came in but when one could get several of them in one day, the payoff was usually handsome. Another feature was the spelling of the word bingo; when those five letters appeared there was an instant $200 pay for a nickel invested. Five nickels or a quarter would give the player $1,000. It was fun to hit.

However, I was not there to have fun with gambling. I was there to feed my passion of wanting to be free and as long as I took it so seriously as to emotionally react to the games, I could not walk away. The task of stepping out to become an observer in the heat of the moment became a difficult one, indeed. At times I would drink a bit too much wine, ending up in the desert incapable of finding my sleeping bag. Several times I would snooze to wake up in an area that would be only a few yards from my sleeping bag, never having spotted it, taunting me.

    Attempts to get away from Las Vegas introduced other challenges. Only in handling challenging situations do we find our strengths and weaknesses. I would go hiking outside of the city for a few days and find the noisy helicopters intruding upon the stillness of the landscape. Some sexual predator would follow me, waiting for me to let my guard down, predators everywhere.

    A guy on a horse comes to mind, coming over to scare me with the horse, questioning me about my presence. Now I had reached the stage of no longer caring about others' opinions or feeling obliged to provide explanations. So I refused to answer his questions and did not respond to his advances, merely indicated I preferred to be alone. When he descended to grab my breast, nothing happened to me. I registered the feeling but regarded it indifferently, no longer controlled by the mechanism of sex. I looked him straight in the eye, felt no fear when he squeezed: no disdain, no anger, no insult, and no victim consciousness. I did not resist so he moved away, calling me crazy.

He reminded me of a warden in the jail. An attractive guy in his thirties, he got assigned to the women section where usually female wardens worked. I sensed his anger towards females and refused to allow him to pat me down before going to the court room. When I caught his eye, he would look away from me. Later on, after I had left, I saw his picture in the local newspaper: he had raped a female inmate in one of the solitary cells where ill women were nursed because there was no supervision there!

Inclement weather would chase me back to the Strip. One night it poured and I slept in a hollow area. Dreaming about the seaside I found the sensation of the water gently touching my body exhilarating. I let my body float. When I fully awakened from my sleep I was soaking wet, lying in a puddle that resembled a drawn bath. So I walked back to the Strip where the action went on unabated day and night. At night there were many places where one could find a good breakfast for only a couple of dollars, places where one could find shelter without being looked upon with the disdain or sympathy of the more fortunate.

I ran into other seekers. One Jamaican man comes to mind; he lived in a shack near some rednecks who regarded me with hostility when I visited. The racial hatred played no doubt a role here and a white woman who kept the company of a dark skinned man was, in their opinion, no good or a misguided slut. No sex, I announced to him, as he offered me shelter for one night. I explained to him that as long as he had no control over his erections at the sight of a (naked) woman, there would be work for him to do. It resonated with him and we parted as friends.

A Christian woman came over to me, upset. Relating to me how she fought with her husband over his gambling their savings away and how this city sucked one in, I agreed. This simple acknowledgment silenced her. She took a long look at me and said with awe that she had never expected to meet somebody like me in this area.

A New Age practitioner announced to me that "all I had to do was think of winning and I would do so" before she waltzed to a machine that did not hesitate to take her money.

Then there were the entertainers I kept running into on the second floor of the Excalibur Hotel. They provided free entertainment every afternoon for families. There was a magician whose closing line of "and wherever you go, there you are" solicited laughter from the crowds. No matter how many times I listened to the songs and watched the tricks, reminding me of my childhood hero, it provided a welcome moment away from the gambling arenas where money ruled.

I also loved two lesbian women who were classically trained and played their instruments, violins, harpsichords, flutes, etc. with feeling and precision. I made it a point to arrive at a time when they would do their fifteen minute performances. We became friends although I could not accept their invitations to visit them. My path was a solitary one marked with the intentions of progressing spiritually and socializing was not on my agenda. Nevertheless, our interactions during their breaks were uplifting to the three of us and we enjoyed each other's company.

There was also a store that featured fine wines where I did my special brand of shopping. I went there so often before I retreated to the desert that I can recall the moments when I got caught by several employees who didn't do anything to stop me, uniformed guards who were called in when they spotted me in the store, etc., bottles I had to put back because I would have jeopardized my (outer) freedom and I wasn't allowed to do so on that particular day, reminding me of the necessity to detach of my habits. An addiction, something that compels you to consume or do something, *takes a part of your inner freedom away*.

Money was everywhere. I found it in the streets, on the floor of casinos, left behind on machines, in discarded purses, you name it. There is a subculture of people who do nothing but walk around looking for cash to make a living. I was not one of them but could be mistaken for one. In the MGM and some other casinos, with the Eye in the Sky watching (every move is monitored in casinos, not surprisingly), security will be on your back as soon as you take a single coin. As they are all brainwashed and hired to defend the property, one can imagine how dense and sour the underlying vibrations are in the casinos. Their own personnel skims off money wherever they can get away with it; this is accurately portrayed in the movie Casino with Robert de Niro, Joe Pesci and Sharon Stone, but all of their venomous antipathy is spewed at the hapless crumb thieves they nab for a couple of bucks.

    I experienced many occasions when I felt down. Then I would walk away from the Strip to inhale some fresh air, uplift my spirits and get another point of view. The University of Nevada, situated a couple of miles from the Strip gave me a place for time out from consumerism. But even there was no relaxing atmosphere. The self-proclaimed King of Las Vegas, a guy whose public relations machine centered on a rare disease that would eventually leave him blind, evoking sympathy based on a lie, dictated to the University what it was supposed to teach, holding its professors hostage to his wishes and financial endowments.

    People who knew him shed light on his shady dealings, a master manipulator who installed judges and politicians who would answer to him. At present, he still rules. In fact, a guy who played the role of a lawyer for the Mafia in the movie Casino actually became the mayor of Las Vegas. Was this a case of irony or life imitating art?

    People who owed him money would be chased after by employees specially hired to search the globe for negligent debtors. One can only imagine what would happen to them once found! I recall a banker from Indonesia who returned to Las Vegas after losing one million dollars in one of his casinos got thrown into the city jail as soon as he got off the plane. The slant of the story, naturally, was in favor of the Las Vegas King who had been robbed but who knows? After they booked him and he promised to pay off his debt, the

King allowed him back in one of his casinos so he could lose some more of his wealth.

    This type of control is not frowned upon, people actually applaud the control this guy exercises because he is giving the robber a chance to make good on his actions. But what does that have to do with anything? The King himself started out with money provided by gangsters who assisted him in increasing his wealth. Not because he was such a model of virtue but according to his agreement to 'scratch their backs when they scratched his.' Does that make him a good person? He may have been good for some people but bad for many others, it all depends on one's point of view.

    No doubt he is a dark predator who wraps himself in a cloak of Light. Smiling in front of the cameras that are usually handy to eternalize his victories and moments of triumph, deserved or not, he evokes an image of worldly success and magnanimity. When close there emerges another picture of this control freak. An employee told me that he would go out in a limousine at night to fuck women who were married to clients he was unhappy with for some reason. Not one but several in any given night he would visit, regardless of the fact that he had a wife. It prompted the person who told me this to quit his job.

    He controlled his office with a panel on his desk, pushing buttons to open and close doors, windows and electronic gadgets, covering his back at all times. That would probably be a good idea when you create many enemies and want to live a bit longer. It also denotes a terrific fear of getting ambushed. He played the Game of Life so well that he could fool almost anybody with his façade of, for instance, being a philanthropist who invested in rare paintings that would adorn his hotels on the Strip so the school children could learn about them. His own total lack of appreciation of art did not come into the picture. He merely invested in those paintings to make a profit and come across as a suave individual for the sleeping crowds. It is like government officials telling the masses they are peacekeepers when, in effect, they rape and kill women and children in countries they invade and bomb.

And he fools lots of individuals. I recall an incident that involved the kidnapping of his daughter. The culprits initially got away with getting him to pay a ransom, then made the stupid mistake of buying an expensive car with cash. The first call of the dealer went to the father to let him know that his money would be returned to him.

Spontaneity is unknown to someone who is bound by rules so if you burst out laughing at something delightful, it may be a cause for dismissal. Here I am exaggerating, but it really is that serious and stocked in the simultaneous spirit suppressor's arsenal of weapons to slay the dragons of affinity, love, joy and individualism. They (and their gophers, human slaves) will not hesitate to put a dumper on one's happiness. They are incapable of love (although they use that word a lot), joy, ecstasy, expressions of the higher chakras. Instead of applauding awakened individuals, they are inclined to destroy them or make their lives miserable.

Thus the charade continues. Our newspapers are filled with pictures and stories of people who are, in reality, suppressing us and using our resources while they are laughing at us as we applaud them. If somebody points out that the emperor is wearing no clothes, they refuse to look for themselves or are no longer capable of doing so, pouncing on the messenger who is spoiling their fun.

When I could finally leave Las Vegas, I was grateful for the opportunity to experience the city but glad to know I would never be back. The excitement and noise would be replaced by a slower pace in an old city in my home country of the Netherlands. The sudden change reminded me of an episode in The Twilight Zone where a man crossed a hill to find himself in a different century!

FORTY-SEVEN

Amsterdam

Right after the bicentennial I returned to my roots. The next two years were mainly spent tying loose ends with my brother, niece and cousin.
The previous decade of primarily walking around had resulted in a dislodged toe that needed to be set and a big toe that needed to be straightened. As I have a double-jointed body with a flexible bone structure that lent little support to my foot arches, the successful operation resulted in a recovery period of four months during which time I could not even put pressure on my leg in the cast. With my estranged brother taking care of me, the set-up was perfect for healing old wounds as well.

As a man who likes to be in control of people while catering to them, it was the only way for us to get together. His sympathy replaced the antagonism my mother, using gossip, had deliberately created in his mind towards his sister, a fact I was not totally aware of but learned about during our time spent together. When he confessed to having stolen my inheritance to buy a car and an expensive vacation for his only daughter, a woman in her twenties, I asked him to take care of me as long as I needed it to compensate somewhat for my loss.

When I got ready to move, the name of the next place popped into my head: Vancouver, Canada. Landing in the winter of 2001, snow welcomed me.

Ayla's Quest

Then I spent a few weeks traveling throughout the province of British Columbia until I came to a dead stop in a ski resort near the Rocky Mountains where my bags got stolen. Immediately, I got assistance with a ride to a truck stop. One driver offered me a ride halfway back to Vancouver to another town where I spent the night in a motel before I got a ride from a man who needed my spiritual assistance. During the hours we talked I knew from the comments he made that I had given him a new slant on beliefs he held.

Stanley Park was my next stop. I found a wayward willow where I found shelter for several months while walking and exploring the city, getting rid of ballast weight I had gained during my sedentary time of recovery from my foot operation. Then, one day, while riding the bus, I felt the strong impulse to get off at a stop near Kitsilano, a former yuppie section of Vancouver where lots of vegetarians and creative people congregated near the beaches. When I stopped to use the bathroom in a restaurant I found my next 'assignment,' a man who invited me over to the house where he lived.

As he had just some teeth pulled the cottons in his mouth made him near impossible to understand, reminding me of the British comedian Dudley Moore in the film Ten. His wife, played by Julie Andrews, thought him to be a burglar when he tried to talk to her over the phone, with a cotton stuffed mouth and called the police.

The main floor was divided in five separate rooms for five single men who shared a kitchen, bathroom and living room. The living room resembled a storage area with items stacked high, making it impossible to use it for anything else. His room matched the living room without light, the windows covered up with carpets, any white spot on the walls covered by some picture, posture or painting. A mattress on the floor formed his bed and I shuddered. There must be some mistake, I thought, what am I supposed to be doing here? It became clearer when three of the most powerful books I ever held arrived in the mail, the Matrix V Gold volumes written by The Author, surrounded by gold energies, the color of Balance, hidden to the dense addicts.

Within one month, the only guy gainfully employed left so there were four of them for several months until a mixed Indian/white guy in his thirties took the empty one, bordering on the kitchen. Without my knowledge, I had now five drug addicts as daily companions.

My assignment, a man in his forties, had the image of a twelve-year-old kid. At that age he had been raped; he remained there, stuck in time. Combined with an issue of having been given away as a baby, a sure fire reason to feel rejected, he drowned out his problems with drugs and alcohol. Now he wanted to kick drugs, completely cleanse out to live a sober life. Apparently, my function was going to be that of a scream tree again.

It didn't take too long before his DNA-programming took over to get rid of me: something got re-activated and he started to scream for me to leave his place without giving me the chance to talk to him. I couldn't snap him out of this re-activated behavior and when he threatened to become violent I left. After two weeks, I ran into his friend who lived in the room adjacent the living room, a tall guy who lived in a huge mess, a room covered with several layers of trash. He told me that my assignment wanted to apologize and ask me to come back.

For me, it was like living in another torture chamber. Daylight did not enter the room, the television was on for hours on end and would have stayed on all night were it not that, after two o'clock in the morning, I could no longer take it. Our quarrels invariably centered on the television if it was still on after that particular time. I could endure a lot by this time but having a television on full blast during the wee hours of the night, stretched my limits too thin. It's like having a head full of chattering only this time it is coming from the outside instead of the inside. It disturbed my inner quietude.

For several months I still had to fetch for myself, gathering food while I saw it in unexpected places with the exception of a number of chocolate cakes he bought. Having kicked hard drugs and cigarettes, he did puff on the occasional herbal variety, giving him the munchies. With little to do and a desire to eat more wholesome foods, he consented to give me money to buy groceries so I could start to prepare some wholesome meals. Of course, I didn't know that food in the refrigerator would represent a temptation for other hungry mouths to feed as paychecks disappeared into the hands of dealers. All of the money went to feed their addictions while they got their regular food from charities, churches, soup kitchens, and the communal refrigerator.

When the half-breed moved in, he immediately claimed to have a Dutch father to score points with me. Since I had never lived with drug-addicts before, harboring a prejudice against them, I didn't know what to expect. What I did notice was a flying mud pie (an image borrowed from Carlos Castaneda who wrote about the Yaqui sorcerer Don Juan) around his head; here I refer to a Dark entity from the fourth dimension that takes possession of bodies of the addicted. In the beginning he would make obscene gestures behind my back while I cooked; I would let him know I was aware of his actions and didn't mind him doing that. This stopped the teasing soon.

With exception from the guy I shared a room with, the half-breed dominated the house. The loud drug-induced laughs fooled me for a while into thinking they were actually having fun. The old guy in the room next to ours became his sidekick whether he liked it or not. He barged into his room at all hours to get money and things he wanted. Their parties would get so loud that several downstairs neighbors moved on account of those two guys. They were inseparable, it seemed. Only much later I found out that the older guy lived by the credo "keep your friends close but your enemies closer." Basically a coward at heart he lacked the guts to get rid of him, knowing he wouldn't go quietly.

Since the half-breed had actually no interests in anything but intimidating others into giving him drugs or the money for them and controlling others through threats of violence, it followed that he terrorized the others. I was not aware of this until later; this is how sly the demon went about it. For me he had a special friendly demeanor, a charming façade hiding his real intentions, the superiority complex of the mud pie mocking me when it took control of his body.

One night I sensed a certain danger and went to the kitchen. He was there wearing his coat, walking around like a wound-up doll, ready to attack. I sat down and caught the eye through which the mud pie glared at mine; it resulted in him turning his back to me, standing still while balancing on one foot, and then going out the back door. Several hours later he returned covered with scratches; he went bike riding and hit a car wondering why that had happened to him.

I did it on one other occasion to keep his violent nature in check. A Baby Boomer couple that lived in the basement witnessed his rage after he hit a bus riding his bike. Bystanders sympathetic to his plight turned away when his obscene cursing – the movie The Exorcist comes to mind – hit them squarely in the chest. Someone called the police and he ended up getting treated in a nearby hospital. The drama never ends with people who are dark inside, addicts who are possessed by entities that like to create havoc.

The atmosphere did not approve when a woman moved in after a mentally slow young guy, under the influence of the half-breed swallowing handfuls of pills and in danger of accidentally taking an overdose, was ushered out by one of his brothers. She immediately made the half-breed and his sidekick her gophers, setting up a rift in the house. She also did not hesitate to use my guy to haul some of her possessions around and run errands for her. She claimed to come from a wealthy background, got temporarily derailed and frequented the same mental health center as the rest of the guys, drinking free coffee and eating cheap meals while being counseled.

On the second day when she stopped in front of our room to demand I tell her how I had spent my day, I told her I had no interest in doing so. This refusal signaled war. From now on, she started the gossip route only to fall silent when I entered the kitchen, our meeting ground. The half-breed began to make insulting remarks whenever I was around and I nipped this in the bud. The time of letting myself become the laughing stock or be victimized by others I had left behind long ago. His expertise in obliquely suggesting being hungry, waiting for me to offer him free meals (see list) did not work with me either. Making provisions for poor drug addicts is a bottomless pit and *feeds into their victim consciousness, making the donor co-responsible for his condition.*

The subject of tealeaf readings arose when she detected one of my psychic abilities and she recommended a reader for me to consult. I went to see her, a young, native woman in her twenties. She asked me what kind of tea I wanted, drank part of it and poured the rest out to create a pattern of leaves she would interpret for me. As the pattern clearly resembled a huge bird flying upwards she impressed upon me that my spiritually progression would be unstoppable. This is the most important piece of information she provided me with. She also saw that I lived with a dangerous man who meant to harm me. She told me that I was the Teacher for the female who had just entered the household, a possibility I disregarded because she was very afraid of my presence but one never knows exactly how others learn, what's between their two ears or the content of their subconscious that can get triggered.

As soon as I got home I got attacked by the half-breed and the woman-two mud pies- in the solar plexus chakra, my power center. This resulted in such pain that I could not comfortable do anything and started walking in the hope that the pain would subside. I concocted a homeopathic recipe for raw beets as an anti-dote. With my attention on the half-breed, I never did see the female who also sported that Dark halo approach from behind so when I turned around they got me off-guard from two separate angles. Apparently, she had recently returned from some voodoo encounters in Brazil where she had been raped; she never related this story to me, it was hearsay relayed by the half-breed, her favorite instrument of destruction.

When the woman asked me about my reading I relayed just two points: her being my student and the fact that the reader had confirmed my knowing that my life would be the last one on this planet. Of course, time zones aside, our incarnations live simultaneously because time does not exist outside the 3-dimensional bowl. She did not like either point and avoided me on most occasions. Living in the house did not match her imagined status in society, thus she never unpacked her boxes and covered up her furniture with plastic. As she had too many possessions to store in her own room, it ended up in the living room. We had just cleared that one after holding a yard sale. What I learned from her presence, observing her interactions with the guys, was how detached I had become from negative as well as positive emotional influences for which I was really grateful.

 The interaction between us sank to a low point after I negated her attempt to exercise control over my actions. While I was cooking and doing dishes, she wanted to take a shower but got upset over a missing hook to hang her towel on. As none of the guys was around to cater to her she ordered me to fix the problem, using her index finger to point and emphasize her words as females can do so annoyingly. The control freak is incapable of taking NO for an answer, and when I told her to take care of it herself, she looked at me without comprehension. She branded me now the bad one or, as the half-breed confided in me, the 'other presence' in the house, never again using my name to acknowledge me.

 For a couple of months she avoided my presence until Valentine's Day arrived; she was scheduled to move to her own apartment in the downtown section of the city. We got an invitation to attend to her party, and shared cheerful mugs with a motif of red hearts filled with hot cocoa and cinnamon. It would have been a happy occasion, were it not that she ran after the guy that was pointed out to me by spirit, to give him instructions on some matter. As he had recently celebrated a birthday on which occasion she had presented him with a card signed by every member of the household except my own, I chased after her to set things straight.

This confrontation turned into an event with the tall guy who, by now, had cleaned out his room entirely, agreeing with me and the two gophers looking at me, ready to attack me to protect their keeper. While eyeing them to keep them in check, heads bowed, I stuck my finger, duplicating her, in her face. She told me to back down which I refused to do while making my point while setting my boundaries.

The antidote to this 'lifestyle' was the presence of the Matrix V Gold book that contained segments that seemed to describe my life. It felt like a Friend who knew exactly what I had experienced.

FORTY-EIGHT

Neighbors

In the meantime, my assignment began to relax and stabilize, attracting admiration for his willpower to ditch the drugs that had held him hostage for most of his life. The best outward evidence of his decision to allow inner Light as well as daylight in the room to enter was the removal of the carpets covering the windows. For the first time since I moved in there I could walk into the room without having to step over things after we removed a load of items that were space fillers.

Comments about how he was now sober and miserable came from the dedicated addicts to lure him back to his old habits but I functioned as a buffer. However, when someone has lived a pattern of hiding behind the haze of drugs, ordinary reality is hard to get adjusted to. As a sober guy he had little to say and offer about his interests or his life's purpose. Most strangers open a conversation with questions about what their new contact is doing, or has been doing, to determine if they have an agreed-upon reality: a wealthy guy does not open up to a poor one but a truck driver will touch base with another one to share moments on the road, their natural habitat.

I discovered the local library had computers so I went over there to learn the basics. Shortly thereafter, I hit upon the site www.trufax.org (where Matrix 5 is no longer being updated) featuring Leading Edge Technologies that offered the Matrix 5 Gold book and two subsequent volumes. These books offered- besides insights far beyond my own experiences- a confirmation of most of my own gained insights so I read it as a positive validation and confirmation of my path. It dawned upon me how *the process is always perfect* because only advanced, or very advanced incarnations will even look at them.

It still didn't explain why I lived with drug-addicts but I found my prejudice disappearing, a necessary lesson on my path. After reading those Matrix books, I also became aware of my own lingering traces of victim consciousness, subtle ones, but nevertheless present. Giving excuses to justify your own actions is another symptom of that state of mind: "I harassed you because I thought it would be for your own good...blah-de-blah; or, giving reasons for not wanting to do something!

The most important segments of the Matrix books for me, were the ones that confirmed that my decision **'never to work again in a job where I was under paid or supporting the system'** triggered the leap of faith from a mid-Advanced spiritual status into one that is very Advanced, hence the subsequent meeting with the spiritual guide who, per another segment, was one of the Friends I had entered the Game with at the beginning!

A girl who periodically lived with the half-breed, stealing her way around the neighborhood in the night to provide money for---what else? ---gave me a card with a perceptive message and I marveled, once again, on the differences of expression between kindred spirits, regardless of what vehicles they operated, and the slave type that missed most of those insights entirely. I could do little for her besides accept her presence in a non-judgmental way, but addicts have no appreciation for anything as long as the drugs are in their system or when they are in need of them....never! A stay in prison got her temporarily off drugs but as soon as she came out she would rush over to the half-breed who would return her to her habit within minutes of arrival. He only associated with individuals he could overpower, apart from his female keeper who still coached him in the mental health recreation room.

    The female neighbor in the basement apartment liked him because he was, just like her, born in the Year of the Snake in Chinese astrology. They were two prime examples of people who would suffocate their victims. As she was well-versed in astrology I thought it may be nice to talk with her but she eyed me so distastefully when I first arrived, I kept my distance until I knew what situation I had landed in. Strangely enough, her face resembled that of a lizard.

    About a year later, after she deigned to ask me a question about spirituality while tanning on the front yard, we started a fragile relationship. This woman was not entirely gone yet, but was a kindred spirit who had taken on many traits of behavior I describe in my list, part of the sequentialization process; therefore it would be impossible to sustain an open, trusting type of connection with her. The mirror (before awakening) was turned inward, making her see herself while talking to others. Her interest in astrology mostly centered on herself and her inability to make herself wealthy, like someone born with the Sun in the sign Taurus should, according to her.

When Barbara Hand Clow, an astrologer I admired came to town for one lecture I invited a girl I had just met to join me. That day I got very ill with a flu, running a fever, making it impossible to attend her lecture. The other woman did go, read the Tarot cards to find out where I was, and learned I was sick. The next day I was healthy again, no fever or other physical ailments bothered me. My path did not include becoming influenced by any particular professional Healer/Guru or Astrologer! Only the anonymous Author of Matrix V who wanted no followers played and still is playing, a definite role in my life.

I made the gesture of buying the neighbor a poster with a dragon on it which she liked and, later on, a book. She never invited me in for a cup of coffee or tea but would go shopping with me when I happened to run into her on which occasions I noticed that her lack of money did not stop her from spending lots of it to satisfy her own expensive tastes.

Months after our fragile introduction they were thrown out of their apartment because they could not pay the rent. She asked me to take care of her mail which I did and went to visit them in their new apartment. That's when I noticed their drinking and smoking habits which is a no-no for someone dedicated to the spiritual life; I got a cup of tea. Later on, after telling me how she had gotten a huge amount of money from her retirement fund she invited me to a movie and supper at her place because, according to her, 'that's the kind of people they were', the sharing kind. Example of how a *Darksider* operates:

I had to take a couple of trains to get to her place. Assuming that this outing would be a nice gesture for taking care of her mail over a period of several months, I got a cold shower. Right before we were supposed to walk over to the theater for the latest Harry Potter installment her companion jumped up to accompany us; he walked in front of us the whole way. When we got there she paid for the two of them and left me to take care of my own ticket.

Then she bought two tacos after I had told her how much I enjoyed that Mexican food, but shared it with her companion. Later on, she sent him back to get two more tacos laughing at him for being her errand boy. She gestured for me to be quiet and would only talk if she initiated the conversation. By the end of the movie I was so disgusted that I told her that I was no longer in the mood to share a supper with them and the rest of the afternoon. When a voucher worth $25 came in the mail for her to spend at a local coffee shop I took it as compensation for my work.

New realization
1) I could no longer be played as a sucker by a wily person but I was still slow in perceiving them: something had to be shown before I got it.

FORTY-NINE

Back to Europe

My brother would send occasionally a bit of money in the mail so I could take my sleeping bag for a few days well-deserved rest on one of the islands on the coast. The first time I did this I went to Bowen Island. It turned out to be against the law to go wild camping near the town so here I was in nature without a possibility to pitch my tent. I did anyway as it was too heavy to carry around and climbed upon a small hill; this spot turned out to be an area where many people walked their dogs so that didn't satisfy my desire to experience solitude.

Climbing upon another hill I found nothing there except a small stream. As soon as I heated some water over a modest fire two helicopters with heat sensors descended upon me; one of the pilots mentioned he saw a woman so before they landed next to me, like in Las Vegas, I doused the fire with the water and crawled back into my tent which I had covered with branches as camouflage. I couldn't believe that in a country like Canada with so much open space one could no longer spent a few days alone without being watched and spied upon.

My stay at the house with the addicts almost came to a violent end. The half-breed started a fight with me on the day the governmental paychecks were expected to arrive in the mail; it was also the birthday of his sidekick, August 24, 2006. I remember it also, due to the demotion of the planet Pluto to dwarf planet. The latter had informed me earlier that he did not even like him and didn't know how to get rid of him. It baffled me as they were always laughing together, almost acting like a married couple; or, maybe, that was the reason why.

    The room across from ours, vacated by the female, had been taken by a friend of the birthday guy, a guy in his sixties who had also spent a lifetime on the escape trip of daily doses of drugs. When the half-breed insisted upon spending the guy's money on alcohol, I tried to stop him but it was in vain. The fights between the half-breed and I got worse as the day progressed, something was in the air. I had just about reached the limit of my patience with him and wanted to get rid of him. On several occasions, when he screamed at a high pitch or kicked visitors out, doing whatever he pleased, we had called the landlord. The latter was merely interested in his money and refused to get him out.

    That night, drunk and hungry, the birthday guy went alone into the kitchen to cook a supper. He put a pot without water on the stove, fell asleep and died from smoke inhalation while the house burned down around him. Unfortunately, there were no smoke alarms in the house. I had to jump out of the window with my books when the flames reached through the door only to find TV-cameras filming the ordeal without anybody offering a helping hand. Seeing an ambulance I grabbed my friend whose arm was badly hurt and asked for transportation to the hospital. Over there I watched our house burn on the morning news with the half-breed half-naked with an oxygen mask over his face, ready to be hauled off to the hospital. Then he went on to say that the older man died of smoke inhalation on his birthday!

We moved to a friend's house near the beach. My assignment was clearly over; synchronistically, a very low-priced, one-way ticket to Amsterdam became available.

My brother wanted to get rid of me as soon as possible so I bought a bus ticket to Reims, a city in the north of France. Crossing the border, there were uniformed cops with dogs that sniffed the luggage in search of drugs; I found that disturbing. About twenty kilometers to the south was a forest of dwarf trees I wanted to see, so I walked over there. Walking through the vineyards I got chased by some old men in cars while people eyed me suspiciously. Poverty is an incentive for men to solicit sex easily: it cost them sometimes nothing more than some food. Apparently, France had now homeless people. The hand of the power-hungry people in government crushing the people resembled the Norse god Thor's hammer.

Wild camping over there turned out to be a whole different kind of experience. The ground was clay and very moist. When I finally found a spot to put my sleeping bag it didn't feel right. In the States I would invariably find a spot with a certain type energy that would be in harmony with my own. Listening to Swan Lake by Tchaikovsky, a CD I had carried with me for months, I suddenly heard the opening notes emanating from the nearby village, delighting me. Instead of finding 'my' spot here was another indication that I was where I was supposed to be.

When the night fell it was pitch dark and I heard a gravelly, hoarse bark coming from an animal I dubbed "The Hound from Hell." The next morning I left for another area where I spent a couple of days but I was incapable of shaking the forlorn looking, sex starved men in Citroens, so I decided to return to Reims. There I found an email from my brother who had had a change of heart and invited me to stay for the winter. I accepted his offer and returned to Amsterdam where I proceeded to write a synopsis of my story based on the impact of the Matrix V volumes for the book Matrix VI.

At the end of March, I bought a bus ticket to Toulouse, a city in the south of France where I planned to walk a pilgrimage to Spain. Most of the refuges were still closed; the season for pilgrims had not yet started. Every once in a while I would stay in a hotel but they were so high priced that I would be out of money long before I reached my destination, wherever that was going to be. I didn't plan on walking all the way to the western part of Spain.

One night when I found another refuge closed, I wanted to keep on walking through the countryside but rain set in, making it hard to get a few hours of shuteye on a grassy slope. Without any lanterns or lights I followed a road until I saw the contours of some trees alongside a driveway that led to a farmhouse. When I was midway, not knowing there was a house looming ahead, I wanted to sit under a tree but got immediately stopped by the whinny of a horse that didn't sound too agreeable so I moved on, only to run into a barking dog that, instead of chasing me away, did just the opposite. It was so starved for company that it slobbered all over me.

A few minutes later headlights shone in the direction of the shack where I holed up with the dog. When the car approached, I got up and swung my arms in the air to let them know that I was unarmed. In my halting French I explained that I was a pilgrim caught in the rain who looked for shelter during the night. One of them gestured for me to keep the dog company, informing me that an old woman lived in the house. Lacking options for better lodgings I was grateful to have a roof over my head even though I had to endure the lickings of the mutt, debatably the friendliest dog I've ever met. When I lifted my arm, the dog whimpered, telling me not to beat him. Sigh. I communicated to him that he could sleep with me but to lay off the slobbering.

In the morning, rain still coming down, I walked through the puddles back to the road and thumbed a ride back to town. The first car stopped but the driver told me to step into the car of his wife who came from the opposite direction because he had to attend to his business. Thus, I switched cars.

After listening to her story, I asked her to stop at the graveyard where her daughter was buried. Apparently, the student had jumped out of a window at the University and her death had been ruled a suicide. When I stood at her grave I got a vision accompanied by the proper French words to explain she had been pushed by another student. With that piece of information, she drove me back to the railway station where she bought me a cup of coffee. She had calmed down. As a Catholic woman, she had been worried about her daughter's soul, but now she felt like a burden had lifted from her shoulders.

    After spending the day walking to the next town I checked into a modest hotel for two days. Then I took a bus to return to the trail but couldn't find it, walked to the library where I was invited by a man and his two daughters to have a cup of tea. I spent most of the day there, connecting with his oldest daughter who expressed an interest in learning Astrology. Asking her father, who was a helicopter pilot, for his birth data it turned out that his chart had strong similarities to mine which impressed him. I told the girl that I considered her a member of my spiritual family which made her beam.

    After I left, I kept walking through the night, took a wrong turn somewhere along the line and ended up in the morning near the same town I had left the day before. Exhausted, I decided to spend the day resting in the same hotel I had vacated the day before and took a train to bypass that particular area altogether.

    After about 450 kilometers walking, I stood in front of a meadow with many bulls that kept the grass fertilized with lots of shit. I called it quits at this point and took a train back to Biarritz, a jewel of a town on the coast of France. From there I contacted an Irish friend to see whether I could visit him in Plasencia,

Spain. After a three week' sojourn with the retired, alcoholic mathematics professor, he advised me to go to Dublin because it would be easy for me to find a job as a translator. There was no sense in explaining to people I could not get a job, but I wanted to give it a try. With the help of an astrologer friend, I determined that it was a soul urge to go there, even if it didn't make sense to me, so off I went. Two offers for a job fell through and I knew it would not yet be my time to pursue employment.

For four months I endured rain in Ireland, from Dublin to Waterford to Galway. After spending my money on the pilgrimage I had not enough funds left to get a home base so once more I had to be creative about finding lodgings. At Dublin airport was an area where comfortable chairs accommodated travelers who stayed overnight. I started writing there and got in touch with new friends over the Internet, ones with whom I had a spiritual connection. They helped me with money so I could buy a tent and keep myself afloat for a while to come. I pitched it in an area next to the highway, obscured by trees, walking through the brambles, an area where nobody wanted to go and where I found several hours a day isolation and energy to keep me going.

When the rain came down too heavily I would go to the airport where people were friendly enough not to bother me. I met another woman who claimed to be on her way to Faro, Portugal, on vacation from a professor husband. However, I found it odd that she was spending several days there if she had a husband who supposedly could easily pay for a higher priced ticket. When I told her that I was living from day to day she criticized me, but it turned out she was in a situation similar to my own, minus the spiritual purpose. A couple of weeks later she was still sitting at the airport to tell me she planned on moving inland to a youth hostel. Shame, regret, and concern about other people's opinions were emotional commodities I left behind long ago.

    A Belgian tourist bought me a bag of French fries, very appropriate as that's where the fries were invented. I told her some story about doing some traveling and writing while she flew back home. Several months later I ran into her and her boyfriend who worked as a teacher for handicapped children and, of course, she looked at me with suspicion, not believing I was still there. Playing with her, I told her that I had flown back to Holland and returned just like she had done. I showed her a pile of papers I had written to let her know that I was for real but didn't feel I had to prove myself to her: if she didn't believe it, oh well!

Note: The fact that I saw the Belgian tourist again reminded me how much faster my 'doubles' were taking place, karma erasers!

    When a priest came over to hand me a brochure that read "You're Special", I laughed. I regard that type of incidence a gift of the universe, a cosmic joke. We talked for a while but when we arrived at the subject of embracing a God outside of me, I explained to him that we had to part here because our different points of view would deteriorate into an unending, unsolvable type of debate.

There was no getting away from the rain but, fortunately, after a while, it had little effect on me. In Galway, a nice town on the west coast of Ireland, I tried to find a spot in the countryside but ended up wild camping across from a street in an area that was flanked by heavy brambles where I had to wade through. The only creatures close to me were some horses and, in the beginning, when I heard them neigh it sounded so close that I imagined them to be standing in front of my tent.

For a couple of months I found a niche at the University where I could use the computers during the absence of the students while I used the facilities at nearby camp grounds to shower and wash my clothes. The coast was beautiful and only one man, in search of forests he grew up with in Poland, knocked on the door of my tent to see who was camping there. Feeling sorry for me, he wanted me to go to the welfare office to get proper lodgings, the brainwashed type of advice, incapable of seeing who I really was, not understanding that I was not in search of a roof over my head. Sometimes the energy of the Earth feels so exhilarating that I simply prefer it to being inside four walls and a roof.

I discovered a casino and went inside to play on some nickel machines for the first time I left Las Vegas behind. It featured fun machines that would provide bonuses just like the Bingo machines I used to play. It was in an area where many locals came to play and it became a diversion for me if I wanted to stay out of the rain for a while on days when the University was closed.

    When I wanted to return to my brother in Amsterdam I heard that he no longer wanted to associate with me so I had to go elsewhere. Again, with the help of the same friend I booked a one-way flight to Düsseldorf, Germany, thinking that perhaps the country of Croatia, welcoming foreigners to invest in business, would be a good place for me to visit. It never came to pass as I tried to hitchhike in that direction and found out, to my horror, that it was virtually impossible to catch a ride. After several hours a Spanish truck driver who headed for Luxembourg offered me a ride. I was so tired of standing on the side of the road that I asked him to take me with him to Luxembourg, forgetting about Croatia altogether. I refused to go that far a distance with that many difficulties in getting rides.

    At the border I did try to get a ride out, but an older, very vocal female came over to ask me what it was I thought I was doing. It turned out I stood in the wrong spot and there was not one car that would stop to offer me a ride. Not having a clue of where to go, I let her rant and rave and guide me back to the restaurant where she bought me a cup of coffee. As soon as I decided to move to a side road I got a ride in a Mercedes driven by a female who worked with handicapped people. The only impression she made on me was the fact that she kept repeating, in German, that the car was paid for and belonged to her.

    After one more ride, very quickly begotten after the female dropped me off, I ended up in Echternacht, the oldest town in Luxembourg, where I camped out near a Boy Scout camp. I got tired of camping out in Europe, and wanted to end it to resume a more comfortable, productive existence. But it was not my time yet.

For six weeks I walked through forests, visited the beautiful town, met few people and basically realized that I was fading out of any society. Serenity and peace of mind were mine and I could create shock effects through minor actions such as getting some clothes that were donated to a local charity. A couple of people who saw me take a coat and some clothes so I would be comfortable for the fall reported this to the charity; thereafter I never saw any other clothes in bags outside of the donation bin. In fact, they added an extra bin to make sure that nobody could enjoy freebees other than the sequential-run charities.

I borrowed a green tarp to keep a bit of heat in my tent while camouflaging it so hikers would not immediately spot it and come to check me out; my tent was pitched on the slope of a hill about a twenty minute walk outside of town. Again, there were camp grounds close by where I could use the facilities to take showers and keep clean. However, this time the tests comprised everything I had learned during my years on the road:

Without any money whatsoever, no Internet connection, no friends or contacts I had to use more wits to survive. I was not allowed to ask anybody any favors so I explored the town and entered a couple of hotels, restaurants, the local youth hostel, stores, and private residences to get what I needed. Occasionally, I even took disregarded left-overs out of trashcans right in the busiest shopping street, not caring if anyone saw me or disapproved of my actions. I answered questions by the local police, told white lies with a smile, countered control freaks without feeling bothered by them, no longer caring about their dumb, intrusive, haughty behavior.

When I started out doing these things separately I would look over my shoulder, feel ashamed if someone shot me a sour look, get physical reactions such as a sinking feeling in the pit of my stomach, nervousness; I also had a mind that worked continuously to come up with explanations for my behavior and now, nothing… **real freedom!**

Getting close to finishing my outdoor existence I found a couple of supermarket carts that I pushed back to the store to get change for a bus ride down to the south eastern part of Luxembourg, close to the airport. I ended up in a forest close to a highway and after only a few days, one side of my tent lit up at night, reminding me of the flames in the house that burned down. When I jumped up, a pickup truck turned, so I wasted no time to pack my stuff to jump into a grassy area behind the trees. Mere minutes later, three men with flash-lights came down but they never saw me. Totally at ease, like a hollow bamboo, they could not feel or find me and I felt vindicated….all of my work in handling so many situations had finally been rewarded with that unshakeable knowledge that I was a powerful being, not to be messed with any longer. At cause, no longer the effect!

I sloppily pitched the tent so as to get some sleep and I woke up with a boar standing in front of my tent. That powerful animal was a welcome distraction. It nodded and strutted off, and then I left. I walked to the other end of town near the railway and, once more, pitched my tent. Two days later I ran into a posse of boar hunters who gestured for me to get out of town. It felt like the very old days, in another life, of being run out of town. Again, I didn't care, no longer interested in offering explanations, knowing the clue meant *'time to move on'*.

When a train stopped I told the conductor I had no money so he told me to get on while writing out a ticket. It turned out that he had meant for me to pay him directly but I really had no money so I got thrown off the train at the next stop, at the edge of the capital….which turned out to be perfect. After a couple more weeks it dawned upon me…**the final AHA moment…that I had achieved my goal of inner freedom…and I could leave my nomadic existence behind. A door to a new consciousness opened…!**

FIFTY

The Doppelganger or Double

A sure sign of ending a loop (doing the same thing over and over again, being attracted to similar people or mates, etc.) is the occurrence of 'the double'. One situation ends, one person drops you, like my brother dropped me, and here comes the doppelganger.

At a given point I had noticed that situations or things occurred twice in the 3-dimensional bowl (2 3). For instance, if I saw a woman with a dog I would see another woman with a dog at the exact same spot if I passed by there again. If I got into a fight with a rugby player, another one would pop up with whom I had another, usually less intense fight. It kept me on the straight and narrow, trying to avoid feeding the fire in the human drama because I knew I had to deal with those situations again. It happens to a lot of people but the time lag is larger, months or years in between the similar/identical situations or items so one does not notice it as easily.

However, I surmised that the numbers in their case, when the persons are not spiritually awakened, would be 3 2 as they would play the 3 dimensional Game without noticing the 'doubles'. In a regressive type of therapy when the counselor asks for 'an earlier time something like that happened, directing the spirit back until the root cause has been discovered of present time discomfort' it is very clear how loops keep people, who are stuck on the time track, doing the same thing over and over again until they become aware of doing it. Once they do, they can break the loop. Identical situations or things, just appearing twice, get erased from the Akashic Records. How do I know this? *I tapped into my inner knowing to get that answer.*

Somehow, through the creative process of being a contributor to several forums on the internet, someone suggested in response to my question as to how to move through Europe without money, to sign up for an organization that featured people who offered shelter to weary travelers. Once I did that, it brought me to the apartment of a British motor-cycling guy, the doppelganger of my brother, who lived in Amsterdam. I knew instantly I would get the opportunity to leave my hometown for good so I moved in. He agreed to give me shelter in exchange for buying food and cooking him three daily meals with the money welfare temporarily provided me with.

Although he did not misappropriate my inheritance for his own use like my brother did, he certainly showed me he had chosen the path of 'service to Self', thus a Darksider. As I had been spared contact with the SSS ex-wife of my brother, this guy was fully controlled by one whom he referred to as an ex-girlfriend, visiting him every single day. After the removal of a brain tumor, he worked at home on his computer where he mostly solicited sexual partners who appeared on the doorstep every once in a while. He created problems for me.

My notebook disappeared, my mail he held back, he sent me away when a woman from Hong Kong arrived for a week's stay so he could indulge in his passion for S&M sex. The SSS-ex tried her usual control method which backfired. I observed myself, remaining calm, setting my boundaries when she entered my room to complain about the food I cooked for the guy. I barged after her, deciding to yell that it was none of her business and that I was a beautiful person. This was for the benefit of my host whose level of courage around her became nil.

    The downstairs neighbor moved out, then the upstairs neighbor followed suit. Suddenly I found myself alone in the building that the owner planned on renovating. He gave my host $10,000 in cash so he could use his storage area on the upper floor. That did not encourage him to diminish my cash input; in fact, the only order I got was 'not to tell his ex'. With a twinkle in my eyes, I made a remark on how easy it was for such women to walk all over wimpy guys like him.

    I passed my final test when I did not react physically when another SSS woman came over in a department store where I listened to music through a pair of headphones, to invade my aura. I stood my ground while her body grazed mine, fingers floated across my face, without blinking of eyes or jerky movements, so she left in silence. It reminded me of the invasion by alien tripod fighting machines in War of the Worlds with Tom Cruise in which the machines scout around for movement of their human preys. In the 2nd to last installment of The Hobbit, Smaug the Dragon speaks words like "I can smell you" when searching for the hobbit!

FIFTY-ONE

Practicing Allowance
The key is not in acting out resistance to the current apparent situation, circumstance and apparent events, but in focusing on the desired outcome. The act of holding the desired outcome within the emotions of desire and idea of the outcome is the application of the Law of Allowance.

Moving by plane from The Netherlands to Vancouver Island near the West Coast of Canada, I rented a room in a downtown hotel in Port Alberni to write my story without interference from friends and acquaintances. This type of reasoning does not enter the world of the spirit where interferences sometimes translate into tests conducted by one's Higher Self. During the first week there, I ran into a reptilian that tested me on my ability to anticipate his every move and I passed.

I already knew that with spiritual progression, the responsibility quotient rose. What would have been an impossible task in the earlier days, I could now handle. A month later, one of the most difficult assignments of my life followed the thought that "it may be nice to be touched."

This desire manifested itself the next day in the person of an attractive man my own age who came to my table to introduce himself while I waited for a take-out order in the bar-restaurant of the hotel where I stayed. As it hardly ever occurred that a suitor presented himself since I had quelled my desires to have a husband and family long ago, I did a double take. His spirit reached out through the haze of a drug- and alcohol- induced aura and my inner bullshit detector went haywire. An electrical current jolted us both when our hands lightly touched. The accompanying vision in front of my mind's eye showed a member of the **Sons of Belial in Atlantis** where I had lived some of my other lives.

    He offered to pay for the meal after I had taken care of it, so I made light of the situation to joke about it. As a regular customer spending his leisure hours in the hotel bar, his face was known in local circles. I knew I could not ignore this man, so I told him to meet with me later that evening. After the consumption of a glass of wine and a twenty-dollar bill he pushed across the table to cover taxi fare, I consented to go over to his house located around the corner, only a couple of blocks away.

    The house was fairly isolated with an acre of grassland on one side and the nearest neighbors, some shops that closed for the nights. Playing loud music was therefore no problem and possible cries for help futile in case of attack. After having spent so many years learning to trust myself in a variety of difficult situations I decided to throw myself wholeheartedly in harm's way, come what may. My only defense consisted of staying alert, third eye open, in an unguarded and rare moment, wrapping myself in the color of Balance, Gold.

Ayla's Quest

The re-acquaintance (I knew his spirit from interactions in that other life where we were downright enemies) turned into an emotional ordeal, hitting me squarely in the heart chakra. The most telling indications of danger presented themselves when he wrote down his phone number in Roman letters on a card, then the data for his astrological natal chart which I erected to compare to my own chart, known in astrology as synastry. The data could be looked upon as an almost perfect match, scanned over lightly, were it not for some horrendous aspects of the Moon and the planet Mercury in his chart.

Several planetary configurations were almost identical, denoting superb compatibility or, again, formidable opposition; both Moons were in the sign of Libra, the sign of partners and/or enemies, in the Fourth House, the House of Home/Self. Listening to him and observing his actions fueled by several 'mudpies', entities on the lower 4th dimension that fed off of dense emotions such as fear and grief, indicated a person whose body ruled his spirit. The intention towards me was a mixture of curiosity, hope, destruction and disdain.

His story included some horrendous, satanic abuse as a young boy by his father who would chain him to a tree for days without food and little water while adults were too afraid or not interested to lend him a helping hand. He also locked him isolated in dark rooms and took beatings from his father. During the three weeks I spent with him I can certainly attest to see him go without food for days while slowly killing himself chain-smoking cigarettes, and periodic intakes of fairly large amounts of alcohol. In total self-denial he insisted upon the view that his father made him strong, prompting him to leave the parental home at the tender age of eighteen.

True to form and ready to get his anger, vulnerability and aggression compensated for, he joined the American forces (he had dual citizenship for Canada and the USA) for a stint in the Vietnam War for one year on the front line where he committed and witnessed atrocities that he related after the consumption of two Black Russians, a concoction of vodka and kahlua. The alcohol awakened the most accessible "personality" in his subconscious, that of the lieutenant who had to steer his troops through hostile territory relying upon the men on his flanks. On two separate occasions he got downright lethal as he attempted to demonstrate on my body to "teach" me killing techniques in face of oncoming enemy forces.

I approached him on this subject when he returned to his regular personality and he admitted that yes, he did have nightmares that would put him back into the fire line, completely out of present time, the here and now, and he would attack the person that was in his close vicinity: that type of touching I had not asked for or specified!

In addition, he confided to be a member of an elite team that functioned as executers for a mafia-style secret organization in present day. He professed not to like this but incapable of leaving the organization on his own cognizance.

Without my inner freedom and strength, I would have made a beeline for cover and run away as far as possible from him after he gave me that information. Surprised that I didn't, he kept asking me over and over again whether I liked him and if I wasn't afraid of him. I reassured him that I would accept him the way he IS without wanting to change him.

He was aware that people sensed the danger in his aura, making him a prisoner of his own actions, guaranteeing a loneliness that would not be possible for his spirit to break through. In a rare moment of trust he confided to be terrified of himself, not capable of self-love or love, knowing that he had been subliminally affected by mind-control techniques in the army while in Vietnam. Observing him, I did notice that he responded to sounds and specific words before he jumped into action: local fights he jumped into to break them up using his army training. What else could he do, a programmed killing machine does not differentiate between war and peaceful times? Invariably, he emerged without a scratch.

A subconscious (or DNA-programmed) overloaded with commands not accessible to his awareness level resulted in behavior described as unpredictable by the locals. I lost some new acquaintances immediately after they saw me in his company. A complicated man, split personality, considered insane, I knew this assignment would be very trying; its success would depend on my accurate application of the Law of Allowance. As seen from a spiritual assessment, he appeared as an immature, simultaneous spirit who got valuable but tough lessons in the school on Earth. *The more immature the spirit, the more human drama!*

His humane side came out when he rescued people on the highway while working as a truck driver. Ironically, his expertise from the army served him and others in retrieving body parts in horrendous accidents; a task that proved beyond the capacity of most police officers who would faint or puke at the sight of a child's decapitated head. He had done it so often that he had been nicknamed Angel of the Highway.

Note-In the spiritual realm I operate on the opposite end of the spectrum with spirits that infuse the alien controlled human slaves. I am an individualist, going my own way, doing what my Higher Self prompts me to do; my opposites are entirely under the influence of puppet masters who control their every move. What is the difference? **INTENT!!!**

With this man I compared as follows: he was a kindred spirit but his body was controlled mostly by puppet masters. His spirit reached out to me, unknown to his controllers and himself (he thought it had to do with finding a friend/lover), indicating that he wanted my assistance to change his life sufficiently to enter a new venue. His approach reactivated my interest briefly in becoming a clearing practitioner. *Real change* is only plausible if a majority of the simultaneous spirits face up to their dark side (fears); put it in perspective and use it at appropriate moments. It is not going to happen in this Endgame on our planet.

The first thing I noticed about the way the Dark entities operated, were the conflicting commands he lived by:
I play to win *(active aggression)*
It was (not) meant to be *(passive, having no control)*
Get 'er done (*the command for a leader who needed to get a job done regardless of personal intent*)
It is not possible for a person *to act against their own intent* unless brainwashed, mentally controlled and/or programmed, the ultimate crime against the human right of exercising individual freedom.

Marvelously to me, showing the strength of his spirit shine through the filters surrounding his body, he actually put the brakes on harming me, a major accomplishment in this case. I did not resist, facing my last fear of getting physically hurt squarely and unabashedly. I was not passive but active in my knowing that I held no longer a trace of victim consciousness. My willingness to be physically close to him combined with the absence of fear, control over my emotions and healthy self-confidence, resulted in the diversion of his energy as a victimizer. Trusting in my Higher Self, I knew he would never intentionally harm me!

When I talked about my first love, a man I was slated to marry in my early twenties and lost, after a couple of glasses of wine produced crocodile tears, he immediately told me that he wanted "someone happy." I explained to him that if my body still held some residual pain in connection with a lost love it would be healthier to let them go! He thought about what I said, not having cried for years, and took the clue to put on the record "First Cut is the Deepest" as sung by Sheryl Crow, assisting me in opening up the floodgates of tears that I still harbored. It only took once as I had done lots of inner work decades earlier, eliminating this past hurt completely. My Higher Self communicated this tidbit to his spirit who would file this information for future actions. No *valid* information is ever in vain.

He grilled me on my attitude, telling me not to fall in love with him (as if that was an option) as he had yet to finalize the divorce between him and his wife of almost 40 years. Then the womanizer would shine through to tell me that he had broken lots of hearts, smiling smugly. He showed his inner programming in a tendency to escape into emotional formlessness, to mistake ego inflation for cosmic reunion. The command "You will never forget me" fell regularly from his lips even before there had been any indication of leaving. I concluded that he had used this line in connection with lots of women successfully, after using and discarding them. There are no shortcuts in eliminating this faulty wiring. I cannot tell a person about what is wrong with them because that would be a judgment. They have to want to change, and then take responsibility for their own actions before they can even start looking at the hornet's nest inside, releasing its content little by little.

He kept warning me about 'having issues' as if to push me away from getting involved with him. A disastrous obstacle to a happy relationship with anyone is for one partner not able to love him- or herself, evident in almost everything he did. As I had walked in those shoes before, I understood the desperation of living without love or a rudder to steer the boat. How could one pass an inner wall preventing an exchange of love vibrations unless one could direct a laser? I could do that but I wouldn't get anything in return which, in turn, would create an imbalance. My contribution to his spirit consisted of fearless companionship.

Laughing at himself, he related that he had hovered near death three times, each time he had the choice of pushing a button on a panel. Twice he had pushed the same button, the one that would secure him of food, not necessarily of love or happiness. *Dense, dark entities will mock you, telling you stories like that to see how you react.*

Basically, a person harboring that many issues is a waste of time for any healer. In my own case, it gave me the opportunity to gauge my own inner strength in a situation with someone who had lost the connection to his Higher Self, yet be able to lift him slightly up through sparse openings. Just the fact to endure someone's presence, allowing them to BE regardless of how insane their behavior seemed to others, without making judgments, will register on a deep level with the spirit!

After a couple of nights on the town which felt more like being interviewed for a job, he insisted on giving me the key to his house so I could enter it at will while he worked or not. I reluctantly accepted the key. Back in my mind I regarded the possibility that if something went missing in his house I would be the designated culprit since I had the key. It turned out he had all kinds of precautionary measures like strings and threads over strategic points to determine whether somebody was checking out his possessions and since I did not do that, a pinprick of trust had been established.

One of the first things he mentioned to me was his interest in having a friend. Getting a woman to alleviate physical tensions and/or sexual pleasure did not fulfill a present need. Despite his marriage he had engaged in many other affairs and one night stands according to him. He had lied his way through but noted that he wanted to try to be honest. I took this as a clue that he regarded me as a sap that would fall victim to the carefully orchestrated scenario that would test my frailest weakness and possibly strongest asset, my open heart and inner freedom.

As an aside I'd like to mention that David Icke mentions in his book Tales from the Time Loop that this man who had been subject to the rituals of a secret society and possibly the ones conducted by the military could very well have been used as a stud. ***DNA programming is done with vibrational codes. These codes are activated via the rituals which occur at all levels*** (even by parents, unbeknownst to them). A desire to join the army is thus also activated.

I decided to forfeit techniques to protect myself so I could remain open and vulnerable to whatever influences and vibrations would enter my aura and chakras. I then fully immersed in the lifestyle of the "assignment" and shared a few glasses of wine with him while listening to very loud music (the house was bugged) and meeting with people he designated as "real" that came to visit. Asking me for permission to smoke or play his music, I reassured him that since he paid the rent for this house, he did not need my permission to do what he wanted to do.

The Law of Allowance reflecting the release of the need to control, through allowance, changes the perception profoundly. It allows transcendence from responsibility for others and recognizes the personal choice of releasing them to their own personal decisions. Rather than bringing forth feelings of separation, this blessing process brings forth an experience of a form of love that has blessed them in a way that will have profound effects on their life.

Evoking memories of my own teenage days of self-indulgence did not quite cut the same picture as it did now; in other words, the alcohol, musical notes, subliminal messages emanating from TV and emotional output no longer had the power to affect me in any way whatsoever. I was free of it. The density of the emotions of fear and grief underlying the superficially induced happy scene did pull my body down a notch or two. My energy level depleted through a lack of rest induced by his demand for undivided attention, waking me up at odd hours, and basically clamping on to me as if he was drowning.

A self-described man of few words when sober, the emphasis on getting to know him was displayed in the photographs that adorned the walls of his living room. The most prominent one was a family picture that consisted of father, mother and siblings and his own family consisting of a soon to be ex-wife and a son and daughter. Then there was a bird's eye view of the property in British Columbia that, according to him, was valued at millions of dollars. It would play a significant role in the uncontested divorce that included a separation of one year. The wife lived only a few streets away in the same town, a similar situation as the one of the wine merchant I encountered in the Napa Valley.

Unfailingly, he made remarks that showed exquisite sensitivity and psychic ability, making it extremely difficult for anyone to bypass the seduction of the compliments to take a thorough look at the source. He would so earnestly tell me what he liked about me and so sincerely sum up my strengths that I was in awe of his observations and clarity. However, things were not well in the body of this 'assignment', a man who ran his program of commands like "taking control of the situation", "getting the job done", etc. Seeing himself as a master in the field of sexual gratification (or the denial of it), heartbreaker, heir to a fortune, helpless abused child, and other personalities inside that acted independently, he dramatized as if his life depended upon it.

There was no silent, invisible clue forthcoming to point me in the direction of proceeding so I asked him if he wanted me to leave. Yes. On the day I got ready to take the bus to the ferry, a gold coin arrived in the mail from a friend who wanted me to visit him in California! Note-*As a guide, I never know what the assignment picks up on. It does not matter, really, as the opening of a closed area or a piece of valid information will find its way to allowing the Light to permeate where darkness reigned before.*

FIFTY-TWO

Observations
'When attitudes and opinions are deliberately programmed within a limited set of rigid guidelines, the activity level of the total pattern of experience begins to slow. The key is the word *deliberately*. This means that the guidelines are imposed, not by the individual through knowledge experienced into wisdom but by the beliefs imposed on the individual by those he/she considers outside authorities. (Law of Allowance)

His indoctrination and membership in a couple of secret societies, not known to me, seeped through in his fascination with genetics. According to him, we were both blessed with good genes and the possibility of a steady relationship got expressed in "money marries money". Even though it had no value whatsoever in my own life, he merely rattled off whatever program had been installed in him.

The female bank president in my family refused to give me a loan to set up my own business, setting the course of my life in an entirely different direction. I often thought about the words "Be careful of what you ask for, you might get it." At the time, I considered it horrible to have a family who opposed my efforts to do my own thing but, in the long run, they assisted me inadvertently in making the right decisions as far as my own unique path is concerned. Much later, having dealt

Ayla's Quest

with those phases my function of being a Guide to specific people became clear.

As a man whose body controlled his spirit and a woman whose spirit controlled her body, we held diametrically opposed points of views; in essence, it pitched us clearly against each other. For me, who had lived with the command "I have to get out of here" for years it was a temptation to do just that. Why would I have to put up with abusive, controlling behavior I had despised most of my life? But synchronicity kept pointing its arrows when I thought of fleeing and one of my personal guidance numbers, the number 11, kept popping up. Eleven cents on the couch, his badge number as an ex-cop started with 11. The house number added up to 13, another guidance number. It simply would not gel if I walked out; things have a horrendous way of going wrong for me when I do that.

On another occasion when he stood me up, I hoofed over to his house to shove a note under the door- the door was always locked before he handed me the key- telling him that if he considered his time more important than mine, letting me wait for him in vain, he could go his own way. Then I found the door wide open. This was so unexpected that I stood for seconds in the opening, watching him move around in the living room. Very clear to me, I was not supposed to give him the note and break off the contact prematurely. It was my responsibility to aid this spirit, even if it turned out to be in a minuscule way.

For a person who is centered and whole within oneself, the necessity of finding an outside partner is superfluous; at best, it is icing on the cake. He coped with the loss of a wife who had walked out on him but still controlled his every move. As a man of habits, he had difficulties letting go. Then, in unguarded moments, he would take on another voice to tell me that he didn't care about anything besides himself and did what he wanted and when he wanted, painting an inner picture of conflict and confusion.

    This knowledge did not negate or stain my enjoyment at being hugged for the first time in years, even if the energies exchanged were incompatible. Walking around hand in hand with somebody had a charm I had long forgotten about. That he went around the area playing mental games with other females showed clearly in their behavior towards him. Again, I hesitated at being immersed in this new endeavor, somewhat feeling like throwing myself headlong in front of an oncoming freight train but the subtleties of synchronicity kept pointing towards involvement.

    As a guide, I never know how my show and tell method is going to affect the student. I give myself in service of another spirit who is ready to enter a new phase on its path, thereby learning in return.

    My Mayan sign is Blue Spectral Hand, Tone 11. Blue Hand is a gateway, an opening, a portal from one understanding to another. A clue to the meaning of Blue Hand is found in the meditation, "I am, by veiled design, the threshold to other dimensions. In my ending is my beginning. The initiatory gateway awaits." Blue Hand is the seventh or last archetype in the cycle of development of primary being; seven is the symbol of mystical power which is also my life path number. It represents the power found in completion. Blue Hand is seen as a closure, which is really an opening to another level of being. Blue Hand is also my Higher Self and Guide (I am guided by my own power doubled.)

White Wizard is my Subconscious Self and Hidden Helper. White Wizard is the magician whose powers are activated by wisdom that emanates from the heart. Such wisdom is not the intellectual understanding known in Western culture; it is the wisdom that comes from an alignment of mind and heart. An open trusting heart is a refined tool of perception. Allowing 'I' to 'not know' opens the door for the mind to a deeper understanding of others and the universe.

In this case I knew instinctively that I would feel the ramifications after time spent in close contact with a person whose energy vortexes (chakras) were shut down. Whatever door needed to be opened here remained to be seen; initially, it struck me as enigmatic to get a programmed, soul suppressed man at this stage in my life. But the process is always perfect; I just needed to *Be There*.

When the tall ships came to town, I hesitated to buy tickets. I had never had a social life or been allowed to do ordinary, touristy-type activities while on an assignment. Perhaps it did no longer apply, I reasoned, and went ahead to find several obstacles to overcome before I could actually get them. On the day we went, holding hands, a young woman sobbing loudly approached us. At first, confused, I thought it was one of his other women who he lied to about undying love but it turned out to be his only granddaughter. I tried to impress upon her that we were mere friends but, through her tears, she indicated that their interlude was none of my business so I left momentarily to allow them their space together. Looking over my shoulder, I saw the back of his wife having joined the group. Returning to him, upset as he was, I ditched the tickets to the tall ships in favor of a long talk.

    His wish to be honest had taken an unexpected turn of coming true, not entirely what he had had in mind. The secrecy of our budding relationship, not in any manner consummated, had a strange way of coming into the open. I did nothing to encourage or discourage his decisions to do or not to do something, just go along with the program without interfering with his lifestyle. But I had nothing to hide or a need to look over my shoulders. He did.

    His guilt complex was his greatest obstacle to happiness as he punished himself constantly in moments of pleasure. It is another control mechanism. His marriage to a Catholic woman, whom he had financially supported all of her life, had been forced upon him to "give the baby a name." His father, the most prominent role model in his life, had implanted many commands for him to live by! His personality had stored them carefully to be used at appropriate times like veils that would remain in place to deny him his own individuality. According to him, his father had been afraid of him while he attempted to break the spirit of his eldest son. Affinity had no prominent place in either the family he grew up or the marriage he had entered. His mother was the ally who had protected him somewhat and he compared most women to her; interestingly, I looked like his mother.

After I moved my possessions into a storage room of his house, I discovered soon that he had a great sense of humor, so often the case with people who hurt badly. A story about winning the Golden Gloves, a boxer's trophy, only to lose them when in the heat of the moment he decked the referee, struck me as hilarious. Five Indian chiefs who came to his parental house to speak to his father about him turned out to be on a mission to honor him rather than punish him, for keeping the braves in line. He also showed me his knack for taking care of people and animals in pain. Those actions would temporarily override his confusions, guilt complexes and mental garbage.

After he told me that his womanizing was summed up in a search for love, I wholeheartedly agreed, having gone a similar route in my earlier days. Amazing but not entirely unexpected, our interactions had a subtle, transformational effect on me as well. Of course, there were alarm bells that went off when he told me that he would protect me and take care of me while his aggressive actions told a different tale. A veritable protector speaks the truth in silence; my heart knows when I feel safe with someone or not and he was not one of them.

In the course of our acquaintance this proved to be correct. His idea of being loved or to love associated with the beatings he had endured as a child, he expressed through causing pain. His touch consisted of aggressive pawing, bites and painful bear hugs. On one occasion when I kicked my leg into the air he grabbed it only to make me lose my balance, fall over and hit a piece of furniture on my way down to the hard floor. The fall resulted in a huge bruise on my inner arm where I had hit the edge of a desk. At that moment, *I was subject to a psychic attack,* due to the pain lowering my frequency instantly. As an expert on dealing with pain, he then guided my attention to a different area of my body to neutralize it, a technique I had also learned decades ago and very effective.

    Not surprisingly, sex between us never happened. Every time he got close to getting in the mood, something interfered with the moment. On a weekend trip to a lake where we camped out for one night, mosquitoes and a car load of children hit the shore. At home the doorbell or the telephone would ring, even the water of a hot bath turned cold when getting ready. My willingness took the wind out of any drive to conquer, while my lack of resistance also served as a shield. How could one win a fight if there is no resistance?

    Divine interference, I finally said, to which he nodded in agreement, putting frustrations aside but not feeling rejected. I wondered if his fragmented personality would grasp this as a signal that no matter how powerful a person thinks himself or herself to be, there was no such thing as being in total control of one's destiny. Outside forces and intentions of conflicting goals postulated by others, did thwart one's own intentions on occasion. For instance, war is an anomaly that I don't want to have anything to do with but it happens regardless of my wishes. Since I surrendered to my Higher Self I don't get to choose what kind of students and people enter my life either.

    The night before I moved in, he lost his job as a truck driver, freeing up his time to experience an intense time in my company. This I clearly saw as an opportunity to dive headlong into establishing a friendship, through the mere act of non-judgmental acceptance. For me personally, there was the added satisfaction that I would assist another incarnation of mine in Atlantis who had interactions with this same soul I worked with in the present. Mine was an astrologer and scientist who opposed him as a member of one of the snake societies, in a similar situation as the present one. My newfound ability to apply the Law of Allowance heralded a major vibrational victory.

    It is important to find positive attributes in the current experience to appreciate and honor, even as a new paradigm of experience is desired. *This is the paradox that is found throughout creation.* In order to have what is new, it is necessary to honor aspects of what is present as a stepping stone on which to stand before creating a new stepping stone to continue the progress. To honor something does not make it necessary to carry it on into the next phase. Again it is necessary to point out that the grateful heart reflects a feeling aspect that resonates with the Law of Attraction that brings into experience more for which to be grateful. It is the way it works.

Going through the motions for decades, it is amazing how a few weeks of quality time can add a whole new dimensional aspect to someone's life experience. Thinking oneself to be happy is not the same as feeling joy. When someone bypasses the inner radar to directly connect with the spirit, when genuine affinity with spirit blooms, the world takes on a different color.

When affinity between two people is reciprocal and sufficiently strong, the universe panics enough to start throwing a wedge between them to drive them apart. Why would this be? Most of us are searching for that affinity and when found, it usually goes accompanied by emotional pain, other people's envy and jealousy and gossip to demean the high vibration it emits. But even a moment's worth of that loving truth can blot out years of pain and misery, transforming the whole experience, giving meaning to it, and putting it into the Light. In this particular case, aside from the affinity, there was the issue of the code activation in the DNA.

There were two TV's and a radio on full blast to drown out the noisy chatter in his own head, all day and night long. While staying with the drug-addict I could not get past two o'clock in the morning when the loud TV started to bother me but, this time, I didn't blink an eye. This changed soon to periodic intervals and only one TV and/or the radio. The mere presence of one awakened person moves and shakes the surrounding pattern; while we were trying to adjust to each other we had an intimate and revealing time together when he

Ayla's Quest

opened up about himself, and his desire to be free, as personified by me, mostly unbound by society's rules. Knowing it would not be in reach for him this lifetime due to the hand that was dealt him, he sighed that "it is hard to be free."

    His wife called to tell him that the family dog they had lived with for eighteen years had died. Did he want to attend a simple funeral conducted at the beach to let the breeze carry his ashes over the ocean? Yes, the family went first, he told me, and that was part of the legacy he would extract himself from, possibly not while alive; the memories are inexorably there, to be dealt with in the mind and heart. On the day he was supposed to go he looked very uneasy. I couldn't exactly put my finger on it until he told me that his wife would pick him up so he sat waiting around for her to show up. The wine merchant and his ex-wife came to mind instantly. The big difference, in comparison, manifested itself by my non-involvement, second time around.

    Later he told me that she had treated him to an afternoon of songs and tunes that used to have some meaning in their lives with the intention of making him feel uneasy. It worked; his day had been thoroughly upsetting even with the distraction of two of his grandchildren's presence. Crawling into a shell where I could not follow him, I let him be. This dysfunctional family represented a snake pit of problems and troubles, reminiscent of my own upbringing. To know that I had left all of that behind me, the relief it brought, I regarded as another gift. **Gratitude catapults one into a**

higher frequency where the lower creatures cannot enter.

    Later, when I showed him a book on Reiki, he opened the book on the page where the author described performing Reiki on her dog. That action reflected a spirit coming through, even momentarily, to connect with the present day issue. It also led to a request of asking the author, an acquaintance of mine, a question on the day I had planned to talk to her over the phone. Right before the call he insisted upon having a couple of drinks, resulting in him forgetting the question he wanted to ask her. Forthwith, he proceeded to interfere with our conversation, demanding my attention like an overgrown and neglected child. But he put himself in check and, again, made a sensitive remark about the relaxing and loving quality of our interaction. The deliberate interference served as a reminder of where one ends up if it is up to the personality to learn lessons through doubts and fears as the mainstay of one's existence.

FIFTY-THREE
Just as removing one pin will cause the failure of a vital piece of equipment, a simple logical statement can change an attitude or perspective that affects how or if a person will act within a given situation. (See Law of Harmony and Balance)

The next day we met his granddaughter again. What are the odds of that? He asked, taken aback by the encounter. For me, it was one of the signals that the experience would come to an abrupt end because my presence pulled in that clear, energetic field. When events or objects occurred twice in a short period of time, like him cutting a second key for the house because the first one didn't fit right, I know that our time together is measured.

This time he introduced me to her and when I asked her if she wanted time out, she shook her head. A bit strained, we had a short talk while he experienced excruciating pain connected to a back problem that happened to kick in at that exact moment. His lack of self-acceptance fueled by guilt, manifested itself in the double edged sword of happy moments immediately tainted by pain and/or misery, hitting his granddaughter with a blast of that dense energy.

She told me to take him to a doctor but I knew well what was *really* going on. He helped injured people and animals and had a gift to understand and guide young people. However, due to mental programming in a childhood filled with trauma that formed his past and influenced his present, self-help or homeopathic assistance could not enter the picture. Many people are aware of how inadequate, even ineffectual or harmful allopathic treatments can be.

Smiling more, he began to do the small things that touch the heart in such pleasant ways by picking scented roses from his yard and buying me a card with a picture of a teddy bear; a simple message adorned its pages, evidence of another pinprick of trust and hope. I put it on the window sill so I could enjoy looking at it. It became the piece of 'evidence' his wife took to her lawyer to use my presence as an indication of adultery, part of the pattern she and her ex-husband held in possibly more lives to come.

The ability to receive and appreciate those heartfelt gifts, reminded me also of the time I would push them away; years earlier I did similar things, like present an old lady walking down the street with a gardenia, a random gift that brought tears to her eyes; buying a glass of milk for someone who accidentally dropped hers, etc. Even though it would give one pleasure to unconditionally extend a helping hand, if the donor cannot grasp a reaching hand in return, to extend that same courtesy to another person who could experience that pleasure, balance is missing.

Playing a tape, his father's voice filled the room, telling a story about how he and his younger brother had built a riverboat that they had built from scratch. The frailty resounded in the voice of an old man who had left a legacy to his eldest son, debatably his favorite. He had even built a replica of the boat, a crude model carved out of cedar wood; it sat on his roll top desk. It was the first time he listened to the tape after his father had passed, stirring up feelings and memories he had repressed since then. Despite their uneasy association, based on forced DNA programming, he acted as if he liked and honored his father, as witnessed in a video where he attended to him at his deathbed until he passed on, right before the wedding of his only daughter.

A drawing of his brother adorned one table. There were three brothers and two sisters in that family and the one who understood him and that he felt close to, found a premature death in the mangling arms of farm machinery gone haywire. It taught him the lesson, underscoring the deaths he had witnessed in the Vietnam War, that everything under the sun was temporary, an unending cycle of beginnings, middles, and endings. Bravely, he admitted that the brother lived on in his heart, the best way to honor someone's life, while now being capable of dealing with his presence on the celluloid of films.

The brother did indeed have a similar type of personality and kindred spirit as detected in certain mannerisms and eye glints. When people are very close it's like losing a part of themselves when they pass on, leaving the ones left behind burdened by heavy weighing emotions and the task of learning to let go.

It triggered the memory of my own brother. Although he had the chance to rectify his deed of stealing my inheritance illegally, the gist of the matter is that his own conscience prevented him from ever getting to know me or being able to interact with me in an ordinary, spontaneous manner. The theft had erected an insurmountable gap between us, never to be bridged. I had to let him go, the memory of the shy, little brother who would giggle in delight at life's promise and who ended up as a bitter, friendless adult, thanks to wrong choices and his own actions. He lacked the ability to take responsibility for his own actions thereby forsaking any possibility to get out of the quagmire, forever pointing the finger to blame someone else for his own mistakes. It was impossible to reach his spirit, cemented as it had become in his body.

FIFTY-FOUR

End of a cycle

He escorted me back to my hotel room. Then I asked whether he wanted to go for a walk to the harbor knowing he could not ask me comfortably. His actions bespoke the story of a man who could not really be decisive in ordinary matters. Perhaps the ideal killing machine in the heat of battle, a competent arbitrator in breaking up fights, and an executor for a criminal and secret society, he felt out of place in matters of the heart and came across as an awkward suitor.

According to him, his heart had belonged to a woman he had enjoyed a relationship with for a period of eight years while he remained married to take care of his obligations. However, as he compared me to both his mother and this woman, apparently the two most important women in his life, a picture slowly emerged of the same controlling predator that had caused great dismay to either one of them. His mother suffered from Alzheimer's disease while his soul mate married several times to 'penalize' him while he remained loyal to this wife.

New realizations
1) I had a clean record
2) I could handle any situation applying the Law of Allowance
3) I achieved my goal of inner freedom, earning me a new name

4) I set a new goal.

Lack of Inner Freedom as manifested in this assignment providing a close look at 'the enemy':
1) Body controlled spirit
2) Fragmented personality
3) Watcher – total withdrawal that has no intentional reason for becoming aware other than curiosity.
4) Victim Consciousness – expressing sympathy for the afflicted ones around the globe is complicity in disguise; supporting feelings of victimhood (see Law of Intention).
5) Bound by rules and societal laws.
6) Blames others for perceived misfortunes.
7) Gives power away to an outside God or other people.
8) Can be subliminally influenced and has limited control over own mind. Can or cannot be hypnotized.

Inner Freedom gained during the quest:
1) Spiritually controlled body
2) Whole within self, integrated personality.
3) Observer – using knowledge gained for an intentional purpose.
4) Lack of victim consciousness.
5) No longer bound by rules; application of natural Laws of Attraction, Intention, Harmony and Balance and Allowance.
6) Responsible for own actions.
7) Uses own power.

8) Has full control over own mind, cannot be hypnotized.

FIFTY-FIVE

Life without influence of the simultaneous spirit suppressor

    Once I understood the workings of our society and could identify the various players in the Game, life has become easier. Fully trusting my Higher Self, knowing who I really am, being like a hollow bamboo without negative thoughts or fears impeding my progress or intent, the world simply does not exist. Whatever I do, spirit is always guiding me with gentle humor combined with irrepressible love.

    Basically, the acceptance of the idea that we always get what we need, not necessarily what we want, an impossibly difficult task for the ego-driven person, lends a pervasive pliancy to my daily existence. Living in the pressure-cooker called the Matrix is no longer applicable to me as the tangled web has been hacked into with an imaginary machete, leaving the strands dangling. The quality of freedom that is attainable while enmeshed inside the body is only available to those who recognize the power of spirit and walk their talk.

    The simultaneous spirit suppressor has no longer a hold over me in any way; it's as if I never met any one of them, in other words, it seems as if they do not exist. I perceive them all around me but they can no longer 'get' to me. Every once in a while my Higher Self puts me to the test, e.g. recently I went to an indoor estate sale. As soon as I entered the living room one of them, a middle-aged female admonished me on walking over a 'priceless carpet' with my shoes. Apparently, she did not work there because she added that 'they had informed the visitors' of the necessity of taking the shoes off. I merely glanced at her over my reading glasses, silently, to which she loudly proclaimed 'that I did not care'. In her mind, she accomplished other visitors registering that I was the indifferent one while she followed the rules (like we all should in her programmed mind.) I simply observed it, smiling.

Decades ago, I stopped watching TV due to the lack of integrity of the media to report what the people need to know, infusing subliminal messages into their programs and their outright lies. I stopped listening to the continual changing faces of politicians who like the sound of their own voices telling the same lies over and over again, wondering how many people know who they really elect? They do not deserve my attention so ***I took back my power.***

EPILOGUE

The quest is over but I still have a purpose to fulfill.

Shortly thereafter, I returned to Stanley Park in Vancouver, B.C. where I met a wonderful man with whom I share many parallel lives. Together, we have started a life filled with positive shared actions that will, ultimately, lead to our magical house of healing: a house where seekers can take refuge, find healing, a place where dreamers can dream, musicians play and artists create. If it does not manifest itself on planet Earth, it will be created on the astral.

Maybe we will meet with you in the future.

For comments and/or questions I can be reached at aylashim@aim.com.

--

Made in the USA
San Bernardino, CA
01 September 2017